P9-CDU-713

Careless at Work

Published with the assistance of the Ontario Heritage Foundation, Ministry of Culture and Communications

Careless at Work

Selected Canadian Historical Studies
by

J.M.S. Careless

Dundurn Press
Toronto and Oxford
1990

Design and Production: JAQ
Printing and Binding: Gagné Printing Ltd., Louiseville, Quebec, Canada

Dundurn Press wishes to acknowledge the generous assistance and ongoing support of **The Canada Council, The Book Publishing Industry Development Programme of the Department of Communications, The Ontario Arts Council,** and **The Ontario Heritage Foundation.**

Care has been taken to trace the ownership of copyright material used in the text, including the illustrations. The author and publisher welcome any information enabling them to rectify any reference or credit in subsequent editions.

J. Kirk Howard, Publisher

Canadian Cataloguing in Publication Data

Careless, J.M.S., 1919 –
Careless at work

Includes bibliographical references and index.
ISBN 1-55002-067-6

1. Canada – History. I. Title.

FC176.C37 1990 971 C90-095727-1
F1026.6.C37 199

Dundurn Press Limited
2181 Queen Street East
Suite 301
Toronto, Canada
M4E 1E5

Dundurn Distribution
73 Lime Walk
Headington
Oxford, England
OX3 7AD

Contents

Acknowledgements:

Some of the essays in this volume have been previously published. The author is grateful to the following for permission, where necessary, to reprint here:

B.C. Studies: "Submarines, Princes and Hollywood Commandos or At Sea in B.C."

Canadian Historical Association: "George Brown and the Mother of Confederation"; "Somewhat Narrow Horizons".

Canadian Historical Review: "The Toronto Globe and Agrarian Radicalism, 1850–67"; "Mid-Victorian Liberalism in Central Canadian Newspapers, 1850–67"; "Frontierism, Metropolitanism and Canadian History".

Canadian Forum: "The Political Ideas of George Brown"; "Limited Identities in Canada".

Holt, Rinehart & Winston of Canada: "Urban Life in the West".

McClelland & Stewart: "The Business Community in the Early Development of Victoria".

Multicultural Historical Society of Ontario: "The Emergence of Cabbagetown in Victorian Toronto".

Royal Society of Canada: "'Waspishness' and Multiculture in Canada".

University of Toronto Press: "Aspects of Metropolitanism in Atlantic Canada before 1914"; "Some Aspects of Urbanization in Nineteenth-Century Ontario".

Urban History Review: "Metropolis and Region: the Interplay of City and Region in Canadian History before 1914".

Photo Credits:

Page 16: Public Archives of Canada (PA 122984).

Page 46: *Globe and Mail.*

Page 66: J.M.S. Careless.

Page 76: J.M.S. Careless.

Page 104: Metropolitan Reference Library (T32897).

Page 130: Metropolitan Reference Library (T14459).

Page 146: Royal Ontario Museum.

Page 166: City of Toronto Archives (9.2.4.6 96a).

Page 192: Metropolitan Reference Library (T13541).

Page 206: Metropolitan Reference Library (T30080).

Page 234: Metropolitan Toronto Library Board.

Page 254: Metropolitan Toronto Library (T10365).

Page 281: Archives of the United Church of Canada, Victoria University, Toronto.

Page 294: City of Toronto Archives (James 8036).

Page 308: City of Toronto Archives.

Page 336: J.M.S. Careless.

Foreword

by Carl Berger,
Department of History, University of Toronto

It is a pleasure to preface this collection of essays by Maurice Careless with a few words of personal appreciation. At one level these studies constitute the outlines of an intellectual biography of an outstanding historian of Canada best known for his portrait of George Brown, his survey of the Canadian colonies in the Union period, and for his efforts to clarify the concepts of 'metropolitanism' and 'limited identities' and bring them to the forefront of discussions about Canadian historical writing. These studies are impressive for their analytical rigour as well as their scope, ranging from explorations of the ideas of mid-Victorian liberalism, the interplay of urban centres and their hinterlands, and business life in towns across the country in the nineteenth century, to appraisals of Canadian historiography and the British Canadian roots of multiculturalism. Because they illuminate so many enduring themes and patterns in Canadian development they deserve the attention of anyone concerned with the country's past.

For all their diversity, these essays possess a significance beyond their intrinsic interest. They exemplify an intellectual temper, a way of seeing, that highlights the interdependence and interplay of historical forces in, for example, the mutual relations of towns and hinterlands, or regions and national communities. Careless has criticized a tradition within Canadian historical writing that exaggerated tendencies working towards national unity and minimized (sometimes denigrated) the persistence of regional, or more exactly, provincial identities. He did not reject national history as such; characteristically, he pleaded, on the one hand, for a more open and sympathetic understanding of particularistic traditions, and, on the other, for an awareness that these co-existed with a larger, more heterogeneous community. It is this sense of complexity and a striving for balance that imparts to these essays a sophistication and wisdom that can never be dated or old-fashioned.

Author's Foreword

THIS SAMPLING OF MY CANADIAN historical studies ranges from the 1940s to the 1980s, and as a result may strike some repetitive notes, or in some degree look dated. History, however, *is* dated. Its very claim is that the past does not fade into nothing, but continues to matter, whether or not the purely present-minded are able to recognize that basic fact. And so, while the selections in this volume may consider issues or put forward conclusions that are no longer new, new, new, that does not mean that they have to ceased to matter, to hold significance. Moreover, if there may be passages within the series of samples presented in this volume which return to points made in a previous piece, this, too, is in the nature of history moving over time – reinforcing or reassessing developments as it proceeds.

All I should try to say is that the items of work which are contained below are meant to display the main lines of my career in Canadian historical scholarship, a field which I have found as demanding as it has ever been fascinating. Others might have made some other choices than the materials I have compiled here. But it does seem to me a reasonably accurate depiction of the scope and interests of my particular kind of writings. What remains, still, is to thank a good many people, who cannot in any way all be named in this foreword. Yet first among those who must be named, is the distinguished Canadian historian, Carl Berger, my long-time colleague (and former graduate student, I am proud to recall) who has kindly provided a valuable Foreword of his own. Then there are those who have done so much to impel me to this present book: especially cherished associates (and also former students) such as Fred Armstrong, David Keane and Colin Read. The list could assuredly be much extended; but at this juncture I would instead like to pick out some deeply remembered teachers, who particularly led me to the scholarly course witnessed in this book (though any blame remains my own). At the University of Toronto, Richard Saunders, Bertie Wilkinson, Donald Creighton and Frank Underhill; at Harvard University, David Owen, Crane Brinton and Frederick Merk. But at the end – as in the beginning and always – there is my wife, Betty, who unstintingly strove for my work while astutely, resolutely, running a home and raising five children, while yet receiving far too inadequate recognition for what has truly been a joint career.

PART ONE

George Brown and His Times

Introduction

AS AUTHOR AND EDITOR COMBINED, I have arranged this selection of my published work in Canadian history within four general sections or subject areas. The areas interconnect, and may at times encroach on one another. Nevertheless, I think the particular articles, essays and papers they present will convey the chief preoccupations of my historical research and writing through more than forty years. A bibliography appended at the close records the much larger body of material from which the chosen items were drawn; though that record properly omits still other published pieces of all too slight scholarly relevance, not to mention an accumulation of talks and papers that never got into print.

The four subject areas that follow here each include a brief introduction to identify the selections it contains and to say a little about the circumstances concerning them. The opening section, on the journalist-politician George Brown, his *Globe* newspaper and his times, deals with the earliest major theme in my writings. It starts, also, with the first scholarly article I ever published, "The Toronto *Globe* and Agrarian Radicalism, 1850–67", which came out in the *Canadian Historical Review* for March, 1948. This piece was initially delivered the year before to an informal, work-in-progress seminar in the Department of History at the University of Toronto, where I had begun my teaching career in the fall of 1945. It sprang, in fact, from the research I then had under way on my doctoral thesis – that constant reliance, or lifeline, for the new staff member who only knows one thing better than his learned colleagues, his own thesis project.

To explain my personal case, I have to note that after undergraduate years at Toronto, I had entered graduate work at Harvard. That led to a proposed Ph.D. on "George Brown and the Toronto *Globe*: British

Victorian Liberalism in the North American Environment", essentially a study in socio-political ideas and climates of opinion, which I had gone into at Harvard. But wartime service intervened. I moved to Canadian Naval Headquarters, and subsequently to the Department of External Affairs in Ottawa (with forays overseas), not to return to my researches until the Second World War was over. Thereafter, back in Toronto, the tasks of coping with strenuous teaching demands during the post-war flood of veterans into universities meant that I did not finally complete my thesis for Harvard until 1949. Meanwhile, however, I worked away at its problems of interpretation, and so came to stress the significance of the rising urban business community of Toronto, with which Brown, the *Globe* and their ideas seemed clearly and closely tied.

This emphasis was reflected in my aforesaid first published article. It sought to put an urban qualification on the "agrarian" character generally attributed to the contemporary Upper Canada liberal upsurge – the Clear Grit movement – which Brown and his journal came so forcefully to lead. Subsequently, and after my thesis had been finished and accepted, I went on to take a wider look at liberal opinions in the mid-nineteenth century urban press of Upper Canada, as shown in the second article exhibited in this section: "Mid-Victorian Liberalism in Central Canadian Newspapers, 1850-67", which appeared in the *Canadian Historical Review* for September, 1950. I originally presented it the summer preceding to a symposium on cultural and intellectual development in Central Canada, during a regional meeting of the Canadian Humanities Association at Kingston. By that time, however, I was already turning towards a full-scale biography of George Brown, rather than pursuing newspaper analysis as such; and hence was moving away from plans for publishing my thesis, although I certainly hoped to incorporate the essence of the latter in the biographical work I had in prospect.

Yet again, other enterprises had to be handled first. I wrote a general history, *Canada: A Story of Challenge*, sent on to the publishers by 1953, and next co-authored three high school text books for Canadian "social studies" – then a popular curriculum fad – all of which meant that I did not get very far into the intended Brown biography until 1955-6. That year my wife and I and our (now) four children spent on leave in Britain; for I had uncovered a cache of George Brown's personal correspondence at the home of his descendants near Oban in Scotland. Their generous hospitality allowed me to visit and work there; and I was also able to begin writing the biography when down at my temporary base in Cambridge. As the outcome, the first volume of the two I projected on Brown was later finished back in Canada for publication in 1959. But meanwhile, I had at least added up, weighed and encapsulated his central body of thought in "The Political Ideas of George Brown", which came out in February 1957 in the *Canadian Forum,* and is thus included below as the third item in this general theme-area. It remains a fairly brief article, nevertheless, tailored as it was to the space limits in the *Forum* of its day. Further assessments of Brown's views may be found in the lecture which I delivered in a public series at Carleton University, Ottawa, and which was published in 1959 in *Our Living Tradition* , edited by R.L. MacDougall. But since only a selection could indeed be put into the present volume, I would have to ask any sufficiently interested reader to consult my bibliographical list below, in order to track down the Lecture just mentioned, or any other additional writings of mine.

I did still other writing and much talking about Brown, before the second volume of my biography reached print in 1963. Here, however, I have included only one further example of those endeavours, the fourth item set out below:"George Brown and the Mother of Confederation", which I gave before the Canadian Historical Association in 1960. Based on Brown's letters that I found in Scotland – letters above all to his wife, Anne, the "Mother" – it illustrates the riches of the material discovered, and has always been a bit of a favourite of mine.

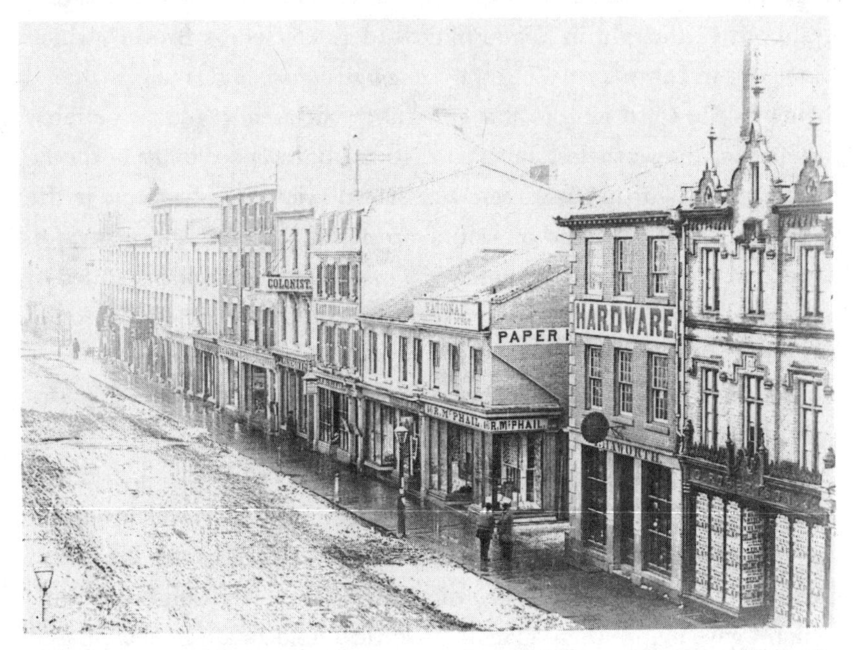

King Street, 1856. The Globe's *office was out of range of this very early street photograph, but the* Colonist*'s office is evident.*

The Toronto Globe and Agrarian Radicalism, 1850–67

It is well established in Canadian tradition that the Toronto *Globe* of the Confederation era spoke above all for the farmers of Canada West. The *Globe*'s constant care for the "intelligent yeomanry of Upper Canada" was repaid by the flattered members of that community in steadfast devotion to George Brown, his party and his journal. An anecdote of the time sought to illustrate this when it depicted a farmer of the Huron Tract replying warily to a remark that it was a fine day, "I can't say till I've seen my *Globe*." At a much later date scholarship has strengthened tradition by demonstrating that the *Globe* under George Brown, like the Clear Grit party under his leadership, was largely an expression of the forces of agrarian radicalism that were at work in Canada West in the years prior to Confederation. "For the essential thing," one authority has said, "about the *Globe* and the movement it led is that it represented the aspirations and general outlook on life of the pioneer Upper Canada farmer. The 'Clear Grit' party was an expression of the 'frontier' in our Canadian politics just as Jacksonian Democracy or Lincoln Republicanism was in the politics of the United States."[1] The Upper Canada Reform Convention of 1859, perhaps the most significant manifestation of Grittism in the two decades before Confederation, and one in which

Brown and the *Globe* figured extensively, has also been characterized according to this view: "One cannot but be struck by the fact that the voice of the assembly was that of an agrarian democracy. . . . Here in truth was the essence of Jeffersonian philosophy springing out of the soil of Upper Canada."[2] Following the same approach, it has been noted how consistently the *Globe* directed itself to the western agrarian interest. It turned away from the corrupt and ignorant mob of the cities – where Grits were seldom elected – to rest its faith in a broad franchise on the independence and native wisdom of the agricultural classes. It steadily championed their cause against John A. Macdonald and those Lower Canadian powers of darkness – Montreal big business and the priest-ridden French. The *Globe*'s campaigns on behalf of the Grits, in the bitter sectional struggle for control of the United Province, show on analysis how strongly it stood forth as the protagonist of the agrarian West, whether, for example, it was opposing Montreal railway, banking, and tariff policies, or was pressing for westward agrarian elements and the commercial, financial, and political power of the more developed eastern regions. Here, it seems, was another case of west *versus* east, farmer *versus* financier, rural democracy *versus* urban privilege.

One can scarcely question the essential validity of this well established interpretation of the *Globe*'s opinions and activities. And yet if followed too narrowly it may tend to obscure other significant characteristics of the *Globe* and the movement it represented. The wholly "agrarian approach," if one may so call it, needs qualification. To explain the complex opinions of the *Globe* even generally in terms of the outlook and aspirations of pioneer farmers is to overemphasize one aspect of the journal and to neglect or misconceive other aspects of considerable importance. For instance, it would be unwise to assume too much from a premise of agrarianism about the *Globe*'s attitude toward democracy, or its views on commerce and manufacturing or banking and railways. It would not be sufficient to identify the *Globe* – and George Brown himself – with the aims and interests of a farming population. And it would be dangerous to accept its Liberal creed simply as an expression of frontier democracy. Of course, cautions of this sort have not gone wholly unregarded. But they have had little weight in judging the policy of the *Globe* as a whole.

Moreover, it may be questioned whether the *Globe* was speaking, as has been affirmed, for a "pioneer agricultural settlement."[3] There is good reason to doubt whether this is a satisfactory description of the western portion of the Province of Canada, during the fifties and sixties of the last century, and therefore to doubt whether it provides the proper frame for examining the newspaper. In many ways the pioneer era was rapidly passing away in Upper Canada by 1850. Even in the western Ontario peninsula, the stronghold of agrarian radicalism and a major source of *Globe* support, the fast dwindling supply of fertile wild land foreshadowed the disappearance of the frontier. In the next decade, the growth of the grain export trade, the increase in local commerce, the rise of the towns, and the coming of the railway began the transformation of the western region. A scattered community of backwoods settlements was becoming an integrated commercial agricultural society, in which the business class was steadily rising to prominence, and through which the metropolitan pull of the city of Toronto was making itself felt ever more strongly. Toronto in 1850 was merely "a fair-sized commercial town," mainly distinguished from other Upper Canadian centres by its administrative functions and its past as a seat of government.[4] By 1867 it was well advanced on its way to economic as well as political hegemony over the entire western section. Between these years Toronto invaded territory formerly subject to the trade of rival Ontario towns, spread out a railway network, became a leading Canadian manufacturing centre, and established capital facilities capable of serving a wide area. It even began to contend, on not too unequal terms, with the older metropolis of Montreal. One could scarcely suppose that the *Globe* would remain isolated from the turbulence, the aggressive self-confidence, and the grand designs of its native city. In fact, its own expanding influence throughout Upper Canada in this period may be read as one striking manifestation of Toronto's rise to metropolitan status. The city's press was coming to dominate the West.

In similar fashion, in politics "Tory Toronto" became the headquarters of Grit radicalism – not a surprising development, for this expression of Upper Canadian sectionalism found a natural focus in the rising western metropolis. In the middle fifties the Clear Grit agrarian movement thus fell under the control of an urban and professional group led by George Brown which was chiefly to be identified with Toronto. The many-headed, loosely led Clear Grit movement was gradually organized under a party hierarchy centred in that city. The mass of agrarian support was joined with influential western business interests, numbers were linked with economic power, and a strong sectional block was built up. The *Globe* played a major role in this process as the voice of the Toronto leadership, and did a good deal to put its views, full of care for business considerations, before the rural community. The proprietor of the journal was himself far from being a member of the farm community. George Brown was a fairly typical member of the Toronto business world; and many leaders of Toronto business were prominent in the party which he dominated. Among them were William McMaster, whose extensive financial and mercantile interests made him the dean of Toronto business, John Macdonald, head of the city's leading wholesale house, A.M. Smith, an urban real estate owner and one of Toronto's wealthiest citizens, John McMurrich, a prominent city merchant and president of two insurance and investment companies, and W.P. Howland, one of the Howland family then outstanding in Toronto finance and industry. All these men appeared as Liberal members of the Assembly or Legislative Council in the decade after 1857; and all but W.P. Howland were in 1867 members of the party's Central Committee (which, however, included H.S. Howland).[5]

Brown had close business ties as well as political affiliations with these urban Liberals. He was one of the leading members of the Toronto group, captained by McMaster and including John Macdonald and the Howland brothers, that formed the Bank of Commerce in 1867 to meet the threat of a Bank of Montreal monopoly.[6] His brother, Gordon Brown, editor of the *Globe* during much of this period, was associated with McMaster, W.P. Howland, and McMurrich in financing the Kennedy expedition "of commerce and exploration" to the Northwest in 1856;[7] and he was again associated with them in the directorship of the North West Transportation Company, organized in 1858.[8] George Brown was also affiliated with A.M. Smith and with two other prominent Toronto magnates, William Gooderham, Sr., and J.C. Worts, as a major shareholder in the Toronto Linseed Oil Manufacturing Company.[9] Shortly after Confederation he appeared with McMaster and John

Macdonald in the directorate of the Toronto Isolated Risks and Farmer's Insurance Company.[10] His private holdings during the eighteen-fifties and sixties, apart from the most widely circulated newspaper in Canada (in 1862 it claimed three times the circulation of its nearest rival,) included a large amount of speculative real estate, lumber workings, saw mills, a cabinet factory, a village, and oil lands in the heart of the western oil-boom districts of Kent and Lambton.[12] From the material interests of its proprietor alone, it would seem to be safer to identify the *Globe* with the Toronto businessman than with the pioneer farmer. Without swinging to this other extreme, however, it does become necessary to consider the journal with reference to the growth of western business generally and of Toronto business in particular. To put it simply, the *Globe*'s dealings with "urbanism" must be treated no less than its dealings with agrarianism.

The fact that the *Globe* had these diverse interests does not necessarily imply any contradiction in its views. One need not look for any inevitable conflict between urban and agrarian interests in Canada West during this time of transition from the frontier era. Instead, dividing lines between town and country were somewhat blurred. Prosperous Toronto citizens turned from their offices to practical farming, as did George Brown on his Bow Park stock-breeding farm, and not to golf clubs or summer homes in beautiful but barren Muskoka. Wealthy farmers like the prominent Clear Grit, Joseph Gould, invested in banking, railway promotion, and new factories in or about the towns.[13] In general, as in the case of Winnipeg and the prairie West in a later age, the farming populace and the local business community that lived by its trade shared many important points of view, particularly in opposition to outside metropolitan forces which sought to dominate the whole region. Accordingly, in Upper Canada of the Confederation era one could find an "agricultural interest" representing the West as a whole in its struggle against Lower Canadian domination, but made up of both urban and agrarian elements. Its prevailing tone might be that of an agricultural society. Its leadership would come largely from town-dwellers, commercial and professional men, and well-to-do farmers with close ties with the urban world of business.

In this context, the *Globe* might speak generally on behalf of the western farming classes; but it would look specifically to the interests of the leaders of western agricultural society, which involved a good deal of concern for matters of commercial significance outside the ken of the ordinary farmer. Approaching the journal by way of agrarianism and frontier democracy obscures the significance of its constant care for business affairs. The final picture of the *Globe* should not be that of an agrarian radical oracle making common cause, on occasion, with the essentially foreign world of Toronto business; but rather one of an urban Liberal newspaper seeking to carry its viewpoint to the rural masses – and generally succeeding.

II

The "urban" view of the *Globe* may be illustrated by specific references to its attitude toward leading issues of the mid-century decades in Canada. There were two closely related issues which played an important part in the sectional conflict of the period: the value of the Union of the two Canadas and the significance of the St. Lawrence transportation system, on which the Union so largely rested. The agrarian and business communities of the West had somewhat different interests in these questions. Western business men and western farmers formed one front in opposing Lower Canadian attempts to exploit the St. Lawrence route at Upper Canada's cost, whether by preferential tariffs or Grand Trunk schemes; but the western business man was more closely concerned than was the farmer with the meaning of that route for the trade of Upper Canada, more concerned with maintaining unhampered communications down the St. Lawrence to the sea, and therefore, more aware of the commercial value of the Union. The western farmer was not so strongly affected by these considerations of trade; union or separation, he thought, his wheat would still go to market. Visions of "the commercial empire of the St. Lawrence" were not for him. The "Erie ditch" would serve his purpose well enough. On the other hand, although the mercantile community of Canada West had ties with New York and the Erie route, and did not intend to sacrifice this alternative system of trade for complete subservience to a Montreal – St. Lawrence monopoly, it was essentially still complementary to Montreal. Its investment in trade by the St. Lawrence was real; so were its fears that a separate French province unfriendly to English commerce might erect interprovincial trade barriers. The western farming community could – and did to a very large degree – agitate for dissolution of the Union as a way out of the sectional problem. The western business community could only view the prospect of losing the unity of the St. Lawrence with deep misgivings. Toronto in particular would have been affected. Success in the city's efforts to control its own trade did not lie in cutting ties with Montreal to become wholly dependent on those with New York. Moreover, on the positive side, the Upper Canadian merchant stood to gain a good deal if the long enduring dream of the St. Lawrence continental empire could be realized in that era when the great American plains were being peopled. Trade between the plains and the sea by way of the St. Lawrence system would pass through Upper Canada's waterways, railways, and towns. Toronto again would be particularly affected as a main junction point between the routes east and west. In the eighteen-fifties and sixties, Toronto business men fully conscious of these possibilities, were striving to improve the city's transportation facilities, with the warmest support of the *Globe*.

In fact, the *Globe*'s whole stand on the significance of the St. Lawrence route and the value of the Union expressed its understanding of mercantile interests. It repeatedly stressed the commercial meaning of the unity of the St. Lawrence for Canada, and it steadily argued for the maintenance of union in the face of a powerful movement for separation springing mainly from the storm centre of Grit agrarianism, the peninsula of western Ontario. George Brown himself summarized the *Globe*'s position when in 1856 he told a large rural audience, "the magnificent chain of inland seas stretching through both provinces from Lake Superior to the Atlantic almost forbid the idea of separation."[14] During the eighteen-fifties, the *Globe* actually fought a major battle within the Grit party against the forces of separation, which can broadly be interpreted as a struggle by the urban leaders of an agrarian movement to bring their followers in line with the interests of the leadership. The *Globe*'s ultimate solution of the sectional problem, federation of the two Canadas, was put forward as a means of saving the commercial benefits of the Union while eliminating those features which made for discord. At the Reform Convention of 1859, the Clear Grits adopted as their platform a compromise which at last opened the door to such a federation. The compromise represented the victory of George Brown and his associates in the party leadership over the policy of outright separation favoured by the majority of delegates at the Convention (but by none east of Bowmanville) and mainly advocated by lesser party members from the western peninsula, the area, in fact, which sent the great bulk of the delegates present. The rank and file of the Convention of 1859, as it has been said, voiced the sentiments of agrarianism.[15] But the policy established there was that of the group about Brown, which included Foley and Mowat, city lawyers, and McDougall and Gordon Brown of the *Globe* editorial staff. It was this group which George Sheppard, a leading advocate of dissolution, accused of "cooking" the Convention in his letters to Charles Clarke, a prominent local leader of the Grit organization in North Wellington, in the heart of the peninsula.[16]

After the Convention, the *Globe* devoted itself to maintaining the victory over dissolution. Its editorial staff was instructed not to mention any alternative to federation in its columns.[17] Considering the journal's widespread influence throughout Upper Canada by this time, such a programme of deliberate silence must have done a good deal to help bury separatism. Ultimately, the Grits' acceptance of the Coalition of 1864, and the greater movement for union which sprang from it, might in part be traced to the success of Brown and the *Globe* in controlling their own party on the question of preserving the unity of the St. Lawrence. It is true that their Liberal-Conservative foes argued that the *Globe*'s policy of constitutional reform (whether representation by population or federation) aimed specifically at the destruction of the existing Union. Yet the *Globe* always contended in reply that constitutional reform was necessary to save the Union from an impossible situation that only created sectional discord, and did so especially because the Liberal-Conservative government used one-half of the United Province to control the other half.[18] Without forgetting the *Globe*'s inflammatory views on racial and religious issues, one must recognize that it did not create the sectional conflict which lay in the nature of the Union; and it seems fair to say that it had some grounds for its contentions in this regard. At any rate, the *Globe's* campaign on behalf of the Union, against separatism in Upper Canada, began early in the eighteen-fifties and went on consistently until the success already noted was achieved at the close of the decade.

In 1851, the *Globe* condemned the "senseless, suicidal agitation for repeal of the Union."[19] The Union, it said, was necessary to Upper Canada which was cut off from the seaboard, in order that the western import and export trade might be carried on effectively; moreover, the Union allowed Canada to develop a great system of internal improvements and enhanced her prestige and credit abroad.[20] These are surely the arguments of commerce. In part they were directed against certain agrarian radicals then pressing for dissolution, members of a group at that time scorned by the urban *Globe* as the "Clear Grits." However, by 1855, Brown and the Grits were being driven together by their common hostility to Conservative and Lower Canadian domination. Thereafter, the *Globe* could hardly find it politic to call dissolution "suicidal" when it was strong in the very area and in the very party which it was striving to control. It came to admit separation as a last resort , if all else failed; but it proceeded to stress another remedy, representation by population. And this was postulated on maintaining the Union[21] – or why seek it so long and so hard when dissolution would cut the Gordian knot? At the same time as the *Globe* pressed for representation by population, it embarked on propaganda for the Union. In a series of articles in the summer of 1855, the newspaper reiterated that separation would put Upper Canada's trade "at the mercy of Brother Jonathan and Jean Baptiste," would close free access to the sea and leave the St. Lawrence route under "an enervated and unambitious race."[22] Not a cordial approach to Canadian unity, but, considering the prejudices of the *Globe's* western constituents, no doubt politically sound. Brown himself elaborated this theme at a reform rally a few weeks later, after a Grit member of the Assembly had advocated prompt dissolution if representation by population could not be immediately secured:

> I cannot think that it would be statesmanlike, because Upper Canada representatives of the hour are traitors to their cause, to yield up forever the solid advantages obtained by the

> present union of the Canadas. I could fancy that if a dissolution were accomplished today that ten years hence we would look back with astonishment at the utter imbecility of 1,300,000 Anglo-Saxons in Upper Canada, and 300,000 in Lower Canada, frightened by some 700,000 Frenchmen into surrendering forever the noble St. Lawrence and all the fertile land it transverses to the domination of Popish priestcraft. (Cheers) For one, sir, I will never be a party to such a transaction until every other remedy has failed.[23]

In 1858, however, the unhappy collapse of "His Majesty's Most Ephemeral Government," the Brown-Dorion ministry, carried with it the hopes of soon obtaining representation by population. Then the *Globe* cast about for a new way to save the Union, and came up with federation. Even before the tragi-comedy of the Brown-Dorion Government, George Brown had expressed in parliament a "conviction that the Union could be better wrought on the federal principle than on the present system"; and in the same speech, it might be noted, he declared that he had always believed the Union to be a great and statesmanlike measure and the concept of the bond of the St. Lawrence a noble one.[24] It is true that for a few months in 1859 the *Globe,* in a mood of confusion and angry frustration, did play with the idea of dissolution. But this was during George Sheppard's brief sojourn on the *Globe*'s editorial staff, and he may well have written the "dissolutionist" articles. In any case, gradually through that year the federal solution was worked out in the *Globe*'s pages; and one may suppose that the lead in this direction came from the proprietor himself. At least, towards the end of 1859, Sheppard was complaining to Clarke that his opinions were being ignored in editorial conferences, that George Brown meant to overcome the "extreme views" of the separatists, and that he would have to resign.[25] Certainly, once the federal solution had been clearly evolved, the *Globe* flung itself with missionary fervour into converting the Grit party to the new doctrine, with the results observed in the Convention of 1859. In George Brown's speech at that gathering, which so effectively mustered the arguments in favour of federation, it is worth noting that the appeal to reasons of commerce which had defended the Union appeared once more: "And the fact can never be lost sight of in the argument – that the scheme of the committee [federation] would secure us free access to the Ocean, and every facility for trading with Lower Canada – while Dissolution would place us in both respects, to a certain extent, at the mercy of Lower Canada. Are you content to hand over control of the St. Lawrence – to have customs officers stopping our railway cars and our steamers at certain points in their downward journey and overhauling all the passengers as if entering a foreign country?"[26] The Convention was persuaded not to hand over the St. Lawrence. In so deciding, it once again defined a common front for western sectionalism. Yet in seeking this front, it should be clear how steadily the *Globe* had been looking to business interests.

Furthermore, the *Globe*'s opinions on the potentialities of the St. Lawrence system expressed more of the merchant's dream of a western commercial empire than the restricted outlook of back-country farmers. The journal indeed agreed with the farmers that "the free and healthy competition at present carried on between the American and Canadian routes"[27] should not be interfered with by tariff measures or bounties aiming at a St. Lawrence monopoly. Western business men would have largely endorsed that too. But, voicing a "sincere desire for the prosperity of the St. Lawrence and all those connected with its trade," the *Globe* advocated further works to improve the system, lower tolls on the canals, and subsequently, the building of railways to facilitate the flow of traffic.[28] Nor were these improvements to be made solely within Canada West. The *Globe* also supported a St. Lawrence-Lake Champlain canal to divert trade from the Erie route;[29] and this in 1855, by which time the Liberal-Conservative coalition was well established in office and the charge that it was levying a toll on Upper Canada to support Montreal's trade was often being heard in the West. The journal voiced its belief, too, in the innate superiority of the St. Lawrence route over the Erie, predicting that "there is no doubt that the great bulk of western produce must come by it."[30] It described the vast potential trade of the American prairies which might be secured to Canada by the St. Lawrence system. However, gradually it became clear that the supposed advantages of a "natural" route over the "artificial" Erie system (to a convinced free trader like the *Globe*, the former adjective virtually implied advantages) would not automatically win the American western trade for Canada. Then the *Globe* put its faith in a plan for steamship navigation in an unbroken line from lake-head to the sea, believing that the advantages of the modern "screw steamer" over canal barges and paddlewheelers would accrue to the broad waterways of the St. Lawrence.[31]

Yet an alternative to the prospects of American western commerce increasingly intrigued the *Globe*: the British Northwest might supply all the trade that the St. Lawrence route could handle. The opening of the Northwest was a project which offered at least as much to the western business man as to the western farmer. That fact was well recognized in the city of Toronto. For example, in December, 1856, the Toronto Board of Trade, under the presidency of W. P. Howland, took the lead in pressing for an inquiry into the Hudson's Bay Company's title to the western lands. The *Globe*, which had been urging this course of action, warmly praised the Board of Trade.[32] "Toronto," it said, "is better fitted by its situation than any other place to be the depot of the business of that country."[33] The connections between Gordon Brown, the editor of the journal, and Toronto business men who led in plans for opening the Northwest have already been noted. In fact, it is evident that the *Globe* in its well-known agitation for the acquisition of the Northwest had in mind the interests of western business as well as the land-hunger of the farmers. Westward expansion, besides meaning new farm-land and increased population to swamp Canada East, meant gaining a rich new trade: "The wealth of 400,000 miles of territory will flow through our waters and be gathered by our merchants, manufacturers and agriculturalists. . . . Every article of European manufacture, every pound of tropical produce will pass through our stores. . . . Our cities will be centres of its business and education, its health and refinement."[34] Here present-day western agrarianism might regard the *Globe* less as a sympathetic echo from an older agrarian community than as the prophetic voice of modern Ontario, looking forward to dominion over the people of the great plains. The newspaper pointed out the future market for manufacturers in the Northwest;[35] it urged that the Upper Canadian canals be enlarged for the great western carrying trade which would surely come.[36] It envisioned Toronto as "the great *entrepôt* between the east and west," exchanging the products of the prairies and the mines of Lake Superior for imported goods.[37] It even sought to arouse Montreal's interest in western expansion, recalling the great days of the North West Company and the fur trading empire built on the St. Lawrence,[38] and predicting, as later history proved, that once again the trade of the Northwest would continue by the St. Lawrence to the city that dominated the great river. Toronto could be the *entrepôt* between east and west; but as for the imperial city, Montreal, "the chief gains of the extension of western and north-western trade must go to the meeting place of ocean and river navigation."[39]

The *Globe*'s comprehension of a St. Lawrence commercial empire – as it actually came to be, over the Canadian, not the American West – reveals once again that its outlook took in more than the concerns of western agrarianism. Another illustration of this fact lies in its ardent support of free trade, although this was certainly a policy strongly favoured by the farmers of Upper Canada. "Let it never be forgotten," the *Globe* said, "that the Agricultural interest is the one great interest of our country; and that while it prospers there cannot be serious trouble."[40] Accordingly, the journal opposed protection for manufacturers, because, Canada was "a farmer's produce exporting country" and a protected home market would only raise the farmer's costs of production and hinder him in competing in the world market.[41] Yet this attitude was no different from that of western business men who lived by the prosperity of agriculture. It would be wrong to assume that, because some agitation for the protection of home industry could be found in Upper Canada during the Confederation era, the business community of the day should be identified with protection. If anything, the major and well established commercial interests, the wholesalers and importers, opposed the protectionist schemes of the newer manufacturing element. One might point to the protectionist movement of 1870, where the commercial leaders of Toronto largely ranged themselves against the industrialists. In a meeting of that year arranged among representatives of big Toronto firms to discuss protection, A.R. McMaster, nephew of William McMaster and himself high in the governance of McMaster interests, repudiated the protectionist trend; while J.G. Worts, whose name is almost identified with the rise of Toronto, asserted that Canada had progressed by adhering to free trade and should not abandon it.[42]

George Brown said somewhat the same thing when he told the Reform Convention of 1857 that free trade "lies at the roots of our commercial progress."[43]

Moreover, the *Globe*'s attacks on government fiscal policies which deviated from free trade were repeatedly couched in terms of the effects of these measures on the commercial interest of Upper Canada. In 1853, it attacked a tariff bill giving preference to the St. Lawrence route, claiming that the preference "was introduced into the bill in order that our [Upper Canada's] trade might be destroyed – that it might pass into the hands of the merchants and forwarders of Quebec and Montreal."[44] In 1859, it condemned a similar plan because it aimed, "to secure to Montreal importers in a single year the command of western markets; inflicting injury on every merchant of Toronto, Hamilton, and London. . . . The trade of this section will be crushed, its energy paralyzed."[45] The *Globe*'s opposition to preferential duties, then, was not solely an agrarian policy. Similarly, its opposition to protection for manufacturing did not mean that it thought only of an agricultural economy for Upper Canada. Instead it felt that Canada was not in a safe position as a staple-producing country dependent on external markets, and needed pursuits "less variable, liable to fewer fluctuations, and which besides would give employment to a greater number of hands in proportion to the capital invested."[46] Consequently, beyond its Cobdenite free trade dogmas, the *Globe* sought to promote "natural" industrial development, in which it included textiles, paper, shoes, and machinery[47] – and even locomotives, since British and American engines built for the Grand Trunk had proved "how inferior they were to those of home manufacture."[48] It urged greater Canadian participation in world industrial exhibitions in order to attract foreign capital, and to this end sought a government grant for entries in the London Exhibition of 1862, for it would be "disgraceful" if Canada did not take part.[49] Remarking on "abundant capital" in 1865, it pointed to new fields of investment in mining and manufacturing;[50] and from time to time painted bright pictures of Lake Superior iron and copper resources, or, in the early eighteen-sixties, of the oil fields in the western peninsula.[51]

But the *Globe*'s chief concern for the development of industry was to see it grow in the city of Toronto. "There can be no question," it said, "that the growth of the city of Toronto. . . depends almost exclusively on the facilities which can be offered for the establishment of manufactures."[52] Hence the city corporation should lease idle land to manufacturers at low rates. The *Globe* rejected the concept of Toronto as an agricultural capital and instead envisaged the city as the commercial and industrial metropolis of Upper Canada.[53] It observed that the local farming population did at one time provide the city with much of its business, but this retail trade was slowly shrinking, thanks to railways, as village merchants took it over. But the wholesale trade and manufacturing had no such limits; their customers were all over the province and would buy at whatever centre supplied the best range of goods and the most liberal terms; and these depended on the wealth and enterprise of each town. Toronto needed more of the wealth and enterprise which would come with manufacturing, if she were to gain control of the provincial market. "Toronto needs manufactures to make her great."[54] Here in the "agrarian" *Globe* was a perfect slogan for rising Toronto business.

The *Globe*'s constant attention to the interests of Toronto can also be seen in its concern with the development of the city's transportation facilities. Toronto was to plan itself as a port "not only for the provincial marine but for the mercantile marine of the empire," and build ships and a drydock to prepare for the flood of commerce that would come if the city realized its position as the key to the West.[55] The chief task, however, in improving Toronto's communications lay in the building of railways: "There is no question that Toronto is destined to be the great emporium of imported goods in western Canada, that its establishments will outnumber those of all other cities in number and importance; but the opening of railways will do more than this – it will make our city the great exporting harbour of Lake Ontario."[56] This was written in 1855, at the height of the Canadian railway boom; and the *Globe* then was thoroughly railway minded. In that year it hailed the opening of the Toronto-Hamilton link of the Great Western and the Grand Trunk's extension from the east into the city, since these two lines would overcome Hamilton's advantageous position as a wholesale centre for the western peninsula. In fact, Toronto could make the whole of Upper Canada its hinterland by building railways.[57] For this purpose, the *Globe* supported the Great Western, calling it "a brilliant success."[58] In the east, it suggested a "North-East Railroad" to divert to Toronto the trade going to the eastern towns of Upper Canada;[59] and in the north it looked to Toronto's first and very own railroad, the Northern, both to bring the through traffic of the prairie West and to extend Toronto's hinterland to the northern limits of the province. Many articles appeared in the *Globe* from 1852 on, defending "the Great Northern Route" from "a good deal of scepticism."[60] The newspaper described the benefits the Northern would bring to Toronto, ". . . when a large proportion of the produce of the prairies, the copper of Lake Superior, and the manufactures and imported goods of the Atlantic cities will pay dues in our harbour and be forwarded by the labour of our railwaymen – when the traveller from the Mississippi to the Atlantic . . . will pause in our city to observe its condition and gain strength for his onward journey."[61]

The height of the *Globe*'s railway fever, however, came in December, 1855, when a great "Railway Celebration" was held in Toronto upon the opening of the Toronto-Hamilton branch of the Great Western. The *Globe* was filled with civic pride: "The mercantile community of Toronto and those who will share in their prosperity consider that the construction of the Toronto and Hamilton Railway is to be to them a great benefit, and they desire to mark their sense of it in a way which will . . . serve as a memorial event. . . . As to the expense, we imagine if the people of Toronto see fit to spend twenty thousand pounds instead of ten thousand dollars in an entertainment, it is nobody's business. . . . Toronto is too large a place in the estimation of its own citizens to permit them to do anything in a shabby or mean manner."[62] George Brown spoke at the ensuing celebrations. He said, "if there is a country or a city that have reason to be grateful because railways are brought into operation, it is Canada and the city of Toronto."[63]

This wholly favourable view of railways seems a far cry from agrarian radical attacks on them as extravagant instruments of corrupt city finance. Yet the *Globe* very definitely took the latter line with regard to the Grand Trunk Railway. How can one reconcile the two sides of its railway policy? In the first place, by noting that the *Globe*'s friendly feeling was for railways which benefited Toronto; in the second, that its unfriendly feeling, to put it mildly, for the Grand Trunk, was for what seemed its mismanagement and corruption, especially when it benefited Montreal at Upper Canada's expense.[64] From the first, both Brown and the *Globe* had wanted a trunk line through Canada. In 1851, the newspaper said that "we are clearly in favour of building the road from Quebec to the St. Clair at all hazards,"[65] though shortly afterwards it objected to the cost of the proposed measures, and,in 1852, thought that Canadian capital should build the line.[66] In 1854, Brown was well advanced in his attacks on the Grand Trunk, but he declared that he would support the granting of aid to ensure the continuance of construction. Commenting on this, the *Globe* explained that Brown had opposed the agreement with Jackson and Company as "pregnant with evil," but now that the public credit was pledged to them felt it his duty to see the railway go forward.[67] The pattern of approving the line but attacking its management was continued in the following years. The *Globe*'s vendetta against the Grand Trunk therefore, was not inconsistent with its general zeal for railways, which may have lessened with the passing of the railway fever in the depression after 1857, but which was permanently linked to broad designs for commercial expansion. Thus in 1867 it was advocating the latest Toronto railway project, a line to reach Grey and Bruce, the westernmost part of the peninsula, saying that, "it is of great importance to the people of Toronto that some road to Grey and Bruce be built as soon as possible."[68] The *Globe* was still concerned with railways that were in the interests of Toronto.

The *Globe* also looked to Toronto business interests in its attitude to financial questions; and the "Silver Nuisance" controversy of 1865 supplies a most revealing example of this. In that year, depreciated American silver coin was flooding into Canada because it was still being accepted there at face value. The consuming public and the retailers were quite content to buy their goods with silver at par; the ultimate loss fell on the wholesalers and the large business men who accumulated the depreciated money. Accordingly, the business leaders in the large towns began a movement to accept American silver only at a 4 per cent discount. In Toronto, the Board of Trade made such a recommendation, and the chief business houses one by one began to put it into effect. But the retail merchants held out, and a popular counter-movement for "silver at par" grew up in the city. In the ensuing controversy of February and March, 1865, the *Globe* wholeheartedly supported the major business group and the silver-at-discount cause, backing it with many a learned disquisition on "sound finance" in the best tradition of classical economics. It rejected any solution which would "artificially" fix the value of silver when its real value had fallen: "If we could only get the idea out of the heads of people that there is something transcendental, mysterious, supernatural about the fluctuations in the currency, we should render an essential service to the country; because then we should soon ensure the conviction that gold, silver or copper coin will not, do what you like, legislate as you will, pass for more than their real value without creating loss. But while the habit is persisted in, of treating the metal dollars as removed above the laws of supply and demand which regulate other marketable commodities, confusion must be the inevitable result."[69] The *Globe* noted that Toronto's trade was controlled by forty or fifty business men, and addressed itself to them, asserting that if they would all adopt the silver discount, the lesser men would be forced to do the same.[70] It briefly advised its agrarian constituents not to deal with retailers taking silver at par, and went on to spend its efforts in the cause of the Toronto Board of Trade. On March 16, it was able to announce that all the banks, all the insurance companies, all the wholesale merchants but two, all the main downtown retailers and "the chief employers of workmen" were discounting silver. These constituted the core of Toronto business. The way in which the *Globe* identified itself with them was exhibited by its reaction to a mass meeting of March 20, which passed a resolution in favour of silver at par. This, the *Globe* said, merely "afforded ample proof of the difficulties of making the general public understand the details of a currency question." The "absurdities" of the silver-at-par enthusiasts had been "eagerly swallowed by a gaping crowd." It was no atmosphere for speeches on "sound principles of finance," such as the able one by Mr. Worts: "No banker, merchant, broker or general dealer spoke in favour of taking money at more than its value. They were all mechanics, with one exception, whose dealings do not enable them to see and understand the evils of the system which we have been pursuing."[71] As the *Globe* prophesied, the opinion of this meeting had no effect. By the end of the month, the power of the discounting group had settled the question in their favour. But the interesting point is that, throughout the "Silver Nuisance," the newspaper had thought it worthwhile to endorse so vigorously the stand of Toronto big business.

The *Globe*'s interest in the financial concerns of the business world appear again in regard to the question of usury, wherein Brown and his journal stood for "free trade in money" against Lower Canadian opposition and against some opposition in Upper Canada, including elements of Grittism. Brown succeeded in having a bill of his own passed in parliament in 1853 which amended the usury laws of the province so as virtually to repeal them, since the legal rate of interest was raised so high that it did not normally restrict the investment of capital. However, through the years that followed there were repeated attempts to lower the legal interest rate, based on wide French Catholic support. In Brown's steady fight against these efforts, we find him making strange allies in parliament, including John A. Macdonald, Galt, Rose, and other representatives of Montreal finance. The *Globe*, of course, echoed Brown's pronouncements. It objected to the usury laws because they turned capital from investment in Canada and sent it to the United States. Brown said the same thing: "If this country is to take its stand as a commercial community, if we mean to carry on great enterprises, individual as well as collective, private as well as public, we can only secure these objects by putting our citizens on the same sound footing as our neighbours."[72] Here was the argument of the capitalist and investing group as opposed to the debtor classes in Canada – and they are often identified in North America with the agrarian community. When opponents of Brown spoke on behalf of the debtors and specifically for the farmers, claiming that they must be protected by fixed low interest rates, he simply replied that legal enactments could not do it, and went to stress the needs of capital.[73] The *Globe* followed by condemning the "old fogeyism" of those who defended the "poor borrowers," and recommended to them "a little work on political economy by Miss Harriet Martineau."[74] As for the argument pressed in the Assembly in 1860, that the farmer could not afford the current interest rate of 8 per cent: ". . . let him not borrow at all if he cannot pay what the owner demands. Why should the capitalist be required to satisfy at a fixed price the possibly fancied wants of the farmer, mechanic or merchant?" The whole idea was "an insane project" smacking of the thirteenth century.[75]

The *Globe*'s financial ideas were generally of this sort: more fitted to the needs of large investors than to those of pioneer farmers. Certainly in its resolute defence of hard currency there was none of the "greenbackism" which has so often appeared in western debtor communities. It remarked that, "Paper money to the financial system is like narcotics to the body."[76] And it rejected the free banking system favoured in the American West in favour of conservative, stable chartered banks.[77] But a precise illustration of the *Globe*'s "sound business" view lies in the field of labour relations. Here George Brown, the farmers' friend, stands out as the Toronto business man, an influential employer of labour in the city, with a somewhat stormy record of relations with his workmen: while his newspaper works steadily to publicize the employer's case. In the eighteen-forties Brown had led in organizing the newspaper owners of Toronto to reduce wages. In the fifties, he fought unionism in the printing trade, again by organizing the employers, and faced strikes at the *Globe* in 1853 and 1854. In the latter year, having combined the master printers, he had the workmen who combined to strike arrested and fined a penny a piece for conspiracy. The sum was nominal, but the precedent was established for Brown's conduct in the great printers' strike of 1872. The *Globe* backed its master's labour policy, often by invoking the inalienable laws of laissez-faire individualism on behalf of the employers. For instance, writing of the failure of the Engineer's strike in England in 1852, the *Globe* said:". . . nearly a million sterling has been deducted from the fund for the payment of wages by those whose great aim was artificially to raise wages. . . . The result of their stupid and blundering machinations has been to humiliate them far below their former level. . . . Such has been the abortive folly and the suicidal mischief of the proceedings of the unionists."[78] At home, however, it was apparently not sufficient to leave the possibility that the Canadian journeyman tailors might combine to resist the introduction of sewing machines to the inexorable operation of economic laws:". . . we trust . . . there will be no combinations among the workmen; if they are formed, it will be the duty of the employers and the officers of the law to resist them to the utmost, and of the community to give its support."[79] Although the *Globe* faced no more strikes between 1854 and 1872, its views remained the same. It warned the workmen against "all attempts to fly in the face of unbending laws of commerce."[80] It cited the horrible example of the British steel industry, which was being overcome by Belgian competition because unionism had raised its costs of production.[81] It proved that the Eight Hour Law of 1867 in New York State could not help the workmen much, though it might "easily betray them . . . into very foolish strikes and very wicked violence."[82]

The *Globe's* care for the common man, it seems, only began at the city limits. The fact that it referred to the "intelligent yeomanry" of the countryside, and to the "gaping crowd" in the city, may indicate less a natural affinity for farmers than a natural distrust of propertyless workmen. Or it might reveal a belief in the harmony of interest between solid rural proprietors and urban men of property that would enable the *Globe* to espouse the cause of rural democracy. In any case, it should be evident by now that, although the urban *Globe* might ally itself with agrarian radicalism, its general viewpoint was not one of Jacksonian or Jeffersonian democracy. Proving this point involves a further question: what body of ideas did the opinions of the journal represent? If the *Globe* voiced urban Liberalism, not agrarian democracy, in what tradition of thought did it lie?

III

Regarding the general pattern of the *Globe's* thought, one must say first that its political ideas could not fairly be called "democratic," as the word was understood in North America of that day. It was liberal, no doubt. But it was even whiggish in its adulation of the British constitution, slowly broadening down from the Glorious Revolution, and in its distrust of the "constitution-mongering," the sweeping democratic programme of the early Clear Grits. From an initial condemnation of the first Grit platform of 1850, which sought to make Canada a complete American democracy with a fully elective government, to the successful campaign against an elective Upper House in the new federal constitution, the *Globe* set its face against "republican institutions." But above all, the journal opposed a doctrine which lay at the heart of North American democracy – universal suffrage, the right of every man to share in the control of government. The *Globe* attacked universal suffrage in France as the foundation of tyranny,[83] and in America coupled it with slavery: "The United States, with universal suffrage, sell their children for slaves in the market place."[84] Essentially, Brown and the *Globe* wanted a limited suffrage embodying some property qualification and recognizing "intelligence."[85] They were at considerable pains to prove that representation by population was not an American principle, but was in some degree observed in Britain;[86] while the acceptance of representation by population by the coalition of 1864, Brown affirmed, in no way implied acceptance of universal suffrage.[87] The *Globe* condemned the American system where, at elections, "The balance of power is held by the ignorant unreasoning mass." It agreed that the franchise in Canada undoubtedly should be widened, but thought increased education should go with its extension, since, "the lower we go in the scale of suffrage the more we add to that dangerous element." "In view of these facts we are not willing to travel quite so fast or so far in the democratic path as some of our friends."[88] This cautious position, tying education and the recognition of property and intelligence into franchise reform, is reminiscent of middle-class Liberalism in Victorian England; and the *Globe* was especially sympathetic to middle-class interests in British politics. Gordon Brown, writing for the *Globe* from England in 1851, described the middle-class Liberals in the House of Commons as: ". . . portly, heavy men, with full bulk and great temples of intellect generally, the merchants, almost always self-made men, who take an enlarged, liberal view of public affairs from the extent of their transactions and scope of action in private business and who yet are eminently practical and attentive to detail. They make the best legislators."[89] In Canada, there was no need for the *Globe* to look so definitely to a similar middle-class, propertied group, because, as it often said, in Canada all could be men of property. Yet its attitude towards the rising urban and industrial proletariat, which contravened that statement, showed that essentially it did not take a democratic position but believed in the political virtues of property. It saw its rural followers as property-owners – they were not "mere leaseholders," it said – and its confidence in their intelligence was largely because they did have property.[90]

Yet does this trust in rural property-owners bring the *Globe* in line with North American democratic thought as expressed by Jefferson?

One could say that once again it demonstrated the journal's reliance on agrarian support; but it did not constitute an expression of Jeffersonian beliefs. The *Globe* had none of Jefferson's distrust of industrialism, or of the commercial classes, and, far from deploring the great power of urban communities, was associated with the rise of the chief city in Canada West. It did not look to the placid rule of simple farm proprietors, and a sort of bucolic Utopia, but to a hard-driving partnership of rural and urban men of property in which the latter led. And, of course, the *Globe*'s feelings for democracy itself were decidedly qualified. Nor does Jacksonian frontier democracy fare any better as a frame for *Globe* opinion. There is too much that will not fit: its rejection of the elective principle – a frequent frontier solution for political domination by propertied groups – its close associations with the business world, its stress on the interests of capital and sound finance rather than those of an agrarian debtor community. Moreover the *Globe* does not fit the Jacksonian tradition as redefined by Mr. Arthur Schlesinger, Jr. He treats three main currents which came together in Jacksonianism – Jeffersonianism, of which we have already disposed, a growing belief in state intervention, and the rising labour movement.[91] To say the least, the *Globe* was unfriendly to the last two.

If, however, the *Globe* does not fit in easily with the ideas of North American agrarian democracy, it falls in readily with the Liberalism of Cobden, Bright, and other middle-class business men in mid-Victorian British politics – the men the journal so much admired. Its admiration for Cobden himself was somewhat restrained by his anti-imperial views. But the imperialist *Globe* found in Gladstone a worthy exponent of all that was best in the Manchester School, together with a proper acceptance of the imperial bond. The *Globe*'s interest in material development and retrenchment at the same time, its stress both on popular rights and on the danger of an unpropertied, uneducated democracy, its concern for laissez-faire business enterprise and its distrust of the labour movement, its devotion to free trade – all these leading aspects of *Globe* opinion accord perfectly with the doctrines of British middle-class Liberalism of the mid-Victorian Liberal thought to the North American scene.

This transfer of ideas is partly to be explained by the character of the men behind the newspaper. George Brown himself was raised in the atmosphere of Nonconformist, middle-class British Liberalism. Associated with him in the early years of the *Globe* was his father, Peter Brown, a Scots merchant turned journalist and a veteran Liberal of the days before the great Reform Bill. The two Browns were Free-Kirk Presbyterians. They entered eagerly into the battle for the separation of church and state in Canada, a question that was exercising Nonconformist Liberals in Britain too, although it hardly echoed in the contemporary American climate of opinion. The *Globe* was kept in close touch with British Nonconformity. This contact, together with others – plentiful copying from English journals, regular correspondence from England, and frequent visits there by *Globe* representatives to cover special events – helps to explain further how British doctrines were transmitted through the pages of the newspaper.[92] Nevertheless, even its close contact with British sources does not fully explain the fact that the *Globe* was such a ready medium for transferring urban British Liberalism to a fundamentally agricultural North American society. If, as the agrarian approach has held, the *Globe* represented the outlook of a pioneer farming community, would this be a favourable environment for doctrines that stemmed from a highly developed industrial and commercial society? However, if instead the *Globe* represented urban business and professional elements in Upper Canada, as well as back-country farmers, then this problem in the transference of ideas disappears. The journal found itself not in the midst of the agrarian frontier, but at the centre of a thriving business community, within a rising metropolis; and it had its interests very much at heart. This is not to equate Upper Canada merchants with the mighty entrepreneurs of Victorian Britain, nor to consider Toronto as a backwoods Manchester. It is enough that the doctrines of urban, middle-class British Liberalism would be naturally qualified to express the interests of the urban, middle-class *Globe*.

The original manifestations of the Clear Grit movement may have expressed democratic impulses common to the North American agrarian frontier, though one might ask how far the transference of British ideas also operated here, to infuse Grit radicalism with the views of the Chartists and philosophical radicals. In any case, even granting that the ordinary Clear Grit was a North American farmer, naturally affected by the common western American environment, the fact remains that the

Globe, despite its strong rural interests and close rural affiliations, dwelt in an urban setting and in a city traditionally devoted to all things British. In such a position, it was particularly open to the transfer of British Liberal ideas, which it then expounded to a western constituency that did not find them alien. In fact, thanks to the *Globe's* prestige in Upper Canada, and to the political eminence of its proprietor, it could do much to direct and re-shape the thoughts of the farming population which it led. That, at least, is one explanation for the decisive change in the character of the Clear Grits between 1850 and 1867. Beginning in 1850 as an extreme radical faction, displaying sympathy for American ideas (for which "Yankee republicanism" they were roundly attacked by the *Globe* among others), by 1867 they had become a respectable colonial Liberal party, devoted to the Crown and the British constitution, and for nearly a half-century after Confederation they controlled Ontario, the most vociferously loyal and British of all the provinces. Surely it is probable that the great influence of Brown and his newspaper over the Clear Grits had a good deal to do with this metamorphosis. The *Globe* took over the intellectual leadership of Grittism as Brown and his Toronto associates took control of the party. In many ways they brought "Tory Toronto" to western agrarianism; and, as Professor D.C. Masters has pointed out, the *Globe* was strongly sympathetic to much that was basic in Toronto Toryism – its pro-British and Protestant predilections and its anti-American and anti-French prejudices.[93] The *Globe's* intellectual home as well as its physical abode was Toronto – the aggressive, energetic western town, with an inferiority complex regarding both Montreal and the United States. That the *Globe* was able to take over the leadership of the farmers of Canada West, to bring them increasingly to look to Toronto, and to influence their thinking along lines of Victorian Liberalism, is in part a demonstration of the growing power of urban and business interests in the western section after 1850, and, particularly, of the rise of Toronto.

These, then, are the qualifications which must be included in any judgment made of the *Globe* on the strength of its close association with the farmers of Canada West during the Confederation era. The newspaper was not the voice of the pioneer settlements, but of wealthy farmers, enterprising western merchants, and Toronto business and professional men, all of whom shared in the leadership of the Upper Canadian sectional interest. The *Globe*'s outlook was not that of the agrarian democrat, but of the urban Liberal. And it spoke not in the words of the American frontier but in the language of Cobden and Gladstone. Thus should the urban side of the *Globe* be used to qualify the view that the newspaper and the movement it led must be described in terms of agrarian radicalism.

Endnotes

1. F.H. Underhill, "Some aspects of Upper Canadian Radical Opinion in the Decade before Confederation" (Canadian Historical Association, *Annual Report*, 1927, 47). But see also F.H. Underhill, "Some reflections on the Liberal Tradition in Canada" (Canadian Historical Association, *Annual Report*, 1946).
2. G.W. Brown, "The Grit Party and the Great Reform Convention of 1859" (*Canadian Historical Review*, Sept., 1935, 253-4).
3. Underhill, "Some Aspects of Upper Canadian Radical Opinion," 61.
4. D.C. Masters, *The Rise of Toronto, 1850-1890* (Toronto, 1947), 2. See this work throughout for the rest of this paragraph, and also S.D. Clark, *The Social Development of Canada* (Toronto, 1942), 223-4.
5. Toronto *Globe*, Apr. 12, 1867.
6. *Ibid.*, Mar. 5, 1897.
7. A. Frazer, *History of Ontario* (2 vols., Toronto, 1907), I, 442.
8. A. Macdonnell, *The North West Transportation, Navigation and Railway Company: Its Objects* (pamphlet, Toronto, 1858).
9. *Globe*, May 8, 1867.
10. *Morgan's Parliamentary Companion* (Toronto, 1869, 1874).
11. *Globe*, Aug. 19, 1862.
12. *Ibid.*, Aug. 18, Apr. 26, 1865. See also *Kentiana* (Chatham, 1939), 99-100.
13. W.H. Higgins, *The Life and Times of Joseph Gould* (Toronto, 1887).
14. *Globe*, July 22, 1856.
15. Brown, "The Grit Party and the Great Reform Convention," *passim.*
16. Public Archives of Ontario, Clarke Papers, G. Sheppard to C. Clarke, Oct. 27, 1859, Nov. 27, 1859.
17. *Ibid*, G. Sheppard to C. Clarke, Nov. 27, 1859.
18. See *Globe*, Nov. 24, 1860, Aug. 17, 1855 (weekly).
19. *Ibid.*, Feb. 11, 1851.
20. *Ibid.*, Feb. 19, 1852.
21. *Ibid.*, June 28, 1855, Brown rejected dissolution as "ruinous and wrong" and sought "a genuine legislative union" through representation by population. Letter to L.Holton, Jan. 29, 1858, in A. Mackenzie, *The Life and Speeches of the Hon. George Brown* (Toronto, 1882), 194.

22. *Globe,* June 28, 1855. See also June 13, 1855 (weekly) and Aug. 24, 1855 (weekly).
23. *Ibid.,* July 27, 1855 (weekly).
24. *Ibid.,* July 21,1858.
25. Clarke Papers, Nov. 27, 1859, Dec. 4, 1859.
26. *Globe,* Nov. 16, 1859.
27. *Ibid.,* July 10, 1852.
28. *Ibid.*
29. *Ibid.,* May 12, 1855.
30. *Ibid.,* Mar. 12, 1850.
31. *Ibid.,* Feb. 26, 1855, Dec. 5, 1856.
32. *Ibid.,* Dec. 4, 1856.
33. *Ibid.,* Dec. 13, 1856.
34. *Ibid.,* Jan. 22, 1863.
35. *Ibid.,* Feb. 5, 1863.
36. *Ibid.,* Feb. 20, 1864.
37. *Ibid.,* Feb. 10, 1855.
38. *Ibid.,* Jan 6, 1857.
39. *Ibid.,* Feb. 3, 1863.
40. *Ibid.,* Sept. 10, 1857.
41. *Ibid.,* Nov. 6, 1852.
42. Masters, *Rise of Toronto,* 105-6.
43. *Globe,* Jan.16, 1857.
44. *Ibid.,* Apr. 30, 1853.
45. *Ibid.,* Mar. 11, 1859.
46. *Ibid.,* Aug.11, 1863.
47. *Ibid.,* July 17, 1865.
48. *Ibid.,* Aug. 26, 1856.
49. *Ibid.,* Aug. 2, 1861.
50. *Ibid.,* Oct. 11 and Oct. 21, 1865.
51. See the *Globe*'s special reports from the oil districts through 1862 and 1863.
52. *Globe,* Feb. 17, 1862.
53. *Ibid.,* Jan.3 and Jan. 10, 1857.
54. *Ibid.,* Feb. 17, 1862. See also Feb. 3 and Feb. 13, 1860.
55. *Ibid.,* Jan. 3, 1857.
56. *Ibid.,* Oct. 26, 1855 (weekly).
57. *Ibid.,* Oct. 12, 1855 (weekly).
58. *Ibid.,* Sept. 14, 1855 (weekly).
59. *Ibid.,* June 1, 1852.
60. *Ibid.,* Aug. 24, 1855 (weekly).
61. *Ibid.,* Feb. 10, 1855 (weekly).
62. *Ibid.,* Dec. 14, 1855 (weekly).
63. *Ibid.,* Dec. 28, 1855 (weekly).

64. The *Globe* attacked the Grand Trunk as a Montreal instrument, levying a toll on every "business man in the Upper Province," Jan. 22, 1867.
65. *Globe, ibid.*, Aug. 11, 1851.
66. *Ibid.*, Oct. 23, 1852.
67. *Ibid.*, Dec. 1, 1854.
68. *Ibid.*, June 7, 1867.
69. *Ibid.*, Feb. 14, 1865.
70. *Ibid.*, Feb. 18, 1865.
71. *Ibid.*, Mar. 22, 1865.
72. *Ibid.*, May 19, 1857.
73. *Ibid.*
74. *Ibid.*
75. *Ibid.*, Mar. 13, 1860.
76. *Ibid.*, Feb. 8, 1862.
77. *Ibid.*, Nov. 4, 1857.
78. *Ibid.*, July 10, 1852.
79. *Ibid.*, Dec. 7, 1852.
80. *Ibid.*, Nov. 23, 1864.
81. *Ibid.*, Feb. 7, 1867.
82. *Ibid.*, May 14, 1867.
83. *Ibid.*, Jan. 1, 1850.
84. *Ibid.*, Jan. 27, 1859.
85. *Ibid.*, Jan. 28, 1851, Dec. 12, 1857, Sept. 23, 1857.
86. *Ibid.*, Dec. 9, 1856, Apr. 12, 1861, July 24, 1861.
87. *Ibid.*, June 23, 1864.
88. *Ibid.*, Sept. 23, 1857.
89. *Ibid.*, Sept 11, 1851. See also Sept. 12, 1857.
90. *Ibid.*, Mar. 31, 1863.
91. A.M. Schlesinger, Jr., *The Age of Jackson* (Boston, 1946), 306-21.
92. F.H. Underhill, "Canada's Relations with the Empire as Seen by the Toronto 'Globe' 1857-1867" (*Canadian Historical Review*, June, 1929).
93. Masters, *The Rise of Toronto*, 80.

The Globe.

VOL. IX. NO. 127 — TORONTO, CANADA WEST, THURSDAY, OCTOBER 21, 1852 — WHOLE NO 934

FRANCIS H. HALL, [illegible]

PATRICK FREELAND [illegible]

J. LEWIS [illegible]

JOHN W. GWYNNE [illegible]

[illegible]

WILLIAM HUME BLAKE [illegible]

SIMMONDS & Co.

LOCKPORT COOPERS' TOOLS.

TURNER & ROGERSON, General Commission Merchants

WELLINGTON HOTEL

REMOVAL.

No. 1, ST. JAMES BUILDINGS, KING STREET EAST.

JOHN TULLY, ARCHITECT, CIVIL ENGINEER, AND PROVINCIAL LAND SURVEYOR, KING STREET EAST.

ELIAS BURNHAM, Barrister and Attorney-at-Law

T. HENRY INCE, ATTORNEY-AT-LAW, SOLICITOR IN CHANCERY, Conveyancer, &c. &c., TORONTO.

MESSRS. LEACH & PAUL, VETERINARY SURGEONS, QUEEN STREET, TORONTO.

J. FOGGIN, DYER AND SCOURER

CARD. MR. R. G. PAIGE. MUSICAL EDUCATION.

HENDERSON & USHER, AUCTIONEERS, And General Commission Merchants

GENERAL AGENCY. Life, Fire & Marine Insurance

MRS. POTTER'S SHIRT ESTABLISHMENT, No. 60, KING STREET WEST.

WHITMAN & WHITLOCK

TORONTO EYE DISPENSARY.

FALL ADVERTISEMENT. M. ROSSIN & BROTHER.

JEWELLERY & FANCY GOODS. GOLD & SILVER WATCHES.

FOR SALE.

L. H. PHILLIPS & Co., LIQUID SALE MANUFACTURERS

WILLIAM ROSS & CO. IMPORTERS OF GROCERIES & LIQUORS, 12, Yonge Street.

Timothy Seed. Clover Seed. Wool.

MR. C. T. [illegible], Historical and Portrait Painter

WINES, &c.

TURNER & ROGERSON

ALEXANDER SMITH

CHURCH OF ENGLAND PROPRIETARY SCHOOL.

The Toronto Ladies' School.

FOR SALE. CENTREVILLE MILLS.

COAL GRATES.

TRINITY COLLEGE, TORONTO. Lectures in the Faculty of Medicine

TRADE SALE of Teas, Sugars, Tobacco, Groceries, &c.

WANTED IMMEDIATELY.

LONDON PUBLICATIONS

WANTED.

THE WEEKLY LINE OF STEAMERS TO ROCHESTER.

ROUTE TO NEW YORK!

THE STEAMER "ADMIRAL"

STEAM COMMUNICATION BETWEEN New York & Glasgow

Toronto Building Society

Home District Building Society. ANNUAL MEETING.

ELECTION OF DIRECTORS.

ONTARIO MARINE & FIRE INSURANCE COMPANY

MONEY!

Provincial Parliament. LEGISLATIVE ASSEMBLY.

[illegible]

The Toronto Globe, *1852. Editorials were on page two.*

Mid-Victorian Liberalism in Central Canadian Newspapers, 1850–67

IT WOULD BE CLEARLY INADEQUATE to assess the cultural life of a modern community through its newspapers. Yet such an approach seems necessary for an understanding of the intellectual development of the English-speaking half of the Province of Canada in the mid-nineteenth century. In the eighteen-fifties and sixties Canada West, the future Ontario, was just emerging from the all-embracing pioneer struggle. A raw young community, it imported the bulk of its books and ideas and was almost without native literary expression. However, it did have its own press. Journalism may often be a rather dubious form of literature, but investigators must work with what is available. Hence the Central Canadian press of the Confederation era is particularly significant because there is little else with which to test the mind of the Canadians in this crucial period when the modern Canadian state was coming into existence. And the thoughts and opinions dominant in these years were vitally important in shaping the future national character.

It is also true that, although much smaller and simpler, the Canadian newspapers of this era were generally of a higher intellectual calibre and of greater influence in their community than most of our modern journals. The nineteenth century was perhaps the golden age of the press, when the reading public, undistracted by the competing charms of radio, movies, and television, gave a single-minded attention to its newspapers. This was the age of great political journalists – in Canada, of editors like William Lyon Mackenzie and George Brown – when readers hung eagerly on the word of these lords of opinion and did not escape to the sports page, the comic strips, or to a confusion of syndicated columnists. The Canadian press of a century ago was of major importance in mirroring the mind of the community, and in helping to shape it as well.

For the purpose of a paper, not a book, any discussion of this press must be drastically limited in scope. Accordingly, it is possible here to examine only the Toronto journals among the many published in Central Canada in these years. There is reason in this, however, even for non-Torontonians. It is useful to choose a complete community of newspapers for analysis, and what more suitable than that of the chief city of Canada West, its political, economic, and intellectual centre, whose principal journals had the largest circulation in the province? Furthermore, during this mid-century period the Toronto press was taking on a metropolitan character and attaining a province-wide circulation, thanks to the advent of railways, cheap postage, and the rise of Toronto itself towards metropolitan stature. The English-speaking Montreal papers could not hope to gain so wide a constituency. Leading Hamilton, London, Ottawa, or Kingston journals might each have a large local circulation. The Toronto press, however, entered all these areas, and two of its members, the *Globe* and *Leader*, stood out over all the province as the giants of Canadian journalism, quite comparable in circulation to important British and American papers of the day.

The other main newspapers in Toronto between 1850 and 1867 were, on the Reform or Liberal side, the *North American* and the *Examiner*, and, on the Conservative, the *Patriot* and the *British* or *Daily Colonist*. The *North American* was established in 1850 as the organ of the new Clear Grit radical movement. The *Examiner* was a much older paper, founded in 1838 by Francis Hincks to fight the battle for responsible government. But by the mid-century mark, its place as the chief Reform newspaper had been usurped by the *Globe*, begun in 1844 by the energetic young George Brown. Largely in retaliation, the *Examiner* tended to make common cause with the *North American* against Brown and his journal. In the early fifties the *Globe* battled hard against the alleged extremism of these Clear Grit partners. In fact, it scorned the very name "Clear Grit," until, after the shattering of the Reform party by the Liberal-Conservative coalition of 1854, the Brownite and Clear Grit groups came together to oppose the coalition ministry, and gradually accepted the name of "Grit" for a watered-down version of original Clear Grit radicalism.

The Toronto *Leader* was founded in 1852 as a moderate Liberal organ. In 1854 it followed the Hinksite Liberals into the coalition with the Conservatives, and henceforth espoused the Liberal-Conservative ministerial cause against the *Globe* and the opposition forces of Reform. Nevertheless for years the *Leader* claimed to be upholding true and pure Liberalism against the wild-eyed, factious followers of George Brown. The *British Colonist* was avowedly Conservative, but more moderate in its Conservatism than the *Patriot* which was, on the whole, the Orangemen's organ, the fervent defender of the British tie and the glorious memory of King William III.

The *Examiner* and *North American* were bought out by the *Globe* in 1855, the *Patriot* by the *Leader* in 1854. The *Colonist* died of malnutrition in 1858. For most of the period, accordingly, the *Globe* and *Leader* held the field between them. The most significant point emerging from an analysis of these two powerful newspapers, the two main organs of the opposing sides in politics, is that they shared the same general framework of ideas. They looked to British institutions and precedents, turned their backs on things American, and accepted the chief political and economic doctrines of contemporary mid-Victorian Britain. In fact, mid-Victorian Liberalism, seems the best term to describe the pattern of their thought and opinions. To the left of the *Globe*, the *Examiner* and *North American* were plainly more liberal or radical than British. To the right of the *Leader*, the *Colonist* and *Patriot* were more British than Liberal. But in general, this pattern of mid-Victorian Liberalism, though admittedly fraying at the edges, may be applied to the whole Toronto newspaper community during the Confederation era. Here was British thought deep in North America, in the most influential press in Canada, and at a critical time in her history. Its meaning deserves investigation.

To make such an inquiry, one might follow many threads of ideas through the questions discussed in these journals, but there is room to deal with only a few main aspects of their opinions. Those most in evidence concern the value which they placed on British political institutions and ideas, their acceptance of Cobdenite economic doctrine, and the stress they laid on issues involving the relations of church and state. Turning to the first of these topics, we are immediately struck by the amount of time spent in the Toronto journals in weighing the relative merits of the British and the American political systems, to the detriment of American democracy. Since Canada had won the right to govern herself in internal affairs by 1850, the question of how to use this right naturally assumed a new importance. Was the British technique of responsible cabinet government, used to win autonomy, a sufficient end in itself or only a means to further political change? Now that Canadians governed themselves, should they adopt new political machinery?

It is true that the *North American,* at least, did accept the American version of democracy. Indeed, it was founded to press for further political change and for new democratic machinery in Canada. This paper and its early Clear Grit associates declared for complete "elective institutions" – an elected governor, upper house, and local officials, and full manhood suffrage. The "aristocratical" forms of the British constitution were deemed unsuited to North America. It was argued that without a written constitution and the separation of powers, ministries were too powerful, extravagant, and corrupt. The state governments of New York or Ohio were urged as the true models to follow.[1] The *Examiner* echoed the *North American* in this Clear Grit crusade, but with less grasp of theoretical arguments and much harking back to the good old days of the Reform party under William Lyon Mackenzie.[2] Mackenzie, incidentally, was a frequent contributor to its pages during the early fifties.

The rest of the press, however, was at least equally fervent in defence of British institutions. The *Patriot* and *Colonist* boiled with indignant loyalty. The *Leader* and *Globe* set out to prove the superiority of the British system in liberty, efficiency, and honesty, and the worthlessness of American republicanism. In fact, these papers were quite ready to indict one another with the most damning charge of all: a leaning towards American ideas. Thus the *Colonist* somehow found that the "prosaic manderings" of the *Leader* were too close to the American "ravings of ultra-republicanism,"[3] even though the *Leader* had earlier been attacking "republican equality" as a state "where all men are born free and equal, with certain black exceptions," and had characterized the position of the President of the United States as "the slave of the Rabble."[4] And the *Patriot,* as always, expressed a most decided faith in Canadian Conservatism, "which clings to the *British constitututional* system of Government as superior to all others, believing it to possess within itself those inherent principles of elasticity and vigor which adapt to the various circumstances of the people, and enable it to meet, with becoming vigor and suitableness, the increased intellectual and progressive knowledge of the country."[5]

Yet since the main concern of this present discourse is with the Liberal side, it is perhaps most significant that the Toronto *Globe* was so definite, so explicit, and so well informed in arguing the case in favour of the British system of government. This was the largest Liberal journal, the one which soon absorbed the heretical *North American* and *Examiner,* but kept no part of their doctrines; the paper which became identified with the Reform cause, but underlined the British affiliations of Liberalism in rebuilding the Reform party. During the years 1850 to 1855 the issue of elective institutions was a major one in Central Canadian politics, although one somewhat neglected by our historians. This issue was exhaustively canvassed by the *Globe,* which tirelessly upheld the British model.

It is true that later, in 1859, the year of gloom and frustration after the failure of the Brown-Dorion government, the *Globe* did toy with written constitutional checks and elected ministries as the solution to Canada's political difficulties; but it soon turned its back on these to offer a combination of responsible government and federation as the way out. And when Confederation became not a distant possibility but a definite project, George Brown's journal again insisted on the British system as the basis for a national government. In fact, it favoured the federal principle as a device which would permit Canada to retain the virtues of the British parliamentary constitution while meeting the North American problem of sectionalism.[6]

The *Globe*'s viewpoint on the constitution appears most clearly with regard to an elected upper house. At the time of Confederation, the paper strongly urged that the new federal senate be not elected but appointed, since under the British parliamentary system a second chamber should have only a minor role of amending and delaying, and should not be able to thwart the national will of the much more significant house of commons. Two elected houses on the American model, on the other hand, might claim a popular mandate, and if opposed to each other, deadlock the constitution.[7]

This was the same stand that the *Globe* had taken in the early fifties when the campaign for an elected upper house for the Province of Canada was the main focus of the elective institutions question.[8] The paper had to fight this battle on two fronts. The Clear Grit journals desired an elective legislative council as a step towards the American democratic system. The Conservative press sought it for other reasons, in part because the existing nominated council was solidly entrenched with Liberal appointees, and also because an upper house elected on a highly qualified franchise would form a stronger bulwark against dangerous radical tendencies. Denying any subservience to Americanism, the Conservative papers could claim that an elected council was not an American innovation since it had been adopted in other British colonies far from the shores of the United States. Still the *Globe* viewed it as the thin edge of the Yankee wedge.[9] A majority composed of Clear Grits and some Conservative and Liberal elements managed to carry an act for an elective council in 1855, but the *Globe* had the satisfaction of seeing the measure undone at Confederation. And it is worth noting that at this later time the *Leader*, now the chief Conservative organ, agreed that an elected council had been a mistake, although it gave as its reason the danger of too much democracy if both houses were elected. And democracy, it said, meant "the dead level of forced and false equality."[10]

It is well to keep in mind that in Canada during the mid-nineteenth century democracy was still a suspect word, with Jacobin, or at any rate American, overtones. The Conservative journals would certainly have none of it, and both the *Leader* and *Globe* pointed to the evils of rule by the masses. "Our form of government is not a democracy," said the *Leader* during the American Civil War, "unbridled and uncontrolled . . . completely in the hands of the mob."[11] Only the *North American* was whole-hearted in its democratic faith. The *Examiner* declared "a plague on both your houses." It condemned indeed the "flunkeyism" of British society and government, but also attacked the "tyranny and slavery of the republican Americans."[12] If Britain had noblemen, the United States had slaves. In this, one is tempted to see the reaction of Mackenzie himself, soured first with Britain and then with the United States – as indeed he said he was, on his return to Canada from his American exile.

Both the *Leader* and the *Globe* in their view of democracy expressed the central position of mid-Victorian Liberalism. Both declared for a wide, popular electorate but still wanted a qualified franchise to recognize property and intelligence, and to prevent the rule of ignorance and mere numbers. The former journal, to be sure, attacked George Brown's doctrine of representation by population as an un-British principle of numbers,[13] but the latter denied that its cherished policy implied universal suffrage.[14] The *Leader* quoted from John Stuart Mill on the tyranny of the majority and urged plural votes for "the virtue of industry and thrift which acquires and preserves property."[15] The *Globe* rejected "that broad and tumultuous constituency which has no restriction in residence or property," and scorned "the unwashed multitudes who boast of universal suffrage."[16] It claimed besides that a limited franchise secured the truest expression of the public mind; while, "the lower we go in the scale of suffrage the more we add to that dangerous element."[17] The *Globe* also agreed with Liberals in Britain that the franchise should be extended no faster than public education, the Liberal panacea, could proceed.[18] In short, there was in this mid-century Canadian press little of the spirit of American Jeffersonian or Jacksonian democracy with their faith in the natural worth of the common man.

The economic views of these Canadian journals approximated as closely to the pattern of British mid-Victorian Liberalism as did their political views. The *Globe* was most fully and consciously Cobdenite in endorsing the British Manchester School philosophy of free trade and the reign of natural economic laws. Cobden, Bright, and their disciple at the Chancellory of the Exchequer, Gladstone, were its economic patron saints. The paper frequently discoursed on the evil of state interference with "the laws of trade," attacking usury laws especially, lectured on sound currency with many quotations from British classical economists, and viewed tariff protection as something between stupidity and sacrilege.[19] It need hardly be said that the *Globe* regularly condemned the United States protective tariff and any heretical protectionist tendencies in Canada.

Its views on labour relations and problems of social welfare were similarly orthodox: labour unions were not to infringe on the liberal right of free contract (this was especially so in the case of strikes at the *Globe* office); strikes could not raise wages artificially, "by flying in the face of nature"; and if the masses suffered in old lands, the only solution was to educate them to understand their lot as dictated by political economy, and to urge them to emigrate in order to enable the labour market automatically to adjust itself. The state should not step in. The *Globe*'s economic individualism was indeed tempered by humanitarianism, and it deplored the doctrinaire rigidity of the more extreme followers of Jeremy Bentham. These same qualifications, however, were being made in Britain within the general context of mid-Victorian Liberalism. In sum, the *Globe* found its authorities, doctrines, and proper practice in economic matters in contemporary Liberal Britain, and condemned any American deviations from the British norm.

The other journals were less explicit and less theoretical in setting forth their economic beliefs. Yet these can be gleaned from the attitudes they assumed towards practical issues in Canadian affairs. In commercial policy, for instance, the *North American* did not accept the prevalent United States model, and attacked "the antiquated notions of American Protectionists."[20] It wanted complete free trade and direct taxation, along with the abolition of customs duties. The *Examiner* shared this general position, praising Cobden, "the lion," for his sound political economy and his programme of free trade and retrenchment in Britain. At the same time it condemned the old protectionist imperial policy as a "clumsy system of mutual monopoly."[21] The *Patriot*, on the other hand, still looked back hopefully to the defunct colonial system, and, as a good old-fashioned Tory, opposed Whig-Liberal free trade in Britain or in Canada. Nevertheless it used the language of current economic liberalism in advocating the repeal of usury laws in Canada. Money should be left "to flow in its natural channels." The legislator had no more power to control profit than to prevent water finding its own level. "He cannot alter the law of nature."[22]

The Conservative *Colonist* held that it was hopeless for the *Patriot* to dream of Britain returning to protection, although it praised the Tories and "honest Protectionists" in England – always excepting Disraeli, whose sudden conversion to free trade in 1852 it thought "indecent."[23] The *Colonist*, however, did think that protection was both sound and feasible in the case of Canada; but felt that the practical course lay between British free trade and the American high tariff, through a tariff designed to create revenue and offer some measure of "incidental protection" at the same time.[24] In this matter the *Colonist* was, as usual, practical in its approach and middle-of-the-road in its decisions, seemingly less concerned than the other papers with the theoretical background of its policies.

The *Leader* also took the practical view with regard to Canadian trade policy: the colony needed the revenue derived from customs duties, and these might well be arranged to offer incidental encouragement to rising Canadian manufactures. In theory, however, it claimed to adhere to the liberal doctrine of free trade and rejected "the exploded theories of protection."[25] The *Leader* thus defended Galt's tariff of 1859 as a revenue measure, and not as protectionist in character, noting that even free-trade Britain still found it necessary to raise a large revenue by customs duties on non-essential articles. Canada could not be charged with adopting "a discarded policy of protection," because she, too, could not afford absolute free trade.[26] But the journal also recognized that "a young community that has just assumed the responsibilities of a separate national existence has many temptations to violate the principles of economic science," and so had to beware the protectionist "nonsense about the desirability of a nation doing everything for itself."[27]

The *Leader* used the proper liberal phrases on currency questions. It too paid homage to the water-level principle by pointing out that "money will go to the dearest market as sure as water flows down hill."[28] Any interference with the value of money was "absurdly injurious," as absurd as fixing food prices by state action; but "this mist of ignorance must soon go in this age of progress, of railroads and steam and sea-spanning telegraphs."[29] Yet towards the close of our period this paper still had to lament the fact that the Toronto Board of Trade was seeking to fix an "artificial" rate of discount for depreciated American silver coins in circulation in the city. Such an attempt showed "an ignorance of those economic laws which no Legislature can overrule."[30]

On labour questions the *Leader* again was orthodox liberal. Disliking the ideas and ideals of trade unionism, it agreed with the *Globe* that the co-operative movement was the true form of unionism for the working classes to pursue, one which permitted them to flourish as capitalists on their own behalf and did not lead them against the immutable laws of economic individualism. The *Leader* noted that co-operative societies were advocated by Cobden, a man "who perhaps did more for the working men of England than any statesman of his time."[31] But greater still, the *Leader* said, was the authority of John Stuart Mill. It gave long excerpts from Mill's *Political Economy* in support of co-operatives.[32] The trade union as a collective bargaining agency was not so well authorized, as far as the Toronto press was concerned, and the *Colonist*, indeed, referred to the strike of the Toronto Typographical Union of 1854 as "a gross and unreasoning assertion of power," an attempt by the strikers to assume arbitrary control for themselves.[33]

But a much more burning topic in the press of the Confederation era than the incipient Canadian labour movement, usury laws, currency questions, or even tariff problems, was the half-political, half-social issue of the relations of church and state. It had many ramifications. It involved in particular, after 1850, the agitation over the secularization of the clergy reserves, the alleged Lower-Canadian Catholic domination of Canadian politics, and the perennial separate school question. The separation of church and state was far from having been achieved in Canada West during this period. The resolve to fight for that principle led George Brown into active politics, brought him and the Clear Grit originals gradually together, and greatly influenced the character of the western Liberal party which grew under his leadership out of this alliance.

The separation of church and state was doubtless to a considerable extent a narrowly sectarian cry, leaving Brown and the *Globe* and their followers open in that day and to this to charges of bigotry. It was also, however, an essential belief in the mind of English-speaking Liberalism in mid-century Canada; and it was associated, above all, not with the

United States, where the separation of church and state had already been accomplished, but with the British background, where the struggles of Nonconformity with the state Church of England were very far from over.

In contemporary Britain, Nonconformity had moved on from an acceptance of religious toleration to a demand for religious equality. It was attacking the principle of establishment itself, urging against "state-churchism" the voluntary principle, that is, that churches should be voluntary organizations without state backing or recognition, so that religion might be kept out of politics and politics out of religion. The battle was joined especially in the field of education, where the "voluntaries" contended against Anglican control of state-supported schools. Voluntaryism (or voluntarism) was strong in British Liberalism, just as Nonconformity was strong in middle-class, Victorian Liberal ranks. Indeed, Edward Miall, a prominent member of the Manchester School, was editor of the powerful *Nonconformist,* a voluntaryist journal founded to work for disestablishment.

Voluntaryism was equally strong, or stronger, in Canada West. The *Globe,* in fact, observed that many of the Canadian Reformers had brought the voluntarist principle with them from Britain.[34] And, of course, George Brown and his father had themselves been vigorous exponents of voluntaryism in supporting the Free Church in Scotland on its break from the established Presbyterian body. In fact, they had come to Canada initially to found a journal (the *Banner*) on behalf of the Free Kirk party in the colony. Accordingly, in Canadian politics George Brown and the *Globe* contended against every manifestation of "state-churchism," and found many supporters.

In the eighteen forties they worked for the removal of the University of Toronto from Anglican control, and against attempts to divide the provincial endowment among sectarian colleges. After 1850 they strove for the secularization of the clergy reserves, and to prevent the passage of an increasing number of Lower Canadian "ecclesiastical bills" which, they claimed, implied state recognition of Roman Catholic institutions. Next they plunged into the rising separate school struggle, determined to defend the secular public school system of Canada West against sectarian inroads and "state-church" designs. And whether it was right or wrong in this regard, the Brownite stand was firmly based on the linked principles of voluntaryism – that no public funds should go to church schools – and the separation of church and state – that popular education was a matter for the state alone. For these principles the *Globe* looked to Britain, and found support for them among Victorian Liberals and Nonconformists.

Brown and the *Globe* made the voluntary movement in Canada very much their own. They began to build a new Liberal party about it. Yet the *North American* and *Examiner* also endorsed voluntaryism. The former early declared for "religious equality to the fullest extent," and on occasion railed against Lower Canadian Catholic influence in the state.[35] The latter became almost as bound up in the religious issue as the *Globe*. "Are we slaves to Popish Prelates?" it asked excitedly.[36] "Puseyite state parsons" of Anglicanism were also attacked.[37] "Let the people of this Province eschew the curse of a State-paid clergy of whatever name."[38] Indeed, the *Examiner*'s motto, from its inception in 1838, was "Responsible Government and the Voluntary Principle." William Lyon Mackenzie, closely associated with the *Examiner*, worked with George Brown in parliament on his return to the house in the eighteen fifties on at least one thing, the voluntaryist campaign. In this he was one of Brown's first parliamentary allies.

The rest of the Toronto press was not so voluntary-minded. The *Leader* approved the principle of the separation of church and state but stressed that the stand of the *Globe* and its followers was bigoted and so, illiberal. We prefer, it said, equality with Roman Catholics to domination by bigots.[39] At the same time this journal sought the secularization of the reserves, and was distressed by separate school bills that cut away at the state education in which it believed. Yet the *Leader* recognized a need of compromise with the powerful Catholic population in the province on the separate school issue. Here it was naturally voicing the view of the governing coalition between French- and English-speaking elements which it supported after 1854.

The *Colonist* could hardly agree with the *Globe*'s voluntaryism since it was the organ of the Church of Scotland Presbyterians who had held to the side of the established church in the old land. It also attacked the "state irreligion" of the *Leader*, and opposed the purely secular common schools that both *Globe* and *Leader* upheld, desiring some religious instruction in the curriculum.[40] The *Patriot* seemed to share the confusion on the religious issue of its Orange supporters, some of whom put "Protestant liberties" first and joined the voluntaryist Protestant Alliance, while others, stressing Tory allegiance, would have nothing to do with this Reform-inspired body. But at length the *Patriot* came down on the side of Toryism; and when Toryism and Orangism came shortly to rest in coalition with the Catholic Bleus, the question was closed for it. It was closed even more definitely by the sale of the *Patriot* to the *Leader* in that same year, the political *annus mirabilis,* 1854. Yet whether opposed or friendly to voluntarism, the Conservative journals like the rest dealt fully with the question of the relations of church and state, and with the frequent references to British precedents and British conditions.

Here lies the key to this major discussion in the mid-century press, to this question, as well as to those of political institutions and economic policies: the constant reference to British ideas. The same reference could be found elsewhere in the journals, on topics of social welfare, sabbatarian morality, and intellectual standards. The plain fact is that these newspapers felt strongly the sense of belonging to a British intellectual community, no less than of belonging to a physical British empire. They were in a stream of ideas emanating from Britain at the height of her power and prestige. Nor was this incompatible with their position in North America.

It is well to make clear that no sharp distinction is intended, or really can be made, between "British" and "American" intellectual influences on Canada at this time. The United States itself was then in many ways still a cultural colony of Britain, and ideas originating in Britain might conceivably come into Canada by way of their American modifications. British and American ideas were hence much of the same kind, but the question of the degree of difference is all important. It has here been suggested that most of the newspapers under discussion received their main ideas directly from Britain, and tended to reject any American differences and modifications. No doubt this was not wholly true. In matters, say, of agrarian policy or public education, Canadian opinion owed much to American inspiration, or to general North American experience. But in regard to major problems of government, economic policy, and the relations of church and state, the influential Toronto press – and hence the mind it influenced – expressed itself mainly in British terms. This fact represents a general transfer of British ideas to Canada, to the North American scene.

Qualifications, of course, are necessary. The *North American* was certainly more American than British in its feeling, in that day, for democracy. Yet this paper also claimed that it cared not if a doctrine was British or American as long as it was useful;[41] and there is reason to think that its democratic ideas had British as well as American roots. The writer who explained the *North American*'s original programme in a series of well-considered articles was Charles Clarke, an Englishman, whose first political memories were those of Chartism; and there were other Chartist affinities in early Clear Grittism.[42] American democratic examples were usually cited; but so they were by democratic radicals in Britain herself at the time, because the United States naturally supplied the working model of democracy.

The *Examiner* also advocated a pattern of democratic government. But much of its thought here went back to the early days of Mackenzie radicalism, which was certainly open to British influences as well as American, stemming from Hume and Roebuck as well as Andrew Jackson. And the *Examiner*, incidentally, was still receiving its British parliamentary papers from Joseph Hume in the eighteen fifties. Furthermore, in its economic and voluntaryist discussions, this journal looked to British, not American, leaders and precedents.

There seems little difficulty in linking the *Globe* and the *Leader* with British Liberal ideas, nor the Conservative papers at least with British ideas. Moreover, one should recall that the radical and Tory wings of the Toronto press in this period soon declined, leaving the essentially moderate Liberalism of the *Leader*, and of the *Globe*, for all its religious zeal, as most fully expressing the public opinion of the day. Whatever advertisements may bring or clever journalists contrive, in that day at least it was the newspapers with the less popular opinions that went under.

We are left, then, with the general view of a press that transferred its main opinions from Liberal Victorian Britain. Why so? The "colonial attitude of dependence" is not an answer, but merely re-words the question. The reaction against the apparent failure of the democratic experiment in the United States, collapsing into sectionalism in the fifties and aflame in civil war in the sixties, is a better reply, but only a partial one. A more complete explanation would first deal with the fact of British immigration. The great mass movement from Britain into Central Canada in the first half of the nineteenth century had virtually inundated the earlier English-speaking population in the country, which had had deeper North American roots. By 1850 the immigrants had firmly established themselves in their new community and thanks to their numbers had risen to the fore. The extent of their ascendancy in the ensuing period may be quickly recognized by noting how many contemporary Canadian public men, party leaders or Fathers of Confederation, for instance, had been born in Britain. Canada, perhaps, never before or since has been so British.

This was particularly true in the newspaper world, where journalists educated and frequently trained in Britain readily came to lead in what was still largely a half-taught, pioneer community. George and Gordon Brown of the *Globe*, Hugh Scobie, first owner of the *Colonist*, James Lesslie, owner of the *Examiner*, were Scots; Ogle Gowan of the *Patriot* and James Beaty of the *Leader* were Irish; Samuel Thompson, later proprietor of the *Colonist* and *Leader*, David Lindsey, editor at different times of the *Examiner* and *Leader*, and George Sheppard, similarly editor of the *Colonist* and *Leader*, were English. Only William McDougall, owner of the *North American*, was Canadian-born. In respect to this journal, there may be something in a name, after all. But the *Globe* boasted that all its editorial staff were from the old country.[43]

Another point of explanation might lie in the fact that in the mid-nineteenth century this Canadian community was, on the whole, more effectively tied into the British imperial system than it had ever been before or was to be thereafter. Responsible government had removed the main grievances of colonialism. Nationalism had not yet really developed. The British tie meant liberty, and security as well against the still threatening United States. Steamships and telegraphs had cut down the barrier of distance from Britain, but transcontinentalism had not yet arisen to turn Canada's eyes inward and along to the West. Central Canada was still a long narrow settlement along the St. Lawrence system that pointed to Britain and channelled every impulse from the imperial centre deep into the Great Lakes country.

And so it was with ideas. They were channelled from Britain by steamship and telegraph, or carried with the immigrants, who so influenced their community that it kept looking to the centre of the British world for the source of its thought. This is not merely to be called dependence. Feeling a unity with Britain, English-speaking Canadians accepted the bulk of her ideas as their own. Their newspapers evidently did the same. The result was the dominance of mid-Victorian Liberalism, seen in the press that has been examined. In the period, therefore, when the modern Canadian nation was being founded, English-speaking opinion in Central Canada was tending away from the exciting extremes of both radicalism and toryism towards a moderate, and no doubt stodgy, cast of mind. Have we lost all our Victorian Liberalism yet?

There is another note to be added. The transfer of British ideas observed in the case of these newspapers suggests an hypothesis for broader use in the study of Canadian history. Such an hypothesis was elaborated some years ago for the United States history by Dixon Ryan Fox.[44] He urged against the frontier thesis, which held that civilization was largely shaped in America by the influence of the West, that the major process in the development of the United States was the progressive transfer of European civilization across the Atlantic and from east to west. This concept of the "transit of civilization" is one of a number of qualifications which have been made to the frontier or native North American interpretation in United States history. One might suggest that the traditional time-lag has been operating long enough in Canadian history-writing. The North American view or stress in our history similarly needs qualifying now by a regard for the transit of civilization. This, in the case of English-speaking Canada, means largely a regard for the influence of transferred British ideas and institutions on our part of the North American scene.

If the history of Canada and the United States may be read broadly as an interaction of the American environment and imported cultures, then surely the transfer of ideas, even if a minor theme, is still more important for English-speaking Canada than for the United States. For we came into the environment later, kept our colonial ties longer; in fact, today we are largely marked off from Americans because we did so. That being the case, we largely exist as Canadians and have a separate identity because of the greater continuing influence which the transfer of ideas has exercised upon us. To such grand suppositions a paper on a few journals during a few short years may lead, though it can only suggest the hypothesis, not prove it.

Endnotes

1. *North American* (weekly), Oct. 30 to Nov. 22, 1850; Jan. 17, Feb. 14, 1851.
2. *Examiner* (weekly), Sept. 5, 19, 1849; May 31, 1854; Jan. 3, 1855.
3. *Daily Colonist,* Jan. 24, 1856. The daily edition of the *Colonist* was so titled. That issued three times a week was named the *British Colonist.*
4. *Leader* (daily), Aug. 14, Dec. 8, 1854.
5. *Patriot* (daily), May 24, 1853.
6. *Globe* (daily), Sept. 14, 1859; July 15, 1864.
7. *Ibid.*, Oct. 8, 20, 1864.
8. *Ibid.*, Mar. 23, 1852.
9. *Ibid.*, Oct. 31, 1850; Apr. 13, 1852; Mar. 24, 1854.
10. *Leader,* Oct. 3, 1864.
11. *Ibid.*, Jan. 25, 1862.
12. *Examiner,* July 25, 1855.
13. *Leader,* Apr. 3, 1865.
14. *Globe,* Apr. 12, July 24, 1861; June 23, 1864.
15. *Leader,* Oct. 3, 4, 1864.
16. *Globe,* June 1, 1850; May 19, 1865.
17. *Ibid.*, Jan.28, 1851; Sept. 23, 1857.
18. *Ibid.*, May 4, 1852.
19. See J.M.S. Careless, "The Toronto *Globe* and Agrarian Radicalism, 1850-67" (the preceding chapter of this book) for economic doctrines of the *Globe* relevant to this and the succeeding paragraph.
20. *North American,* Mar. 7, 1851.
21. *Examiner,* Jan. 30, 1850.
22. *Patriot,* Nov. 18, 1852.
23. *British Colonist,* Mar. 19, June 29, 1852.
24. *Ibid.*, Mar.19, 23, 1852.
25. *Leader,* Dec. 20, 1850.
26. *Ibid.*, Nov. 24, 254, 1859.
27. *Ibid.*, Feb. 18, 1862.
28. *Ibid.*, Jan. 2, 1857.
29. *Ibid.*, May 20, 1857.

30. *Ibid.*, Mar. 14, 1865.
31. *Ibid.*, May 5, 1865.
32. *Ibid.*
33. *Daily Colonist*, June 3, 1854.
34. *Globe*, Apr. 2, 1853.
35. *North American*, May 31, June 4, Dec. 13, 1850.
36. *Examiner*, July 11, 1855.
37. *Ibid.*
38. *Ibid.*, June 14, 1854.
39. *Leader*, Sept. 1, 1853.
40. *Daily Colonist*, Jan. 9, 24, 1856.
41. *North American*, Oct. 31, 1851.
42. Charles Clarke, *Sixty Years in Upper Canada* (Toronto, 1908), 13, 45, 58, 61.
43. *Globe*, Nov. 23, 1861.
44. See D.R. Fox, *Ideas in Motion* (New York, 1935), and D.R. Fox (ed.), *Sources of Culture in the Middle West* (New York, 1934), especially his introduction.

George Brown, circa 1858.

The Political Ideas of George Brown

CANADIAN POLITICAL FIGURES HAVE generally skirted the discussion of ideas and doctrine by wide platitudes. Not George Brown, however, the journalist-politician and Clear Grit Liberal leader of the Confederation era – he was born to argue principle. In his powerful Toronto *Globe*, the most widely circulated newspaper in British North America, he had the ideal instrument for expressing his mind, and for over three decades, from the first *Globe* issue in 1844 to his death in 1880, it presented a massive documentation of the thinking of George Brown. Others, of course, shared in writing its columns, especially after Brown entered parliament in 1852. Yet he kept such strong control that the journal regularly exhibited the consistent pattern of his thought, consistent too with his lengthy, closely argued speeches in the House and about the Ontario countryside. This pattern may be best described in terms of three main threads that ran through it: his creed of anti-state church Protestantism, his belief in free-trade, economic liberal doctrines, and his rooted preference for British parliamentary institutions over American republican models.

But to trace these threads to their beginnings, one must start in the classic way with the early life and family background of George Brown.

Born in Edinburgh in 1819, he grew up in the fervent atmosphere of reform movements that were striving to pry loose the dead hand of the eighteenth century from the Scottish church and state. On one side was the struggle against the old narrow oligarchies in the boroughs that triumphed in the Reform Act of 1832. On the other was the mounting protest against the power of lay patrons "intruded" into the Church of Scotland, a protest which led ultimately to the disruption of 1843, when the "non-intrusionist" faction withdrew from the established Presbyterian church to set up the Free Kirk. Brown's own Edinburgh middle-class family were Whig-Reform in politics, evangelical and non-intrusionist in their Prebyterianism. And both stands were ardently expounded to him by his father, who undoubtedly did more than anyone else to mould the mind of his son.

Peter Brown, a prominent wholesale merchant active in civic affairs, was well acquainted with the capital's literary and Whig social circles, and well acquainted besides with constitutional history, the writings of the masters of Scots Presbyterianism, and contemporary liberal political and economic doctrine. From him a receptive George Brown learned the significance of the separation of the church and state for progress, liberty and truth: that a church-connected state suffered from sectarian strife in politics and the danger of clerical domination, while a state-connected church was degraded by sordid struggles for worldly power and squabbles over benefits from the public purse. He learned as well of the natural laws of economic freedom so indisputably determined by Adam Smith and his successors. And he came to know the merits of a balanced liberal constitution, wherein the forces of the selfish aristocracy and the unenlightened masses could both be held in check by the weight of the responsible, respectable (and middle) classes of society.

Though he was not quite eighteen when he left Scotland, Brown continued under this sort of tutelage; for in 1837 he accompanied his father to New York to help prepare the way for the rest of the family. There he began his career in journalism by assisting Peter Brown to publish the *British Chronicle*, a little weekly for the emigrant Scots community, very Whig-Liberal in its full reports of British politics. At the same time both Browns began to react sharply to the American political scene. As they saw it, republicanism boasted of liberty but practiced slavery, scorned the hide-bound ways of Europe but kept up the old fallacy of tariff protection. Then too, its devotion to the false ideal of universal-suffrage democracy had merely led to the corrupt power of machine politicians and rule by the passions of the mob. And finally it seemed evident that Britain's parliamentary monarchy, cabinet system, and unwritten constitution were far superior to the unwieldy mechanism of American government, with its inflexible written prescriptions and jarring division of authority. George Brown did acquire a lasting respect for the vigour and free spirit of the individual American; but holding views such as these he could hardly live contentedly in the United States. Consequently, when in 1843 the Browns received an invitation to found a Free Kirk journal in Canada (thanks to the *British Chronicle*'s glowing support of the non-intrusionists in the disruption of the Scottish Church), the son was quick to urge his father to make the change.

Moving to Toronto, they began the *Banner* as a Presbyterian sectarian paper. But within a few months their strong political convictions had all but committed them to the Reform side in the contemporary Canadian struggle over responsible government, and George Brown launched out with his own secular Liberal political journal, the Toronto *Globe*. From the start in March of 1844, it expressed the basic ideas that he had acquired in his British background and American experience. Thus the principle of the separation of church and state resounded through the *Globe*'s attacks on Anglican-controlled King's College, and determined its support of a wholly secular provincial university, the University of Toronto as erected by the Act of 1849. Thus Brown's free trade ideal made his paper welcome the ending of the old imperial preferences in the late forties, and look forward to the attainment of reciprocity with the United States as a step towards the rational removal of all tariff barriers. And hence as well, his enthusiasm for parliamentary institutions brought the *Globe* to view the pursuit of responsible government essentially as an effort to gain the crowning excellence of the British cabinet system for the colonial constitution.

The fifties brought the rise of sectional strife in the province of Canada, the collapse of the old Reform party, and the emergence of George Brown as leader of a reconstituted Upper Canada Liberalism. His ideas were modified by existing conditions, but still the underlying pattern remained. Devotion to the British parliamentary model was expressed in his hostility to the new Clear Grit radical movement of the early fifties, whose demands for fully elective institutions he ardently condemned as republican and democratic, and destructive of the parliamentary principle. Furthermore, he kept up a rear-guard resistance to the widely supported proposal to make the upper house elective, on the grounds that two elected chambers would upset the workings of British cabinet government, which could hardly be responsible to two possibly opposed sets of representatives of the people. On the economic side, he fought protective tariff measures, not only as the evil consequences of government extravagance and the lobbying of special interest groups, but because they flew in the face of the great truth of free trade. As for church-state relations, above all he identified himself, first, with the agitation that finally brought the abolition of the clergy reserves in 1854 – on the principle that there should be no state endowment for religion – and, second, with the opposition to mounting Roman Catholic demands for separate school provisions – in the contention that state-supported education must be secular and not denominational in character.

In this last strenuous campaign, Brown has often been accused of simply giving vent to anti-Catholic bigotry. The harsh language of the *Globe* adds colour to the charge, though vehemence was by no means all on one side in an age that violently expressed its religious and political antipathies. It is worth recalling that his stand against "Catholic aggression" in the matter of separate schools was based on a general political principle, which actually sought to take religious strife out of politics by denying any form of state connection to churches in a land of many different denominations. Yet Brown's fierce opposition to Catholic demands undoubtedly indicated more than the defence of a principle: rather, the influence of particular Canadian circumstances on the general pattern of his thinking. Canada then was an uneasy union of two discordant sections, the largely Protestant, English-speaking Upper Canada of the West and the strongly Catholic and French Lower Canada of the East. In terms of population Lower Canada was over-represented in the union parliament, and the compact power of French Canadian votes there could work to impose separate school legislation on the West against the will of its Protestant majority. And so, fired with Upper

Canada's indignation at "French Catholic domination" and filled with his own Free Kirk evangelical Protestant fervor, Brown could readily translate his concept of separation of church and state into militant anti-Catholicism.

Canadian circumstances brought another adjustment in his attitude, when in the mid-fifties he came to terms with the Clear Grits who had been among his most bitter foes. The change came out of the final break-up of the old Reform party in 1854, that put the Liberal-Conservative coalition, and soon John A. Macdonald, in control of the government. The Brownite and Clear Grit Reform fragments left in opposition gradually joined to build a new Liberal party, a potent combination appealing to western sectional discontents that brought together Brown's talents for leadership, the strong voice of the *Globe*, and the growing weight of Grit numbers in the agrarian West. Brown, however, achieved the reconstruction largely by turning the erstwhile Grit radicals from ultimate projects for democratizing the constitution to the immediate question of Upper Canada's wrongs. His past differences with the Clear Grits were laid aside, but he by no means became a democrat himself or gave up his objections to elective institutions on the American plan (though he did accept the American party convention). In fact, he virtually grafted British middle-class urban Liberalism on to Grit agrarian democracy, so that the end-product was the staid and moderate Victorian Liberal party in Ontario which passed on to Oliver Mowat's keeping – a far cry from the root-and-branch democracy of the early Clear Grit radicals.

Nevertheless Brown did identify the forces he directed with the demand for representation by population to end Lower Canada's preponderance of power; and this was a demand that had an ominously democratic ring, and was so attacked by his Conservative opponents. But Brown and his journal frequently asserted that applying this just principle to the allotment of parliamentary seats in no way involved the wholesale introduction of democracy. The *Globe* explained, moreover, that while it was possible to have a good deal wider franchise in Canada than in England, this was because there was a far higher proportion of respectable property-holding "yeomanry" in the population – which still sounded more like the British middle-class Liberal approach to the question of suffrage than the American democratic belief in the inalienable right of one man to one vote.

Yet the North American problem of sectionalism led to a further adjustment of Brown's thinking: to the acceptance of federalism, not closer legislative union, as the solution for Canada's problems. The result was the plan he advocated at the Reform Convention of 1859, a federal union of the two Canadas without the "organic changes" in political institutions which some Grit back-benchers still sought. British parliamentary patterns would be preserved, but combined with the federal principle: it was significant that the *Globe* termed this a "British-American" scheme of government. Within a few years Brown's Canadian federal plan was merged in the wider project for general British North American federation; but at the Quebec Conference of 1864 that drafted the design for Confederation he made clear that he had not forgotten his basic concern for the British parliamentary model. He again opposed an elective upper house in the new constitution, this time successfully. It was not that he expected great things from an appointed federal Senate. He stood rather on the ground that the American type of Senate, part of a system that divided power between President and two houses of Congress, could not be imported into a constitution that gave unity of power to a cabinet organically linked to a single elected chamber. Sectional feeling in the provinces might require a second federal chamber; the principles of British cabinet government no less required that it should not be a competing elected body.

In short, in Confederation as in other political issues, Brown sought to maintain British institutions while adapting them to Canadian needs. He could be sharply critical of things British on occasion, but always within the limits set by his acceptance of a British heritage as fundamentally valuable to Canada. In a sense, this attitude dictated his whole approach to questions in Canadian-imperial relations. Treating imperial affairs as family affairs, his paper was ready to make scathing criticisms of British politicians and policies, in a manner that allowed conveniently shocked Conservative opponents to denounce it as subversive and republican, ignoring the repeated proofs to the contrary, and the *Globe*'s inherent belief in the value of imperial connection. Brown and his journal, in fact, saw Canada as a new nation in North America ("We too are Americans," he declared), but a nation still within the framework of the British Empire and subordinate in its immaturity. Such a view could be assailed both by the more conservative, as trenching on disloyalty, and by the more radical as timid and old-fogey. Both attacks were made before Confederation. Afterwards, in the new national enthusiasm roused in the early years of the Dominion the noise of battle rose chiefly on the left, from idealistic nationalists contending with the *Globe*. As that paper lashed back at the Canada First group of the seventies and their ally of the moment, Goldwin Smith, it might have seemed that Brown had grown colonially-minded with advancing age. Actually, however, even in his most angry moments of denouncing imperial bumbling in times gone by, he had never really felt the impatient yearning for national recognition which now infused some of the "four millions of Britons who are not free." No doubt the simple truth was that times were moving on, and what had seemed a progressive viewpoint in Brown's own generation was becoming old-guard to its successor – which only further indicates that the basic pattern of his thought remained unaltered.

In similar fashion his views on economic policy remained in much the same form that he had brought them to Canada, though once more there might be some adaptation to fit them to the Canadian situation. He conceded, for example, that full free trade on the British plan was inapplicable to Canada, since in an undeveloped country the main source of government revenue had still to be the tariff. Yet this should be kept as low as possible, without "artificial" protective rates, and government expenditure accordingly be held to the minimum. His belief in reciprocity with the United States persisted; though when in 1865 the Americans made clear that they would abrogate the Reciprocity Treaty of 1854 he was not willing to seek its renewal at all costs, and on this specific issue even left the coalition government formed to carry Confederation. Nevertheless it was notable that in 1874, after he had been out of active politics for seven years, Alexander Mackenzie's Liberal government sent him to Washington to negotiate a new treaty; and while his efforts failed, they signified his abiding interest in the project.

Just as abiding was his faith in the doctrines of economic liberalism, which the *Globe* preached with ceaseless zeal. Its editorials – and his speeches – frequently expounded the revealed natural laws of economics: not only with regard to tariff matters, but in respect of the abolition of usury legislation, the falsity of legal-tender schemes for paper currency, and the wrong-headedness of trade unionism. In this last connection Brown spoke with particular feeling as a newspaper proprietor who had to meet some of the first manifestations of organized labour in Canada. When the *Globe* faced printer's strikes its readers were favoured with specially full critiques of collective bargaining. In this Brown's reaction was merely that of most large employers of his day – and as an employer it seems that on the whole he was a fair-minded one. His trouble was that he was sufficiently well read in the prevailing canons to add intellectual horror to business annoyance over trade unions, and had the *Globe* in which to make it plain.

This comes close to a general conclusion on Brown's thinking. Many of his ideas were shared by large numbers of Canadians in his day: his distinction was that, as a leading journalist, he had the *Globe* in which to propound them so thoroughly. Yet this was not the full story. Brown's opinions were far more coherently organized on the basis of set principles, his ideas much more explicitly rendered, than were those of many of his contemporaries – including, specifically, most of his political colleagues and opponents. He may not have had the flexible practicality and intuitive understanding of a Macdonald. He may have lacked the depth of learning and intellectual grasp of a Goldwin Smith. But Macdonald had good reason to regard him as his ablest adversary, Smith to bewail his paper's "literary despotism". No one could dispute the force of Brown's mind, reasoning in supreme confidence from what were to him logical and tested propositions. And when one finds his views echoed by the multitude of the *Globe*'s faithful, reshaping Clear Grit Liberalism, and working to precipitate the decisive sectional crisis that issued in Confederation – who can deny that the mind was a vital influence on the emerging character of a young Canadian nation?

Anne Brown and baby in the 1860s.

George Brown and the Mother of Confederation, 1864

FROM MY TITLE ONE MIGHT assume that I was striving to fill a grave gap in our national genealogy on the ground that everybody needs a mother. Such is not my high purpose, however. I am simply utilizing a happy remark made by Frank Underhill in a paper he delivered to this association in 1927. Speaking of Brown's willingness to come to terms with his enemies in the cause of Confederation, in 1864, he observed that Brown's recent marriage had had a remarkably mellowing influence on the Galahad of Grittism: "Perhaps the real father of Confederation was Mrs. Brown."[1] I am merely altering the characterization to restore to Mrs. Brown her rightful sex.

Should I admit my title is devised to trap an audience? I do not really propose to prove that Brown's activities in the conceptual year of Confederation were directed by a feminine hand. What I do seek to show is that his public conduct was so much affected by his private concerns, centred in his wife and family, that the former cannot be properly described without reference to the latter. No doubt much the same is true of other men, not excluding Fathers of Confederation. All the more reason, then, to try to fill in every detail we can find on the day-by-day and personal existence of the chief participants in the Confederation movement, in order to bring our record closer to reality. And in George Brown's case, we have an ample source of information in the letters which he sent his wife Anne almost daily through long stretches of the year 1864, while he was engaged in the crucial political proceedings that led to Confederation. This paper will seek to trace his own share, as he himself portrayed it to his wife.

His letters, of course, can now be found in the Brown Papers at the National Archives in Ottawa. A number of them have been more or less in print for years, in the selection of Brown's correspondence included by his first biographer, Alexander Mackenzie, in *The Life and Speeches of Hon. George Brown,* published in 1882. But in reproducing some of Brown's letters to his wife, Mackenzie as literary executor kept pretty closely to political comments, and thus cut out a large part – and in many ways the best part – of the correspondence. The affectionate exchanges, the homely details and private small-talk were virtually eliminated in a gutting process that left the end product about as flat and flabby as a filleted cod. On occasion, moreover, Mackenzie cut out or altered political references; and some of the letters that dealt with public as well as private affairs, he did not publish at all. Hence there is good cause to examine the original letters again, now they are available, without heed to the excerpts that Mackenzie put in print.

Brown had met Anne Nelson, daughter of the late William Nelson, the celebrated publisher, in Edinburgh in the autumn of 1862, while he was making his first return to his native land in twenty-five years. He had been out of parliament since his defeat in the general elections of 1861, and had not attempted to find another seat largely because of a serious illness, which had also contributed to his defeat. At length, after a long and gloomy convalescence, he had decided to seek full recovery in a trip abroad; and in Britain, certainly, in the summer of 1862 his health and good spirits seemed rapidly restored. In London he encountered Thomas Nelson, an old school mate of Edinburgh High School days and was invited to spend a week with the Nelson family in Edinburgh.[2] There, in the opulent but easy comfort of the Nelson home, Abden House, he met Anne, one of the lively and attractive Nelson sisters.

She was a strong-minded, intelligent and cultivated young woman, who had not only made the necessary grand tours of Europe but had lived and studied extensively in Germany. Neither a blue-stocking nor the semi-mythical Victorian shrinking violet, she knew what she wanted and saw what she liked in the forty-two year old publisher and politician from Canada. George Brown himself, like many another so-called settled bachelor, fell suddenly and sweepingly in love. He stayed on in Edinburgh, he went to the island of Arran with Anne and the family, and early in October their forthcoming marriage was announced. They were married at Abden House late in November, were well established in Toronto before 1863 began.

It was a properly blissful yet no less busy first year. George was proudly displaying his bride in Toronto society, showing her his beloved country estate, Bothwell, in the far south-west of Upper Canada, taking her to Montreal to stay with his old friend and political associate, Luther Holton, and his wife – and aside from all this, re-entering politics himself. He agreed to stand in a by-election in South Oxford in March, and won handily. He won another campaign for the seat that summer, in the general elections that were called by the weak Sandfield Macdonald Reform government in an attempt to strengthen its position. But though the government made gains in Upper Canada, it lost in Lower Canada, and if anything, was in a worse state than before. The ministry dragged uneasily over the end of 1863 and into 1864, with little hope of more than bare survival. The forces of Macdonald and Cartier, strong in the east, virtually balanced those of the Reformers, strong in the west. The course of politics was set straight to utter deadlock, as the session of 1864 neared. Yet George Brown seemed singularly unconcerned. He had a first child born to him, a daughter, Margaret, in January of 1864. His life was revolving about his wife and home. He could hardly drag himself away from Anne and baby Maggie as parliament opened at Quebec on February 19.

During the opening debates he was writing to Anne from his seat in the house, "Already I long to be back with you and will grudge every day I am kept from your side. . . . Don't fail to write me every day if only a single line to say that you and Maggie are well. Tell me all about your doings and baby's – the smallest incident will be anxiously perused".[3] His whole view of politics seemed markedly detached. Undoubtedly this was a different George Brown from the vehement sectional leader of the

1850s. Perhaps the sobering effects of parliamentary defeat and exhausting illness, a new perspective from his British visit, after long years in the confines of a colony – and surely the marriage that had given a new breadth and focus to his life – had all combined to make the change in Brown.

His letters to Anne from his first re-entering politics the year before had indicated that he had largely done so from a sense of duty and a sense of business yet unfinished. Assuredly in his mind Upper Canada still had to be freed from grave injustice, from sectional domination: the constitutional problem of the Canadian union still had to be settled, whether through 'Rep by Pop' or a federation of the two Canadas. Yet he was not the party leader, and did not seek to be; nor was there the old bubbling optimism, impetuosity, and indeed, impatience. His only impatience was with politics itself, that kept him from his wife and family: "I hate this parliamentary work. . . . I think what a fool I am to be here."[4]

At the beginning of his by-election campaign in South Oxford he had told Anne, "I find a wonderful change in my feelings about all this since the olden time. I am persuaded that had I stayed out of it for a year longer I would never have returned – and I would have been right".[5] It was rather unlike the old Brown when he informed her, "It is very pleasant to find how kind everyone is to me – even those who are going strongest against me – not a harsh word".[6] From Quebec, moreover, he wrote to Anne's mother, "I am half sorry I came back to parliament and yet it would have been difficult for my political friends to get along without me under the present circumstances. Anne says, however, I am not to run again, and as I always do as she tells me I suppose this parliamentary life will not trouble us long".[7]

His position in the assembly was not much less detached than his state of mind. He felt little confidence in Sandfield Macdonald personally, or in his ministry – which did not intend to tackle the constitutional question. Even when the government was reconstructed more to his liking, with his old friend Dorion as co-premier, Brown saw it as far too weak, far too concerned with mere survival, to be able to do anything positive. Accordingly, outside the cabinet as he was, but with a name that still carried great prestige among Grit Liberals of the West, he began to chart a broadly independent line of policy, seeking in a resolution free from partisan tone to establish a select committee that would examine the constitutional question in its own right, and not as a party issue. Otherwise, his letters exhibited little interest over parliamentary matters and manœuvres, only a desire to see them all wound up so that he could get home. He was not even in the assembly for some of the most violent clashes. He wrote to Anne on February 25, "There was an awful scene of abuse in the House last night, McGee, O'Halloran, Ferguson and others pitching into each other like fury. Fortunately I stayed home to nurse my leg [he suffered from sciatica], played a couple of games of chess with John Macdonald and went off to bed at one o'clock. . . . The debates so far have not had one hour's common sense in them. . . . There ought to be a shake up and I hope there will be".

Not that he had any personal ambitions in this regard. He wrote: "Gordon [his brother] is entirely wrong in fancying that I would for a moment entertain the idea of 'going in'. Lots of people here talk of that, but nothing would tempt me to commit such an act of folly. No, my Anne, we will pay off all our debts, have two or three years of quiet enjoyment with our little pet, lessen our labour – and then *perhaps* think of such work. But now – it would be arrant folly. At any time, it would be – well I won't moralize. But *you* are so ambitious!"[8]

He turned to another subject, dear to both their hearts: a projected holiday in Scotland that coming summer. Anne had been diffident in raising the subject, and George responded, "'if we should go home in [the] summer' . . . I can fancy the half-pleasure, half-sadness with which that 'if' was written. I believe Anne, you are the best wife that ever lived. You think it will be inconvenient for me to cross the herring pond this summer – and you are constantly saying kind little things to make it easy for me to say so. But Madam, you may as well make up your mind to the fact at once. There are others concerned besides you and me and Baby. Our words are pledged to go, and go we shall. . . . I would say this whatever business detentions were in the way – but really there never was a time when so little was in the way".[9]

The partisan debates he had once entered with such zest he now found merely boring. "Rose", he said, "has just risen to speak and he has said the only sensible thing that has yet been uttered. . . . He hoped that the debate would now be brought to a close without further waste of time – and that we may get to the business of the country". As for Cartier, "Would you believe it . . . the little wretch screetched – is that the way to spell it? – thirteen hours in one speech! They use to charge me with being long-winded – but Cartier outdoes all the world, past, present or to come". He also sent along a photograph received from a former political ally, D'Arcy McGee, who now sat on the other side of the House. "I enclose you a carte of D'Arcy McGee, and think you will say he never looked so well in his life. It was a great thing in him to give it to me – but I believe he does not think me quite as bad as the rest of the ministerial party – but rather as a redeeming point."[11]

He stayed quietly by himself as much as possible, often in his lodgings, waiting for his wife's letters. "Near three o'clock and Anne's letter not come! That horrid Grand Trunk. For the last two hours every foot on the stairs has made my heart beat a little faster – there come my letters – but it always goes past and I go to work again. Perhaps you won't believe it, but I am very industrious these days. Never go out till the house meets and work like a beaver at letters and all sorts of things. I have a very comfortable room, indeed, with a glorious view of the St. Charles, and read a little, write a good deal, look out a little and think and muse of darling Anne and our little Baby all the while. You won't be vexed if I confess that I am not a bit unhappy – separated though we are?"[12]

In the House, his chief efforts were being spent in the committee rooms. "I am working very hard – something like old times. They have put me on all the leading committees – on eleven I think – and I expect to do some good work upon them. The members (even the French) are all very kind and civil to me this session – particularly so – and I find it very pleasant."[13]

On March 14 he was finally able to move his resolution for a select committee to inquire into the constitutional question. "I was delivered from my responsibility on the Representation question last night – having spoken out my whole mind on the subject. I spoke for once an hour and kept the rapt attention of the house the whole time. What I said seems to have satisfied my own friends very well. . . . The opposition took a wretched course in the debate. Galt, Cartier and John A. throwing aside entirely the importance of inconsistency – John A. was especially mean and contemptible. He attacked Mowat and myself very bitterly – but I think he got it back with interest . . . I don't think we will carry the committee but we will have at any rate a very large vote upon it – and if we don't get the committee we will bring up the question in several different shapes."[14]

He did not get the chance immediately. After hopeless efforts at reconstruction, the Sandfield Macdonald ministry resigned on March 21. Parliament was adjourned; the composition of a Liberal-Conservative ministry under Taché and John A. Macdonald was announced by the end of the month. By-elections followed, and the session did not reopen until May 3 – although Brown himself did not arrive back in Quebec till May 11, having stretched out his Toronto visit as long as he could.

One thing had been decided during the recess: he would not accompany his wife to Scotland, but would follow later, for the political situation had not yet sorted itself out and showed small signs of doing so. In Quebec, he found "the party in an uproar – dissatisfied with the conduct of the leading men and urgent for a test vote".[15] To all intents, the Reform rank and file had turned against Sandfield Macdonald and his former ministers. The party was virtually leaderless. Brown himself was not in favour of a direct test of confidence, but the party caucus had already determined to seek it before he arrived. "It may possibly come on tonight", he told his wife on May 13, "and if so you will have the results before this reaches you. Whatever it is, we are pretty certain to have a general election this year – and then to be done with parliamentary life!"

The test was tried. On May 16, he reported, "our vote of want of confidence has commenced and will be continued tonight. What the results may be is still uncertain, but I expect we will be beaten by from one to three votes. Things are very unsatisfactory. No one sees his way out of the mess – and there is no way but my way – 'rep by pop'. There is great talk today of a coalition – and what do you think? Why, that in order to make the coalition successful the Imperial Government are to offer me the governorship of one of the British colonies! I have been gravely asked today by several if it is true that I have been offered it and whether I would accept! What do *you* say, Madam, will you condescend to be 'Her Excellency the Governess of the Windward Islands, or of the Province of British Columbia?' My reply was, and I think my Anne will endorse it, that I would rather be proprietor of the *Globe* newspaper for a few years than the Governor-General of Canada, much less a trumpery little province. But I need hardly tell you the thing has no foundation." Nonetheless talk of coalition was in the air, and openly being voiced in parliament.

The want of confidence debate dragged on, and before it ended, Brown at last carried his motion for a committee to investigate the constitutional problem. On May 18 he noted, "I brought on my motion for constitutional changes this afternoon and we had a capital debate upon it. The best debate on the question we ever had in parliament, calm, temperate and to the point. . . . I feel a very great desire to carry my motion. I would give a good large sum to carry it. It would be the first vote ever carried in parliament in favour of constitutional change, and even that would be some satisfaction after my long fight for it". Then on May 20 he could gleefully tell Anne, "it was indeed a great success and took Cartier, McDonald [sic] and Co. by intense surprise. They had no conception that there was a probability of my motion being carried . . . my committee had its first meeting at noon today. Sixteen members of the Committee were present – and we had a very useful and harmonious discussion".

While this weighty committee of leading men on both sides deliberated – and while the Conservative ministry survived the want of confidence test by a one-vote margin – Brown himself was as much concerned with plans for getting Anne away. There was so many last-minute details to attend to, to write about. On May 25 he left Quebec for Toronto, to take his wife and child to the steamer at New York. A few days later they went down to stay at the Astor House, until, on June 1, Anne sailed. She was travelling with George's brother, Gordon, whose own state of health required him to take a sea voyage. George and Gordon's wife, Sarah, saw them off, and returned to Toronto together. "We got safely ensconced in a sleeping car", George wrote in the first letter he sent across the ocean, "and were soon sweeping along the Banks of the Hudson northwards". The setting was entrancing in the soft summer night – "but for the wandering of our thoughts seaward . . . "[16] Still, he estimated hopefully, "the session will not likely last more than ten days".[17]

What he found, however, when he returned to parliament in Quebec made him change his estimate. "There is no prospect of an immediate termination to the session", he now declared, "It will probably not close before two or three weeks. Ministers are very weak and dare hardly make a motion – but there is an unwillingness among the opposition to push things to extremeties . . . "[18] He found time to take Mrs. Mowat off to a grand concert in the music hall, since Oliver Mowat was ill with a sore throat. "If you had only seen the crop of glasses directed at us when we took our seats, from Madam Duval downward!"[19]

But as he busied himself again with his constitutional committee, the climax was at last approaching. "Cartier announced on Saturday", he wrote on June 13, "that the government desired to bring the session to an end that day week – but the thing cannot be done. An effort is to be made to defeat them tomorrow night and if Dunkin comes up to the mark it will be successful. . . . If the government is beaten tomorrow night no one can tell how long the session may last."[20]

It was beaten. On June 14 the Cartier-Macdonald ministry was defeated by a margin of two votes. Another government had fallen, though with small hope for a successor. Yet, just a few hours before, on that very day, Brown's all-important committee had reported – and reported "a strong feeling among members of the committee in favour of changes in the direction of a federated system applied either to Canada alone or to the whole British North American provinces".[21] Twelve committee members stood behind the report: only three rejected it. This was the key to solution – evidence that leading men on both sides of the house could agree on a remedy to the constitutional problem: men like Cartier, Galt, McGee, Chapais, Mowat and Holton. Of the leaders, only the Macdonalds, John Alexander and John Sandfield, had signed the report in the negative.

The rapid and momentous succession of events that followed is too well known to need detailed examination here. Sufficient is George Brown's hurried synopsis to his wife (drafted at one o'clock in the morning on June 18 by "your own sleepy husband"): "On Tuesday we defeated the government by a majority of two. They asked the Governor-General to dissolve parliament and he consented. But before acting on it, at the Governor's suggestion, they applied to me to aid them in reconstructing the government – *on the basis of settling the constitutional dif-*

ficulties between Upper and Lower Canada. I refused to accept office but agreed to help them earnestly and sincerely in the matter they proposed. Negotiations were thereupon commenced and are still going on with considerable hope of finding a satisfactory solution of our troubles. The facts were announced to the House today by John A. Macdonald amidst tremendous cheering from both sides of the House. You never saw such a scene. . . . But as the whole thing may fail – we will not count our chickens just yet."

On the 20th, he sent another hasty note, scribbled as he sat waiting in the Governor-General's office for Lord Monck, and promising a longer letter if he could get away in time to catch the steamer mail for England. "If he is short I will write to you. If he is long-winded I will not be able to do so. But meantime I may say that I have closed the negotiations for the construction of a new government pledged to carry constitutional changes – and I have the offer of office for myself and two others to be named by me. I call a meeting of the party tonight to accept or reject this offer – and I must abide by its determinations. I am deeply distressed at having this matter thrust upon me now – but dare not refuse the responsibility with such vast interests at stake. How I do wish you were here to advise me. You cannot tell how I wish you had been. But never mind, I will try to do my duty to the country in such a manner as you, my dearest Anne, will not be ashamed of."

The next day, the 21st, the Upper Canadian Liberals insisted that Brown should enter the government himself. "You will see from the published proceedings", he told Anne earnestly, ". . . that my course was sustained almost unanimously. You will see that the meeting passed a resolution urging me to go into the government – but that did not influence me much. Private letters from many quarters did far more. And the extreme urgency of the Governor-General did still more. His Excellency sent a very kind letter urging me to go in, of which I will send you a copy by the Cunard Boat. The thing that finally determined me was the fact ascertained by Mowat and myself, that unless we went in the whole effort for constitutional changes would break down. . . .We consented with great reluctance – but there was no help for it – and it was such a temptation to have possibly the power of settling the sectional troubles of Canada for ever!"[22]

"It is great fun", he added brightly, "the unanimity of sentiment is without example in this wooden country".[23] The session was quickly wound up. The weather was "fearfully hot" now, and members were already trooping from Quebec. On June 30 parliament was prorogued, and immediately following George Brown and his Reform associates, Mowat and McDougall, were sworn in as ministers of the Crown. Then he departed for Toronto to prepare for the by-election campaign that now awaited him in South Oxford. Within a week it was in full swing.

His sweep around his constituency was almost a triumphal progress. He was returned by acclamation in mid-July, and thereafter went on to Bothwell, presumably both to examine the progress of the crops and to have a rest. Then he came back to Toronto to arrange for the move from Church Street to a new home on Wellington, where they were to take up residence on their return from Scotland. There was new furniture to contract for, wallpaper and hangings, and a whole host of decorating details that Anne had partially commissioned before she left, and which George was to see carried out. As he solemnly affirmed, " . . . we *must* think of wallpaper and carpets, whatever comes of the constitution".[24] He sent her details of the furniture ordered from Jacques and Hay for the drawing room – "the whole of black walnut – and to match and got up in the best style. . . . Before I leave I will order the painting and papering – so unless you speak soon you may be put to shame by my horrid bad taste".[25] As he saw things now he should be able to leave to join Anne early in the autumn. He was to go on to the Maritimes in the cause of federal union at the end of August, following cabinet discussions in Quebec. "The convention of provincial delegates is to be held at Charlottetown on the 1st Sept. and I will either leave immediately after that or return to Quebec and here first and then leave for England in October."[26]

On returning to Quebec in early August he was caught up in a round of cabinet meetings, as plans were readied for the coming discussions of British North American union in the Lower Provinces. Things went rather smoothly, he was glad to relate, and prospects were most hopeful. "I am happy to tell you that all fear of our compact not being carried out in good faith had now pretty well passed from my mind, and I feel very confident that we will satisfactorily and harmoniously accomplish our great purpose. Taché, Cartier and their colleagues have behaved very well and showed no inclination to swerve from their bargain."[27] It was also notable that he was getting on quite amiably with John A. Macdonald, his ancient enemy. They had the month before, in fact, gone together to campaign on McDougall's behalf in his by-election in North Oxford. He now could write casually to Anne of a Governor-General's party: "John A. and I were the only civilians – we had great fun."[28]

But relations between old opponents could not always run on smoothly. Indeed, on the very eve of the Canadian expedition to Charlottetown the great coalition almost fell apart. The story is best told in Brown's own words in his letter of August 28.

"Do you know you were very near being stripped yesterday of your honours of Presidentess of the Council? Would not that have been a sad affair? It was in this way. The council was summoned for twelve and shortly after that we were all assembled but John A. We waited for him till one – till half past one – till two – and then Galt sent off to his house specially for him. Answer – will be here immediately. Waited till half past two – no appearance, waited till three and shortly after, John A. entered bearing symptoms of having been on a spree. He was half drunk. Lunch is always on the side table and he soon applied himself to it – and before we had well entered on the important business before us he was quite drunk with potations of ale. After two hours and a half debate we closed the important discussions of three days on the constitutional changes and arranged finally all about our trip to Charlottetown and our course when there. John A. then declared he had an important matter to bring before us – the dispute with the Ottawa building contractors. You should know that the original contract for these buildings was $700,000 – but when the Liberal party got into power they found that $1,200,000 had been spent – and $550,000 being due to the contractors they were already over paid, and there the matter has stood ever since – nearly three years."

Now that Macdonald was back in power, Brown said, his friends, the contractors, were making a new attempt to secure their claim. "I was quite willing to send this thing to arbitration – but determined that men only of the highest character and position should be entrusted with it."

Macdonald proposed to appoint three men, two of them unknown to Brown.

"I asked that the matter should be delayed until I made inquiries – John A. would not hear of delay and insisted loudly, fiercely, that the thing should be settled then and there. His old friends in the Cabinet saw of course that he was quite wrong – but they feared to offend him and pressed for a settlement. Matters came to a point. He declared that if the thing was done then I would not sit in the council one moment longer. Mowat stood firmly by me and McDougall partly – moderately. Galt got alarmed and proposed a mode which in effect postponed the matter till Monday. I agreed to it and the council all but John A. adopted it. It was declared carried. Thereupon John A. burst out furiously declaring that his friends had deserted him and he would not hold office another day. The council adjourned in great confusion – John A's friends trying to appease him. . . . I don't imagine for a moment that . . . [these arrangements] will be pressed. It will be utterly ruinous to John A. if the whole affair goes before the public. He will not think of it when he gets sober. To say the truth, were our visit to the Lower Provinces and to England once over, I would not care how soon a rupture came. The constitutional question would then be beyond all chance of failure – and I would be quit of company that is far from agreeable."

Here is a foreshadowing – and perhaps a partial explanation – of George Brown's actual withdrawal from the government at the end of the following year. At the time of his writing, however, the breach was successfully closed. He told his wife, "I have written all this for your eye alone . . . there can be secrets of no kind between Anne and me".[29] And then he was off by the government steamer *Queen Victoria* to "that queer place Charlottetown".[30]

It was a pleasant cruise down, as Brown described it (this, incidently, in another long and most valuable letter to Anne completely missing from Alexander Mackenzie's collection).[31] The weather was fine, the ship comfortable; the company proved agreeable. There was "a broad awning to recline under, excellent stores of all kinds, an unexceptionable cook, lots of books, chess boards, backgammon and so forth".[32] Brown was up at four on the morning that they neared Charlottetown, to see the sun rise and have a salt water bath. "We had just reached the northerly point of Prince Edward and were running along the coast of the prettiest country you ever put your eye upon."[33] About noon, "amid most beautiful scenery, we came suddenly upon the capital city of the island. Our steamer dropped anchor magnificently in the stream and its man-of-war cut evidently inspired the natives with huge respect for their big brothers from Canada. I flatter myself we did that well. Having dressed ourselves in correct style, our two boats were lowered man-of-war fashion, and being each duly manned with four oarsmen and a boatswain dressed in blue uniforms, hats and belts, etc. in regular style, we pulled away for shore and landed like Mr. Christopher Columbus, who had the precedence of us in taking possession of portions of the American continent".[34]

The Maritime delegates were already on hand and the Canadians, of course, came merely as unofficial visitors. "The conference was accordingly organized without us. With that being done, we were formally invited to be present. . . . Having gone through the shake elbow and the how-do-you-do and the fine weather – the conference adjourned until the next morning at ten, then to meet for the serious dispatch of business."[35] That evening, Governor Dundas gave a large dinner party. Brown enjoyed it, and found Dundas "a very nice fellow".[36] He himself stayed with Pope, the Provincial Secretary, and his wife – not to mention "a large family of strong vigorous, intelligent and good-looking children – eight of them, all steps and stairs, kicking up a precious row occasionally".[37]

The next day, Friday, September 2, they met in conference. "Canada", said Brown, "opened her batteries", as John A. and Cartier set forth the general arguments in favour of Confederation. There followed a grand buffet supper, courtesy of Mr. Pope. "This killed the day and we spent the beautiful moonlight evening in walking, driving or boating as the mood was on us. I sat on Mr. Pope's balcony looking over the sea in all its glory."[38]

The following morning Galt discoursed to the conference on the financial aspects of British North American federal union; and then it was the Canadians' turn to entertain the delegates at luncheon on board the steamer, in what Brown termed "princely style". "Cartier and I made eloquent speeches – of course – and whether as a result of our eloquence or of the goodness of our champagne, the ice became completely broken, the tongues of the delegates wagged merrily and the banns of matrimony between all the Provinces of British North America having been formally proclaimed and all manner of persons duly warned then, there and then to speak or forever after hold their tongues – no man appeared to forbid the banns and the union was therefore formally completed and proclaimed!"[39]

It was Brown's turn on Monday to address the conference. He took the whole session, talking of the constitutional aspects of a federal union, "the manner in which the several governments, general and local, should be constructed, how the judiciary should be constituted, what duty should be prescribed to the general and local legislatures respectively and so forth".[40] That evening, though, he spent quietly playing chess aboard the ship and engrossed in the intriguing sport of catching lobsters over the side.

Then on Wednesday, September 7, the Canadians heard that the conference was unanimous "in regarding federation of all the provinces to be highly desirable *if the terms of union could be made satisfactory*".[41] There was a final grand ball the following night, given by the inhabitants of the island in the parliament buildings. Brown, however, escaped about midnight as the supper was coming on. "After the supper the Goths commenced speech-making and actually kept up for two hours and three-quarters, the poor girls being condemned to listen to it all!"[42] Then in the early hours of the morning the rest of the Canadian party came parading back to the ship, and they set sail for Pictou. Thus closed one of the gayest whirlwind courtships in Canadian history.

In truth, the festivities went on in Halifax, Saint John and other points thereafter, but the essential end had been accomplished and the pace was less hectic. Brown found himself "unusually nervous" before his major speech at the public dinner in Halifax – "people expect so much".[43] But it went off very well, and he was in high spirits – hopeful and enjoying himself, well pleased with the country and the people. Furthermore, "we have got on very amicably – we Canadians – wonderfully so!"[44] They ended with a delightful run up the St. Lawrence. "Our expedition has been all and more than we could have hoped".[45]

He stayed in Quebec for only a few days after returning there on

September 19, "up to the ears morning, noon and night", [46] drawing up reports for council, signing minutes, and catching up on a pile of accumulated correspondence. It was now evident that he would have to postpone the longed-for trip to Scotland even further, since the Maritime meetings had resulted in an agreement for a further conference on British North American union to convene in Quebec on October 10. It would only sit a week, he hoped in his impatience, and then he would finally get away.

In the meantime, he went up to Toronto to look after private affairs. The *Globe* was moving to a new office, just as the Browns were moving to a new home. There was much to do, both to attend to the newspaper business he had hardly thought of for long weeks (though now the *Globe* was quite big enough to run itself for a considerable period) and to deal with weighty matters of new house furnishings and decorations. He lived an austere existence by himself – "doing Robinson Crusoe"[47] he called it – in a silent empty house, where all the carpets were up and the crockery, linen and drapes packed away in barrels. "I breakfast at Sarah's and dine downtown at a restaurant, and Sarah sends one of the girls to make up my room. I get home in the afternoons and work without interruption, I put on my own fire, draw water and brush my boots. There was not a morsel eatable or drinkable left in the house but plum cake and two bottles of champagne! The latter are gone and the former is fast going!"[48]

Back in Quebec, once the conference had opened, he was far too busy even to write to his wife until the weekends. "We have had such a week of it!" he reported wearily on Saturday, October 15, at 2 a.m., "Council from nine to eleven – Conference from eleven to four – Council again from four to six and sometimes till seven – every day – and then letters and Orders-in-Council to write at night. It has been very hard work. However, the deliberations of the council go on harmoniously and there is no appearance yet of any insurmountable obstacle." But he still managed to exclaim glowingly and at some length over baby Maggie, who was now "a great girl with six teeth".[49] The next week was even busier. Even so, because it was mail day for the British steamer on October 17, Brown brought Council to adjourn at four so that he could write to Anne.

"The Conference proceedings get on very well", he told her, "considering we have a great deal of talkee-talkee, but not very much practical administrative talent among our Maritime friends. We were very nearly broken up on the question of the distribution of members in the Upper Chamber of the Federal Legislature – but fortunately we have this morning got the matter amicably compromised after a loss of three days in discussing it. We have eight or ten other points of great difficulty yet to be got over – and if the talk goes on as heretofore on each of them it is impossible to say when we will get through". Yet distressed as he was at the constant postponement of his departure, he knew that his wife would not "wish me to imperil all my work and ruin myself with my political friends throughout the country by abandoning this great scheme at the very moment when a firm hand was most needful".[50] He was sure of it. "How painful, my own Anne, would have been our long separation but for this perfect confidence that we could not misinterpret each other. For me I enjoy continually the most agreeable quiet chuckles when I think how perfectly lovable and loving my Anne is."[51]

Somehow, in the midst of all the weighty deliberations, the formal dinners and balls, the sense of great historic moment at the Quebec Conference, he moved in a world of his own, resenting any interruptions ("pestering") of his letter-writing, snatching glances at his Maggie's photograph in Council meetings; showing it, and probably making a nuisance of himself, on all possible occasions – as when Mrs. Pope "coaxed him" to exhibit it to the ladies of the Maritime delegates at the Executive Council's ball. "They were all perfectly charmed and declared there never was so beautiful a photograph before!"[52]

And then on October 27: "All right! ! ! Conference through at six o'clock this evening – constitution adopted – a most creditable document – a complete reform of all the abuses and injustices we have complained of!" He was dashing off his note in a moment just before starting for Montreal – "They are crying to me to hurry and my baggage is gone down. There they are again! You will say that our constitution is dreadfully Tory – and so it is – *but we have the power in our hands* (if it passes) *to change it as we like!* Hurrah!" These, then, were his chief reasons for jubilantly accepting the new scheme. The evils of the old union, the old domination, had been ended. The new union, he confidently expected, his party would be able to mould as it saw fit, thanks to the representation by population that would give Upper Canada the largest block of seats in the federal legislature. It goes without saying that he expected that Clear Grit Liberals would continue to occupy the great bulk of those Upper Canada seats.

Now in Toronto, as he went on tour with the Quebec Conference delegates, he again voiced his satisfaction to Anne. "The Constitution is not exactly to my mind in all its details. But as a whole it is wonderful – really wonderful. When one thinks of all the fighting we have had for fifteen years – and now finds the very men who fought it every inch now going far beyond what we asked – I am amazed and sometimes alarmed lest it all goes to pieces yet. We have yet to pass the ordeal of public opinion in the several provinces – and sad indeed will it be if the measure is not adopted by acclamation in them all. For Upper Canada – we may well light bonfires and build monuments the day it becomes law. Nearly all our past difficulties are ended by it – whatever new ones may arise."[53]

He was, he said, "determined to sail by the *Persia* on the 16th of November".[54] He settled all his business matters for two months to come: he scribbled "half a thousand letters";[55] he had the new house well in order with their servant, Jane Campbell, "fairly domiciled" there; and the wallpaper all ordered for their return, including for Maggie's room, "a bright lively pattern for the little darling to wonder at, and a pretty border around it".[56] And then, at long last he could leave.

"In two or three days from the time this reaches your hand", he wrote on November 11, I will, if all is well, be with you at Abden House! . . . Sunday the 27th is the anniversary of that happy, happy day when Anne Nelson became mine – and if I can reach Edinburgh by that day you may depend on my doing so. But it is pretty safe to calculate confidently on being with you on Monday – and so, as great events happening on Sunday are always kept on Monday, why we will just celebrate our great event on that day". It was only unfortunate that he could spend but a day or two in Edinburgh on arriving, before leaving on official business to London. "I am sorry to say they have piled up lots of matters for me to negotiate with the Government folks in Downing Street during my short stay in England."[57] But he would hurry through it – and this was only a small cloud on the bright anticipation of their meeting.

He finally did get away on the 16th. The great Confederation scheme which he had done so much to carry forward through this critical year of 1864 – and yet which was in many ways an impediment to his closer, warmer, private interests – could impede him no longer. When next we hear of him, he is in London on December 3, negotiating with the Imperial government.[58] But this largely represents the opening of a new phase in the Confederation movement, and need not be considered here. It seems enough, in conclusion, only to hope that George Brown did reach Anne in Edinburgh by the anniversary of their wedding day.

Endnotes

1. F. H. Underhill, "Some Aspects of Upper Canadian Radical Opinion in the Decade before Confederation", *Canadian Historical Association Annual Report for 1927*, p. 59.
2. Thomas Nelson to Anne Nelson, August 11, 1862. Though found among George Brown's papers, this letter remains with others pertaining to the Nelsons in the possession of the present Brown family at Ichrachan House, Taynuilt, Argyll. All other references to Brown Papers in this article are to those deposited at the Public Archives of Canada.
3. Brown Papers, George Brown to Anne Brown, February 22, 1864.
4. *Ibid.*, February 29, 1864.
5. *Ibid.*, February 26, 1863.
6. *Ibid.*, February 28 (?), 1863.
7. *Ibid.*, George Brown to Mrs. Nelson, October 2, 1863.
8. *Ibid.*, George Brown to Anne Brown, February 27, 1864.
9. *Ibid.*, February 29, 1864. All following references are to 1864.
10. *Ibid.*, March 1.
11. *Ibid.*, March 2.
12. *Ibid.*, March 4.
13. *Ibid.*, March 12.
14. *Ibid.*, March 15.
15. *Ibid.*, May 13.
16. *Ibid.*, June 2.
17. *Ibid.*, June 6.
18. *Ibid.*, June 11.
19. *Ibid.*, June 13.
20. *Ibid.*
21. The *Globe* (Toronto), June 15.
22. Brown Papers, George Brown to Anne Brown, June 23.
23. *Ibid.*
24. *Ibid.*, July 28.
25. *Ibid.*
26. *Ibid.*

27. *Ibid.*, August 8.
28. *Ibid.*
29. *Ibid.*, August 28.
30. *Ibid.*, August 29.
31. *Ibid.*, September 13. (Compare this long letter on the Charlottetown Conference with the account, largely based on newspapers, in W.M. Whitelaw, *The Maritimes and Canada before Confederation*, pp. 220-226. See also D.G. Creighton, *John A. Macdonald, The Young Politician*, pp. 363-368.)
32. *Ibid.*
33. *Ibid.*
34. *Ibid.*
35. *Ibid.*
36. *Ibid.*
37. *Ibid.*
38. *Ibid.* (Compare Whitelaw, p. 221.)
39. *Ibid.* (Compare Whitelaw, p. 222.)
40. *Ibid.* (Compare Whitelaw, p. 223.)
41. *Ibid.*
42. *Ibid.*
43. *Ibid.*; September 12. This letter from Halifax was actually meant to be Brown's report on the Charlottetown meetings to his wife, but he was compelled to close it hastily, and thus sent his long letter – just discussed – the next day.
44. *Ibid.*
45. *Ibid.*, September 19. (Compare Whitelaw, p.228.)
46. *Ibid.*, September 23.
47. *Ibid.*, October 1.
48. *Ibid.*
49. *Ibid.*, October 15.
50. *Ibid.*, October 17.
51. *Ibid.*
52. *Ibid.*
53. *Ibid.*, October 31.
54. *Ibid.*
55. *Ibid.*, November 7.
56. *Ibid.*, November 11.
57. *Ibid.*
58. *Ibid.*, December 3.

PART TWO

The Metropolitan Approach

Introduction

WHILE CLOSING IN ON THE Brown biography during the earlier 1950s, I also shaped some wider notions about assessing major patterns in Canadian historical development: notions which grew ultimately into the conceptual approach termed metropolitanism, and focussed on the power of the great city. In this respect, the organizing of my general Canadian history text, and the broad-to-tenuous social science texts that followed, probably had a certain amount of influence. Yet other influences shared plentifully as well. For instance, there was work I had begun at Toronto and carried forward at Harvard on the play of frontier and sectional forces in North America; similarly, various inquiries regarding the sway of leading urban communities over extended areas outside them, whether exemplified by French or English medieval towns or a transport-ruling Montreal metropolis. Also, beyond these, there were implications from my own thesis research showing the many interactions between the hinterland community of Ontario and the increasingly ascendant city of Toronto. Add yet again the structuring ideas of metropolitan economic dominance, and the phases in its emergence which I derived from the writings of N.S.B. Gras Throw in even further inspirations received from Innis, Creighton, Lower – plus, in his own way, Underhill – and it is quite evident that the metropolitan approach I was to espouse myself became almost a foregone conclusion: virtually a Gestalt completion for me.

This none the less remains an insufficient account, leaving out the sizeable influence of contemporaries, former students and still more; but I did promise brief introductions. Accordingly, I will merely go on to note that the first piece which follows in this, my "metropolitan" section (the seminal article itself) was originally drawn up in 1953 as a lecture for a historiography course at the University of Toronto, and was meant to explain to students what I considered to be broadly significant stages and trends in the writing of Canadian history. It was then revised and published in the *Canadian Historical Review* for March, 1954, as "Frontierism, Metropolitanism and Canadian History".

But as usual in my writing career, much was to interpose before I went ahead with this conceptual approach: my biographical endeavours in particular. And so it was not till 1966 that I produced a serious follow-up piece, "Metropolitanism and Nationalism" – which is not included here, since it now seems rather old-hat and bypassed: unless in underlining a medieval feudal analogy with the societal functionings of metropolitanism. In any case, after finishing my dealings with George Brown I already stood committed to a volume in the Canadian Centenary Series on *The Union of the Canadas*, and soon to other literary celebrations of the hundredth anniversary of Confederation. Hence I did not really get back to matters of metropolitanism till the late sixties and into the seventies; although the next item contained in this section below first sprang from one noteworthy kind of centennial celebration, a special series of regional seminars held in 1967 by the Canadian Historical Association to mark the great occasion. Thus came the second item here presented, "Aspects of Metropolitanism in Atlantic Canada before 1914", which was given to the special seminar meeting in St. John's, and was in due course published in 1969 in *Regionalism in the Canadian Community, 1867-1967*, edited by Mason Wade.

From the mid-fifties, I had developed a growing interest in regionalism (so basic to metropolitanism in Canada as well as to Canada itself), evidenced both in my teaching the long-lasting graduate course in Ontario history which I started then, and through almost as long a span of cordial membership on the province's Archaeological and Historic Sites Board or its successor, the Ontario Heritage Foundation. But if the Ontario workings of regionalism were so to speak my home grounds, I equally marked its presence elsewhere in Canada: marking, besides, that it was not necessarily antithetical to either nation-alism or metropolitanism, since it could be complementary as well as competitive. And so I was brought to examine other regions beyond Central Canada where metropolitanism was no less in continual play. Thus, treating the Atlantic region and its principal cities as a case-study for my St. John's seminar paper, I strove to show how metropolitan factors had operated here on regionalism, both from within the area itself and from without.

The third item comprised below appeared near the end of the 1970s as a sort of conspectus of my metropolitan approach, following a number of more specific, close-up applications. Entitled "Metropolis and Region: the Interplay of City and Region in Canadian History before 1914", this paper came out in the *Urban History Review*, third issue, for 1978; but it was originally delivered to a research symposium at the Australian National University in Canberra, where I was a Senior Fellow while on leave from Toronto during that same year. Since a previous visit to Australia in 1958, I had stayed intrigued by the comparisons between Canadian and Australian historic experiences of both frontiers and dominant big cities – metropolises. Accordingly, this paper was first offered at Canberra in contribution to a symposium debate on that inevitably wide-ranging topic.

The final piece in this section, "The View from Ontario: Further Thoughts on Metropolitanism in Canada", has not been published heretofore. It was initially composed for (and read to) a conference of the Atlantic Association of Historians held at St. Francis Xavier University in October, 1985. Its contentions and examples were therefore oriented to an Atlantic seaboard setting. A subsequent proposal, however, to include it in a collective volume where an Ontario setting would seem more appropriate impelled me to revise the piece considerably by 1987: essentially, by altering its cases and demonstrations – but not the ideas or arguments behind them – to suit such a changed venue. Nevertheless, its projected "Ontario" publication did not come to pass; the revised version being seen as perhaps too argumentative in pursuing certain criticisms of my metropolitan approach; or at any rate, not wholly in keeping with the book as purposed. I have, all the same, decided to run the piece here in this present selection, and for three main reasons. First, it is a fairly recent reappraisal of a paramount theme in my writings. Second, if it is argumentative, then it is a pretty authentic expression of how I have thought and argued in much of my work. And third, I do not imply (nor at all intend) any personal attacks by way of it. My critics have constantly been courteous, helpful, sometimes commendatory – while I would always prefer to be criticized than ignored. Hence I only return the favour to them, believing as I must that recorded exchanges of views are central to the growth of scholarship.

Halifax in the 1830s: the Atlantic garrison base and the emerging Maritime metropolis.

Frontierism, Metropolitanism and Canadian History

LIKE ANY OTHER HISTORY, that of Canada has been written within the framework of intellectual concepts, some of which have been consciously applied by historians, while others have shaped their work more or less indirectly through the influence of the surrounding climate of opinion. It would obviously be impossible to draw out and catalogue all the concepts that have affected the writing of Canadian history, even in the most general way. Yet it does seem possible to discern certain underlying ideas or patterns of thought that have given character to various phases of Canadian historiography. And in more recent times, in particular, one can note the powerful influence of what might be called (for want of a more precise term) "frontierism" in the history of Canada.

The idea of the dynamic frontier as a great and distinctive force moulding North American development has left an enduring mark on the writing of history in Canada, just as it has in the United States. No doubt this frontier idea is no longer as fresh and vital in its application to this country as it was in the period before the Second World War: indeed, it is largely because its original influence has declined, and the concept has thus become an historical phenomenon in itself, that we are entitled to discuss and assess its influence. Nor was the frontier thesis proper, as propounded by Frederick Jackson Turner and elaborated by his disciples, ever adopted as fully or dogmatically in Canada as it was in the United States – and there, of course, it has long been the subject of qualification and criticism. Nevertheless, the frontier interpretation broadly affected the thinking of a number of distinguished Canadian historians who in the main began their work about a quarter-century ago.[1] Today we can hardly examine the current state of Canadian historiography, and perhaps project its lines of growth, without giving heavy weight to the North American-environmentalist view of our history which stemmed originally from Turner's frontier thesis and which still leaves a rich heritage on both sides of the Canadian-American boundary.

There were other approaches to Canadian history before the rise of frontierism, and at present there are still others, which may involve the modification, complication, or even the virtual reversal of the frontier concept. Accordingly, in order to put frontierism in its proper context, it is first necessary to generalize – rather alarmingly, perhaps – on several "schools" of Canadian history. Each of these had some sort of interpretive approach, or at least some underlying assumptions, which gave a broadly similar character to the works its members produced.

These schools, however, are being set forth merely for convenience in tracing the general patterns of Canadian historiography and not as an all-inclusive filing system; for when individual historians are considered they do not always fit neatly into one particular classification. Some may change their school allegiance with the passage of time, while others, so to speak, may fall between schools. Furthermore, since the writing of history in French- and English-speaking Canada has largely been carried on as two separate enterprises, it would be of small consequence to try to link French-language schools with the English ones to be established below. And yet, despite these limitations, it can still be asserted that at various stages in Canadian historiography certain general approaches have been followed by important groups of historians, so that the designating of "schools" to illuminate that fact is by no means an unprofitable exercise.

I

The first school to be so designated might be termed the Britannic, or Blood is Thicker than Water School. The writers of this group were often convinced imperialists of the later nineteenth or early twentieth centuries and were closely attached in sentiment and background to Great Britain. They tended, as William Kingsford, that dull dean of Canadian historians, said he did, to make their theme the emergence of a new Britannic community within the empire, a part of one imperial organism, whose people enjoyed the British institutions of their forefathers and were worthy members of that indefinable company, the "British race."[2] This Britannic School was inclined to ignore North American forces except when they were concentrated in the threatening power of the United States. The defeat of American pressure from without in 1776, 1812, and 1867 had "kept Canada British." So much for North America: a foe to be resisted.

Yet this group contributed something of lasting significance to the thought of Canadian history: the idea that Canada represented a declaration of independence from the United States, an attempt to build a second community in North America outside the American republic, and one marked off from it, indeed, by the longer persistence of the imperial tie. For some time this Canadian community would look to the bond with Britain to offset American dangers. But in the young twentieth century, when the days of actual threat had passed, that bond seemed to change increasingly in its implication – from protection to subordination. It was now that another school of Canadian Historians began to arise, who viewed the imperial tie more critically in the light of the growing spirit of nationalism. And their main theme now became the march of Canada to political nationhood, through many a parliamentary manœuvre and struggle of words as colonial limitations were progressively overcome.

This new School of Political Nationhood chiefly concentrated on the paper-strewn path to national status, directing Canadian history to Colonial Office dispatches, the records of imperial conferences, and tense questions of treaty-making powers. Two phases, however, may be discerned in the writings of this school, though both were concerned with the peaceful and piecemeal evolution of Canada to nationhood.

The first of these mainly treated the achievement of responsible government and confederation, and on the whole was favourably disposed to things British, since leading historians like Chester Martin and R.G. Trotter saw these national advances as being considerably aided by British advocacy and still as taking shape within the general framework of British institutions.[3] As this indicates, there was really no sharp break here between the Britannic and Nationhood schools, and contemporary opinion in Canada largely tended to think in terms both of national development and of maintaining some degree of connection with Britain. Yet gradually a watershed was being crossed, as more and more stress was laid on the winning of national rights. Thus came the second phase, which dealt primarily with the achievement of autonomy in external affairs, and the motto of most of its authors might well have been, A Canadian Citizen I will Die.

Sometimes, it is true, these historians might welcome the emergence of the new British Commonwealth as the concomitant of Canada's advance to nationhood.[4] But generally they were less friendly to British influences, and the nationalist note was clear, as in the writings of J.W. Dafoe or O.D. Skelton. British influences, in short, were largely equated with imperial leading strings, and the more nationalistic writers were ever on guard against imperialist designs to enmesh pure young Canada in a web of power politics – though one might wonder why gentlemen so keenly perceptive of the harsh realities of power in the European world could not recognize, in fixing their watchful eye on the British menace, that, after 1918, at least, the fearsome British lion had become rather a straw-stuffed beast. Still, this preoccupation with straw men or straw lions may perhaps be explained by the fact that much of their writing was done amidst the somewhat unreal atmosphere of Mackenzie King's bold crusade of the 1920s for Canada's right to have no foreign policy. And these authors were often strongly Liberal in sympathies. At times they seemed to write as if Canadian history was in essence a steady Liberal broadening-down of freedom to the ultimate end of national status – after which absolutely memorable History would come to a dead stop.[5]

Nevertheless the Political Nationhood group, first phase or second, did solid service in uncovering the process whereby Canada obtained the various attributes of self-government. Moreover, in stressing the theme of nationhood they were themselves expressing the basic truth that a society distinct from that of Britain had taken shape in Canada and was demanding recognition and the full right to manage its own affairs. As these historians, however, generally talked in political and constitutional terms, they did not effectively analyze the social, economic, and intellectual forces within North America which were creating a Canadian community increasingly conscious that it was far from being an overseas projection of Britain.

To fill this gap, a new school of historians began to take shape in the later 1920s, although it is important to note that its members were often closely related to the nationalist authors of the day. Indeed, this was nationalism in another sphere, seeking to demonstrate that Canadian desires for nationhood were rooted in the native North American environment: that Canadian institutions and viewpoints were not simply British, but were in their own way as American as those of the United States. The environment had done it. This, then, was the Environmentalist School, or North Americans All.

It was this group that built particularly on the concept of the frontier in North American history derived from Turner and his followers in the United States. The frontier, where man came most immediately into contact with the North American physical environment, was the great seed-bed for the growth of a truly North American society. From the start, as the United States and Canada had spread across the continent, environmental influences that first began on the frontier had worked to shape a native American character different from that of the Old World, left far behind. Here was the key principle to be applied by Canadian environmentalist historians: that thanks to the continuous process of adaptation to the environment, an American content had steadily grown in Canada within external forms of government, society, or culture inherited from Britain or France.[6]

It followed that Canadian history could be most fruitfully compared to that of the United States in its essentially North American nature and course of development. In pursuing this promising theme, however, these writers took over the general approach and mood of Turner and company – the frontier and its agrarian population as emblematic of native democratic, progressive, perhaps even of "Good" forces in the history of the continent – rather than the precise frontier thesis, which received little direct application in Canada. Yet because that original thesis was so powerful in its impact and so pervasive in its influence, it requires examination here; although, admittedly, the subject is hardly a new one.[7]

II

Turner had held in his frontier thesis that "the greatest formative influence" in American history had been the long existence of "the open frontier, the hither edge of free land," continually moving westwards.[8] The conditions of frontier society had determined the character of western institutions, and these in turn had reacted on the East. Out of the frontier, in fact, had come American individualism, democracy, inventiveness, coarseness, and idealism. Turner wrote that the seeds of American democracy were not carried to the New World in the *Mayflower* but sprang up out of the native forest. The effect of the frontier was to make Americans out of Europeans. In brief, the West was the true America, that ever taught the populous but effete East the American way of life.

This was the environmental determinism at its most forthright. The wilderness and the men it produced had made America. Defenders of Turner might claim that he had not proposed a frontier hypothesis as the only key to American history, but it was widely seized upon as the only true explanation, especially as its nationalist and romantic implications gripped the American imagination.[9] Its effects may still be found today, on different cultural levels in the United States. Indeed, it may not be irrelevant to note that Hollywood, that lowest common denominator of the American mind where myths are mass-produced, still pours forth a flood of highly technicoloured Westerns each purporting to touch the very soul of America, as some pioneer rugged individualist with iron hands and blazing guns "carves out an empire" for the nation at various points west, while Indians in their thousands from Central Casting Office go down before the onward march of democracy.

Of course Hollywood is a far cry from the academic world of history, and here there have been repeated and detailed criticisms of the frontier thesis as applied in the United States. Nevertheless the stimulus it gave to the environmentalist – at times even isolationist – study of American history remained a powerful one. Moreover, a broad survey of the opinions of American historians made a little over a decade ago revealed that the majority would still accept the frontier thesis, with qualifications, although the trend seemed to be turning against it.[10] In this trend were men like Carleton Hayes, who asked, concerning the American frontier, "frontier of what?" and answered that America was essentially the western edge of European civilization. Accordingly, its story could be read as part of the expansion of Europe; and its culture and institutions should be studied not solely in national isolation as native products, but rather as elements transferred from Europe, adjusting – no doubt – to a somewhat different environment.[11]

Dixon Ryan Fox also pursued this theme of transfer, finding that the ideas and institutions transmitted from Europe bulked far larger in American development than any modifications of them or new contributions made on this side of the Atlantic. He observed, in fact, that ideas and institutions had steadily been carried west to the frontier, and considered that the East had far more shaped the West in America than *vice-versa* – that the real story of the United States was the progressive turning of pioneer Wests into developed Easts.[12] Further in this vein, Arthur M. Schlesinger Jr. sought to demonstrate that the upsurge of Jacksonian Democracy, long regarded as the very incarnation and triumph of the free farming frontier, was instead far more strongly based amid the urban masses of the East.[13]

The frontiersmen among American historians have, however, struck back. One of them, W.P. Webb, has recently launched a most dazzling counter-attack on all fronts by proclaiming that the whole expansion of Europe since 1500 was one "Age of the Great Frontier."[14] He contends that most of modern Western European civilization as we know it, with its characteristic capitalism, democracy, and individualism, is the product of world frontiers that opened up to Europe when its peoples began to go adventuring across the oceans. He speaks of a four-hundred-year frontier boom, now ended, when Europe grew rich and developed the twin luxuries of freedom and the all-important individual, a boom that resulted from the "windfalls" of vast natural resources that were found in the empty Americas, Australasia, and South Africa. Europe became a dominating metropolis – a word we shall return to later – organizing, controlling, and exploiting these tremendous overseas frontiers, but in consequence having its development moulded by them.

How does all this relate to Canadian history? To some extent there have been similar stages in the use of the frontier interpretation, though these, indeed, might overlap. In the first stage, there were stimulating applications of frontierist themes and concepts to the Canadian half of the North American environment, seen most clearly perhaps in W.N. Sage's paper of 1928, "Some Aspects of the Frontier in Canadian History." This treated Canadian expansion across the continent as an integral part of a total North American frontier movement that ignored the international boundary.[15] Then there were the valuable investigations of F.H. Underhill into the nature of Canadian political parties, and especially the Clear Grit Liberal movement directed by George Brown and the Toronto *Globe*. With regard to Canadian parties, Professor Underhill traced their development according to conflicts between western agrarian areas and eastern business interests, in sound Turnerian fashion (1935).[16] With regard to the Clear Grits, he saw them as "an expression of the 'frontier' in Canadian politics" (1927).[17] E.H. Oliver applied frontierism to Canadian religious development, and in his *Winning the Frontier* (1930) depicted the Canadian churches as being moulded by a frontier environment.[18] Somewhat later A.S. Morton emphasized the dominant power of the environment in the extension of settlement into the Prairie West (1938).[19] And A.L. Burt effectively used a frontier interpretation to show how the people of New France were shaped by North American forces to become truly an indigenous people, not just a seeming copy of Old World "feudal" France (1940).[20]

In the second stage, there came criticisms and modifications of the frontier interpretation, although the environmentalist emphasis was still much in evidence.[21] A.R.M. Lower noted in a paper of 1930, "The Origins of Democracy in Canada," that "There can be little question but that American democracy had a forest birth." Yet he went on to assert that frontier equality might not result in political democracy unless "theoretical positions as to its nature" had already been projected into the frontier environment. In Canada's case, the egalitarian conditions of pioneer life had interacted with traditions brought from across the Atlantic; and Canadian democracy had developed more slowly than American because of Canada's briefer, more limited frontier experience, its stronger attachments to the Old World, and the long-enduring, overriding power of the imperial authority in Government.[22] Nevertheless, despite this recognition of non-environmental, transferred influences, Professor Lower, in his *Colony to Nation* (1946) continued to stress the power of the New World "to change old institutions and give them new form and spirit."[23] North American democracy, he reiterated, was "forest-born." In short, though this was modification, environmentalism sprung from the frontier concept still remained strong.

In the third stage, as in the United States, new emphasis was given to the role of eastern rather than western forces in Canada, to urban interests and to the dominating power of the organizing, controlling metropolis. Thus Professor Underhill, for example, noted in 1946 that the original frontier agrarianism of the Clear Grits had subsequently been qualified by urban and business leadership introduced to the party by George Brown and other Toronto worthies.[24] And Professor Lower in his same *Colony to Nation* paid marked attention to the economic power wielded by metropolitan centres like Montreal and London, which, he made clear, did much to affect the course of events in raw Canadian settlements.[25] On another tack, Professor Fred Landon, in describing the frontier era in western Ontario, gave chief place to the transmitted influence of American democratic ideas and practices rather than to actual frontier conditions in forming the outlook of the pioneer community.[26] But this only pushed the influence of the environment one stage back, to patterns of life worked out in the former frontier states below the Great Lakes. In any case it was evident that, despite qualifications and shifts of emphasis, environmentalism was still flourishing in Canadian history.

Still, it should be plain from this discussion that Canadian environmentalists did not generally follow any rigid frontier dogma and did show regard for other than native or western forces in analysing Canadian developments. After all, in a country which had obviously maintained many trans-atlantic ties and long continued as a colony there could not be as strong an assertion as in the United States of a separate

North American growth in isolation from the world. And yet there was an inclination for environmentalists to see as much as possible of the history of Canada in terms of common North American experience in driving back the wilds – to suggest that the really important features in Canadian development had in truth been "forest-born"; in other words, that the various Wests had been the principal source of transforming energy and of national progress, in which they had pulled along and supported the conservative, exploitative East.

There was, moreover, a certain tendency to fix values. Thus pioneer society, the West, and simple farmers became virtuous and forward-looking to the beholder, while town society, the East, and un-simple business men became selfish and reactionary. There might be an element of truth here, but moral overtones somewhat coloured the picture, so that western farmers who wanted free trade established in their interests were Good, while eastern business men who wanted a protective tariff enacted in theirs were Evil. Similarly, the West appeared as the true home of Canadianism, while the East, which worked out a distinctive Canadian economic nationalism in railway and tariff policy, was hardly Canada at all. No doubt powerful eastern business interests fattened themselves considerably through these arrangements. But could environmentalists properly become moral about business elements adjusting themselves to problems of the environment in their own way?

In sum, Canadian environmentalists frequently displayed the compelling mood of the frontier school, with its moral implications of a struggle between sound native democratic forces and elements that clung to privilege, exploitation, and empty Old-World forms. In so doing they often oversimplified a conflict between West and East, or better, between pioneer agrarian interests and exploitative urban centres. As a result, major Canadian movements for political change might be viewed too narrowly in the light of frontierism. For example, Upper Canadian radicalism of the 1830s, Clear Grit Liberalism of the mid-century, and Progressivism of the 1920s might all be explained in terms of the upsurge of the then newest West, as western forces of pioneer individualism launched crusades against privilege and urban business domination.[27] Yet it could also be shown that Mackenzie radicalism was probably more influenced by the working model of American political democracy and the ideas of British radicalism; that Clear Grittism was closely organized about the rising urban centre of Toronto; and that Western Progressivism was not based on self-sufficient pioneer farmers but on organized grain specialists engaged in a highly complex kind of agricultural business, whose goals involved not the triumph of individualism but the replacement of a set of unfavourable government controls centred in the tariff with another represented by Wheat Boards and government provision of major services.

Furthermore, it might well be a result of frontierism, sprung as it was from the mid-western heart of the continent, that a viewpoint characteristic of mid-western isolationism often appeared among environmentalist writers in Canada. Their view of the environment, like Turner's, was primarily continental. Thus it tended to neglect the influence of the seas beyond, the "maritime environment" that had always tied the continent to Europe. Canada might be treated as a northern extension of certain continental physiographic provinces, without due consideration of geographic and historic forces that had from the beginning of white penetration made this country an east-to-west projection from Europe. And logically it would follow that geography – in the continental sense only – had shaped Canada as a number of disparate American regions, held out of the American republic by mainly emotional forces and by the chance of history: in short, a loose grouping of less well-favoured, somewhat backward, American states. A rather paradoxical basis, this, for the nationalism environmentalists usually professed.

However, it is worth repeating that leading contemporary historians who have been referred to here in connection with the vigorous environmentalist phase of Canadian history have themselves, in more recent writings, not only shown awareness of the shortcomings of interpretations stemming from frontierism but have also done much to reconsider and to correct them. Nor, certainly, have their ideas ceased to develop beyond this one approach. None the less it may be hazarded that the effects of frontierist teachings remain strong today in suggesting for Canadian history, and doubtless for its readers, certain stereotypes about the dynamic West and the torpid East, and about the nature of Canada as a more restricted backward version of the American model to the south. And frontierism may still leave a tendency to overvalue the influence of native North American forces and the material environment, and a tendency to undervalue forces transferred from Europe and the non-material environment: that of ideas, traditions and institutions. Yet these latter factors were particularly important in a portion of North America that did not undergo a revolutionary upheaval, emotional as well as political, to break ties with Europe, and which continued to place a special premium on the word "British" as applied to institutions and ideas. In fact, it is these very things which chiefly mark off the development of Canada from that of the United States. They give validity to the study of a separate Canadian history, one which is not just a counterpart of United States history in having a similar North American content.

Accordingly, while in no way underrating the very great contributions which frontierism and environmentalism have made to the understanding of Canada as a part of North America, it does seem necessary to look for a wider framework for Canadian history. But this, indeed, was already taking shape while the frontier interpretation was being usefully applied, and to a certain extent grew out of it, as an examination will show.

III

This next framework was in some ways a qualified version of environmentalism and in others the frontier concept reversed. It has appeared in most explicit form in the writings of D.G. Creighton, particularly in his *Commercial Empire of the St. Lawrence* (1938) and *Dominion of the North* (1944), but its foundations were laid in earlier works by H.A. Innis which broke rich new ground in Canadian economic history, notably *A History of the Canadian Pacific Railway* (1923) and *The Fur Trade in Canada* (1930). These studies of major Canadian economic enterprises, which were essentially great systems of continent-wide communications, pointed the way to a new general interpretation of Canadian history that would be forcefully developed by Professor Creighton.

His approach, in fact, has been said to establish a "Laurentian School" of Canadian historiography, since it largely rests on the idea that the long St. Lawrence water route and its connections across the continent became the basis of an extensive communications system around which Canada itself took shape. The commercial empire of the St. Lawrence, the broad domain of Montreal, first flung a Canadian fur trade across the continent, then competed vigorously with New York and the American seaboard through canal and railway enterprises for control of the trade of the midwestern heartlands of America, and finally built a new economic dominion across the northwestern plains to the Pacific that was, in fact, the Dominion of Canada. It followed that the existence of a separate Canada was not just a fortuitous result of the American Revolution, of French determination to survive, nor of Loyalist emotional resolves to "stay British" – despite the hard facts of the environment – nor again of the mere continuance of the imperial tie. It was also rooted in powerful factors of geography and commerce that underlay the whole Canadian development.

This, in a sense, was environmentalism, since the St. Lawrence was as real a feature of the North American environment as the North American forest, and a good deal more permanent. Environmentalists had stressed before that the main natural lines of North American geography ran north and south, linking the regions of Canada more effectively with their United States counterparts below the border than with their Canadian neighbours to east and west. But the St. Lawrence, the Great Lakes, the Saskatchewan, and the Fraser traced lines across the continent that were quite as natural; and, as the writings of Professors Innis and Creighton indicated, they made possible the east-to-west linking of Canadian regions from the earliest days of the fur trade, as communications spread by the lakes and river valleys from sea to sea. Perhaps we could even call this the Waterways school, especially since it made clear that the environment did not stop short at the Atlantic edge of North America. For the St. Lawrence system that funnelled traffic from the continental interior out to the sea was closely connected with British finance and markets across the waters in an east-west trading network that thus reached halfway around the world.[28]

Yet the Laurentian interpretation did not mean just a new emphasis on material environmentalism, since it also revealed that this huge communications and transport system could transfer immigrants, ideas, and impulses in one direct channel from Britain deep into the heart of the continent. As a result, the Ontario frontier of the earlier nineteenth century might actually be in closer contact with the sea and the mind of Europe than were the mid-western regions of the United States, more isolated behind the Appalachian barrier in a Mississippi Valley world of their own.

The Laurentian School, however, tended to go even further, and to reverse the earlier environmentalist position in this respect: it looked not from the forest-born frontiers for its perspective of Canadian history but from the developing eastern centres of commerce and industry. Indeed, it primarily studied the effects of the East on the West, and largely regarded business men and conservative urban political elements as agents of national expansion who might well be more far-sighted in their outlook than were their agrarian opponents. Here then was a metropolitan rather than a frontier viewpoint. Moreover, this Laurentian view could be effectively linked with the monumental studies of H.A. Innis on the organization of the staple products trade of broad North American areas through costly and complex transport systems controlled in large urban centres.[29] The result was virtually to establish "metropolitanism" in Canadian historiography, the study of the role of metropolitan forces in this country, a vitalizing approach that may yet undergo considerable development.

Metropolitanism is at root a socio-economic concept that has already seen some application in Canadian history. As mentioned earlier, Professor Lower has made use of it in *Colony to Nation*, and elsewhere as well,[30] but it has been most closely applied in D.C. Master's work, *The Rise of Toronto, 1850-1890* (1947).[31] In this he traced the rise of the city to a position of metropolitan dominance over Ontario, while at the same time it entered into vigorous competition with Montreal business interests for control of a broader Canadian hinterland. Toronto's climb to metropolitan stature is an instructive particular theme in Canadian history, but the rise of the metropolis in general is one of the most striking features of modern Western society. Briefly this implies the emergence of a city of outstanding size to dominate not only its surrounding countryside, but other cities and their countrysides, the whole area being organized by the metropolis, through control of communications, trade, and finance, into one economic and social unit that is focussed on the metropolitan "centre of dominance" and through it trades with the world.[32] Political activity, too, may often become centred on the metropolis.

London and New York are the classic examples of modern metropolitanism. But the metropolitan relationship is a chain, almost a feudal chain of vassalage, wherein one city may stand tributary to a bigger centre and yet be the metropolis of a sizable region of its own. Thus, Winnipeg is Montreal's subsidiary but is the metropolis of a large area of the prairie West. The Toronto metropolis is a subsidiary of both New York and Montreal, while Canada's main metropolitan centre, Montreal, has traditionally been bound to London. These facts are not new in themselves; but when it is remembered that the metropolitan pattern includes not only economic ties but social and cultural associations also, then many effective lines of inquiry may present themselves. One might suggest that the survival of British customs sometimes noted in the English-speaking ruling class of Montreal, or Toronto's split personality, whereby it strives both to be a minor New York and to maintain its "British" character, may be comprehended through the weighing of various metropolitan connections and influences in these cities' history.

At present, however, the chief point to observe is that the rise of metropolitanism is the other side of the coin to frontier expansion. One may speak of the constant expansion of the frontier, or of the constant extension of the metropolitan power that is pushing out the frontier. What Webb called the "Age of the Great Frontier," might just as well be called the "Age of the Great Metropolis," when western Europe in general, by spreading out its system of communications and commerce, organized the world about itself. The age of this great European metropolis has passed away. Its predominant focus, London, has yielded in primacy of economic power to New York – though now there is no one main world metropolitan region, since, despite the rise of North America, Europe still maintains a vast overseas economic network, while a far-flung separate trading system is emerging in the Communist-dominated world.

Returning to the frontier itself, one might say that it is developed by a metropolitan centre of dominance which supplies its capital, organizes its communications and transport, and markets its products. The frontier's culture, too, originally stems from a metropolitan community; at root, learning and ideas radiate from there – and thus is Turner answered. True, there may be frontier religious movements, but these begin with preachers going out to the frontier and end in the focusing of the sect on the city.[33] The economic and cultural metropolitan processes go hand in hand, as newspapers, books, and men of education spread from the centre. Frontiers may often supply grievances for political movements. Urban centres as often supply the intellectual leadership; so that frontier demands take form at the hands of urban journalists and professional men.

It may be seen when this analysis is carried through that the frontier, far from being essentially independent and self-reliant, is in the largest sense a dependent. It constantly requires metropolitan aid and control, though by the same token it may come to resent and resist it. Frontier protest movements are a natural accompaniment of the extension of metropolitan power into new areas. The dynamic, organizing, hard-pressing forces of metropolitanism bring reaction on themselves. This may occur either at moments when the frontier as such is rapidly expanding, and full of problems of adjustment, or when it is actually declining; that is, becoming organized into a more mature and integrated region with a new metropolitan centre of its own, which hopes to wrest control of the local economy away from the older centre, and therefore gives voice and leadership to a regional protest movement.

How does this pattern fit Canadian history? No good historian would try to make it fit too exactly: if we reject a frontier determinism we should hardly replace it with a metropolitan determinism. Still, there may be an approach here as instructive for Canadian historiography as the frontier interpretation was in its day. For example, one might examine the unrest in Upper Canada in the 1830s, when this frontier area was rapidly expanding with the tide of British immigration, as a result of the vigorous extension of powerful business interests into a broad new domain, and of the spread of educated men and stimulating ideas from older communities, displayed notably in the rising power of the press and the journalist on the Upper Canada scene. On the other hand, the Clear Grit movement of the 1850s would appear as the organizing of the maturing western community around Toronto, the rising young metropolis, in a common campaign against the domination of the region by Montreal, the older centre. In this campaign Toronto supplied both intellectual leadership, in the form of the *Globe*, and strong party direction, in the form of George Brown and other wealthy and prominent business or professional men: the urban element was critically important. And as for Western Progressivism in the 1920s, was it not bound up with the rise of Winnipeg as a prairie metropolitan centre, was not a good deal of intellectual leadership centred in that city, and is there not evidence that here was a maturing western community now ready to contest outside metropolitan domination on a large scale?[34]

Metropolitanism can be seen operating even more clearly in Canadian history where there are no frontiers of actual settlement to block the view, so to speak, and by their undoubted colour and liveliness rather steal the centre of the stage. In the Canadian fur trade, from earliest French times on, the role of the dominant organizing metropolis is plain: Montreal and Quebec the metropolitan centres for the posts of the whole fur-trading West, Paris and later London the metropolis for these Canadian towns. On the Canadian lumbering and mining frontiers, in our present northern expansion, the directing, extending, organizing, and exploiting functions of metropolitan interests are evident once more. In fact, metropolitanism has shown itself even more clearly in Canadian development than in American, precisely because we have had far less fertile acreage for agricultural settlement than has the United States. Hence the agrarian frontier of the sort that Turner described has played proportionately less part in our history. This, then, is a distinctive attribute of Canada's own version of the North American story.

Furthermore, in Canada, with its small population heavily concentrated in certain areas, metropolitan influences have had a particularly free sweep. The United States, of course, has much bigger metropolitan cities like Chicago, Philadelphia, and New York. But it also has many more large centres, each organizing its own region, though all ultimately subordinate to New York. Canada, however, has only three first-ranking metropolitan centres today: Montreal, the greatest, Vancouver, which by organizing effective communications has extended its hinterland eastward into the prairies, and Toronto, which controls wealthy southern Ontario and is steadily advancing its empire in the mining North. In

Canada, therefore, metropolitan power is in comparison to the United States more directly centralized and more immediately apparent.

Historically speaking, the functioning of metropolitanism may do more to explain the course of Canadian history than concepts of frontierism borrowed from the United States and set forth before the significance of the modern metropolis was clear. For example, the greater conservatism of Canada as compared to the United States may be read as a mark of the much stronger influence exercised in this country by conservative-minded eastern urban centres – which were certainly far removed from any impulses of forest democracy. Moreover, the stronger influence of British ideas and institutions – and even of colonialism – must have been fostered in Canada by its long and close focusing on the British metropolis itself. Finally, the fact that Canada has pioneered not so much in democracy as in the large-scale combination of public and private interests to overcome the problems raised by a difficult environment, again suggests the greater power throughout Canadian history of the forces seeking to organize communication systems and extend commerce. One might well say that the building of the C.P.R. so far ahead of settlement, and Macdonald's policies of economic nationalism in general, were plain manifestations of the power of metropolitan influences in Canadian politics. And many other instances might also be brought to mind.[35]

It could be objected with regard to some of the foregoing examples that applying a metropolitan interpretation only restates old problems in somewhat different terms. It may be so: but what is particularly needed is a restatement, a new perspective that may disclose new vistas and produce new patterns for Canadian history. At any rate, frontierism, along with earlier schools and approaches, has had its use and its day. Environmentalism needs recasting, and is being recast. The metropolitan approach largely recognizes what is already going on in Canadian historiography and provides a new framework – one which pays heed both to the distinctive features of the history of this country and to a notable modern phenomenon, the rise of metropolitanism all around the world.

Endnotes

1. It is worthy of note that the *Canadian Historical Review* for September, 1932 (XII, no.3, 343), in recording the death of F.J. Turner in March of that year, observed: "His emphasis on the importance of the frontier was the greatest single influence in the re-interpretation of the history of the United States during the past generation. The application of his views to Canadian history has scarcely begun but it is safe to say that they will have a profound effect – perhaps not less in emphasizing the differences than the similarities in the development of the two countries."
2. William Kingsford, *The History of Canada* (10 vols., Toronto, 1887-98). For his declaration of purpose, see particularly the prefaces to volumes VII, VIII, and X. Other historians who might be named to the Britannic school are Sir George Parkin, J.C. Dent, A.G. Bradley, Archibald MacMechan, and James Hannay. Of the works of the last-named, see especially *How Canada Was Held for the Empire: The Story of the War of 1812* (Toronto, 1905), a later edition of his *War of 1812* (1901), whose very title is significant.
3. See especially Chester Martin, *Empire and Commonwealth* (Oxford, 1929) and R.G. Trotter, *Canadian Federation* (Toronto, 1924). Others who might be considered members of this school are Adam Shortt, in his writings outside the specialized field of economic history, William Smith, G.E. Wilson, D.C. Harvey, Chester New, and perhaps G.M. Wrong. It will be seen, of course, that one school may overlap another in point of time, and draw its members from more than one generation. It bears repeating, however, that no attempt will or can be made to classify all major historians in one school or another. Some by virtue of fairly specialized subject matter may defy a broad classification, despite the importance of their work. Scholars primarily concerned with the French régime, the federal system, or regional developments, for example, may not fit easily into a general school, though some aspects of their writings may suggest a possible affiliation. Then again, some authors may display elements of more than one school. In this regard, the imposing figure of G.M. Wrong seems to stand between the Britannic and Nationhood schools, and indeed suggests the transition from one to the other. Professor Wrong assuredly wrote with a

consciousness of developing Canadian nationalism. But perhaps the "Britannic" element in his thought was well expressed in these words from an article of 1920 discussing the sometimes difficult advances made by Dominion nationalism during the First World War: "Yet in spite of this the British peoples were one. Probably we tend in smooth and easy days to underestimate the effects of the deep roots of unbroken tradition which nourish the life of a nation. The liberties of Canada have come, not without struggle, slowly from precedent to precedent based on parallel changes within Britain herself. It is the same in Australia. What these young states thus prize most in their own life is what Britain herself prizes most and it has involved no rupture of the long past or with the parent state. There is among all of them a continued unity in tradition and in political development." *Canadian Historical Review,* I, no.1, "Canada and the Imperial War Cabinet,"23.

4. For example, W.P.M. Kennedy. See particularly his many reviews of the 1920s, and annual review articles of the earlier 1930s, in the *Canadian Historical Review* on aspects of imperial constitutional law and Canada's relations therewith.
5. See particularly J.W. Dafoe, *Laurier, a study in Canadian Politics* (Toronto, 1922), and *Canada, an American Nation* (New York, 1935); and O.D. Skelton, *The Life and Letters of Sir Wilfrid Laurier* (2 vols., Toronto, 1921). See also, of course, the work of J.S. Ewart, who although a lawyer – as Dafoe was an editor, and Skelton became a civil servant – no less followed a nationalist historical approach in dealing with questions of autonomy. Writers of the young *Canadian Forum* "school," rather left of Liberalism, also expressed a deep suspicion of British imperial entanglements. (see the unpublished M.A. thesis by Margaret Prang at the University of Toronto, 1953, "Some Aspects of Political Radicalism in Canada between the Two World Wars.") Others less nationalist in tone but still notably concerned with Canada's developing autonomy were A.G. Dewey (*The Dominions and Diplomacy,* 2 vols., London, 1929) and R.M. Dawson (ed. and introd. to, *Development of Dominion Status, 1900-36,* Toronto, 1937). G.P. Glazebrook and F.H. Soward might also be mentioned as later "affiliates" of this school, but only in the sense that they did valuable work in its field of primary interest, the development of Canadian external relations, rather than that they carried on its earlier mood of eager nationalism.
6. The work of this school will be discussed in detail in subsequent pages, but for now let it be said that, at one time or another, its membership might be held to include W.B. Munro, F.H. Underhill, W.N. Sage, A.R.M. Lower, F. Landon, A.S. Morton, and A.L. Burt. Qualifications will of course be necessary, but at any rate the above authors made good use of frontier-environmentalist concepts in various writings, whatever else they may also have done. Furthermore, J.B. Brebner worked in the environmentalist vein to

some extent, and might be regarded as an "affiliate" of this school during much of the 1930s, while W.L. Morton might be deemed a somewhat later affiliate. It should be plain that no tight determinism is intended in thus naming these authors, nor, on the whole, did they display any. Yet the influence of environmentalism upon them may well be remarked, and hence it seems instructive to try to class them in this fashion for the purposes of this paper, even though many of them might subsequently move on to different perspectives when the peak of the Environmentalist School had passed.

7. See M. Zaslow, "The Frontier Hypothesis in Recent Historiography," *Canadian Historical Review,* XXXIX, no. 2, 1948, for a fairly recent examination.
8. Turner's thesis was first embodied in his paper, "The Significance of the Frontier in American History," read before the American Historical Association in 1893, and reprinted in his *Frontier in American History* (New York, 1920). I am indebted here to the succinct description of Turnerism in G.F.G. Stanley's paper, "Western Canada and the Frontier Thesis," *Canadian Historical Association Report,* 1940, 105. See also Zaslow, "The Frontier Hypothesis," 154-5.
9. See F.L. Paxson, "A Generation of the Frontier Hypothesis, 1893-1932," *Pacific Historical Review,* II, no. 1, 1933, and also H.N. Smith, *Virgin Land: The American West as Symbol and Myth* (Cambridge, 1950), especially the concluding chapter on Turner.
10. G.W. Pierson, "American Historians and the Frontier Hypothesis in 1941," *Wisconsin Magazine of History,* XXVI, nos. 1 and 2, 1942.
11. C.J.H. Hayes, "The American Frontier – Frontier of What?" *American Historical Review,* LI, no. 2, 1946.
12. D.R. Fox, *Ideas in Motion* (New York, 1935). See also his introduction to *Sources of Culture in the Middle West* (D.R. Fox, ed., New York, 1934).
13. A.M. Schlesinger, Jr., *The Age of Jackson* (Boston, 1945).
14. W.P. Webb, *The Great Frontier* (Boston, 1953).
15. *Canadian Historical Association Report,* 1928. See also M.L. Hansen and J.B. Brebner, *The Mingling of the Canadian and American Peoples* (Toronto, 1940), for a general integration of Canadian settlement into the whole theme of North American frontier expansion. Professor Brebner also followed this approach in his essay, "The Survival of Canada," in *Essays in Canadian History Presented to G.M. Wrong* (R. Flenley, ed., Toronto, 1939). In this he ascribed Canadian survival to the cross-pulls of American sectionalism and to the British connection rather than "predominantly to Canadian resistance," so that the emergence of a Canadian nation was largely an externally produced modification of the general North American process of settlement: for, ". . . to the student of population the settled regions of Canada, with the great exception of Quebec, appear on the whole to be

outward projections of the settled regions of the United States . . . rather than interlocked units of a separate people which has systematically expanded its occupation from Atlantic to Pacific" (272-3).

16. F.H. Underhill, "The Development of National Political Parties in Canada," *Canadian Historical Review*, XVI, no. 4, 1935. See also W.B. Munro, *American Influences on Canadian Government* (Toronto, 1929), for the influence of frontier environment on party organization and politics.
17. F.H. Underhill, "Some Aspects of Upper Canadian Radical Opinion in the Decade before Confederation," *Canadian Historical Association Report*, 1927, 47. See also G.W. Brown, "The Grit Party and the Great Reform Convention of 1859," *Canadian Historical Review*, XVI, no. 3, 1935.
18. E.H. Oliver, *The Winning of the Frontier* (Toronto, 1930).
19. A.S. Morton, *History of Prairie Settlement* (Canadian Frontiers of Settlement, VII, part 1, Toronto, 1938). See also, but to a lesser extent because of its largely pre-settlement theme, A.S. Morton, *A History of the Canadian West* to 1870-1 (Toronto, 1939). The attention paid to environmental forces at this period is well suggested by the whole Canadian Frontiers of Settlement series of the later thirties, a nine-volume project under the Canadian Pioneer Problems Committee, begun in 1934.
20. A.L. Burt, "The Frontier in the History of New France," *Canadian Historical Association Report*, 1940. See also his *Short History of Canada for Americans* (Minneapolis, 1942), 23-31. In a more recent work, however, his presidential address before the Canadian Historical Association, "Broad Horizons" (Report, 1950), Professor Burt sought a broadening of approach, beyond the continent of North America, to take in Canada's background in imperial history. And he noted that wider views in history had largely been replaced in Canada after the First World War by a heavy concentration on developments in the narrowly Canadian scene, thanks to "the rising tide of Canadian nationalism" – a statement which might well sum up the whole environmental phase. See also his study, *The United States, Great Britain, and British North America from the Revolution to the Establishment of Peace after the War of 1812* (Toronto, 1940), which rejects a frontier expansionist view of the causes of the War of 1812, stressing rather the maritime clashes between Britain and the United States.
21. Examples of criticism of the application of the frontier thesis to Canada are J.L. McDougall, "The Frontier School and Canadian History," *Canadian Historical Association Report*, 1929, and G.F.G. Stanley, "Western Canada and the Frontier Thesis."
22. *Canadian Historical Association Report*, 1930, 66-70. "It must therefore be a modified or adapted version of the [Turner] thesis which can be fitted to Canada" (66). See also Professor Lower's paper, "Some Neglected Aspects of Canadian History," *Canadian Historical Association Report*, 1929, 67-8. These articles indicate that from the start, so to speak, the author was con-

cerned about the weight to be given to tradition and political structure as well as to environment in explaining the course of Canadian history.

23. *Colony to Nation* (Toronto, 1946), 48-9. See also J.B. Brebner, "Canadian and North American History," *Canadian Historical Association Report*, 1931, in which the author noted the "identities of contour between Canadian history and North American" produced by the continental environment (42), but also remarked on points of difference, for example, in the administration of justice, where "The frontier theory of North American history, that enthusiastic elaboration of Prof. F.J. Turner's reasonable suggestions, obviously will not serve" (45).
24. F.H. Underhill, "Some Reflections on the Liberal Tradition in Canada," *Canadian Historical Association Report*, 1946.
25. *Colony to Nation*, 198-200. See also Professor Lower's *North American Assault on the Canadian Forest* (Toronto, 1938), in which organizing, dominating, metropolitan economic forces are shown in action in the forest environment. Another significant volume bearing on the relation of frontier areas to urban business interests in his earlier *Settlement and the Forest Frontier in Eastern Canada* (Canadian Frontiers of Settlement, IX, part 1, Toronto, 1936).
26. Fred Landon, *Western Ontario and the American Frontier* (Toronto, 1941).
27. Note, for example, W.L. Morton, "Direct Legislation and the Origins of the Progressive Movement," *Canadian Historical Review*, XXV, no. 3, 1944: "It [Progressivism] was the latest upsurge of agrarian and frontier democracy" (279).
28. The growing emphasis on "maritime factors" in Canadian and indeed North American history was a major development of the 1940s that extended and greatly recast environmentalist thinking, or – as it might also be put – marked the transition to a newer, wider interpretation of Canadian history. Perhaps the growing recognition of "extra-continental" forces could be linked to the impact of the Second World War, which sharply checked isolationist tendencies in Canadian thought, as the outside world was borne in upon it: a different result from that of the First World War, already noted, which enhanced a rather inward-looking nationalism. The significance of broad strategic factors, many of imperial or at least extra-continental origin, was newly observed in Canadian history, largely owing to the rise of a "military" school if the name be permitted, in which the rather neglected military and naval side of Canadian development were dealt with by such historians as C.P. Stacey, G.S. Graham, and G.N. Tucker. On the primarily economic side, H.A. Innis' *The Cod Fisheries* (Toronto, 1940) was of critical importance in showing the Atlantic not as a dividing waste of waters but as a linking network of waterways that served an international and intercontinental economy. As Dr. J.T. Shotwell said in its preface, "It extends the frontiers of North America over a vast area that we

have never thought of before as constituting a part – and a fundamental part – of the continent." In more general terms than just the economic, G.W. Brown had answered the question of whether the Americas had a common history by asserting that they had, as integral parts of an Atlantic world ("Have the Americas a Common History? A Canadian View," *Canadian Historical Review*, XXIII, no. 2, 1942). And J.B. Brebner, in closing and climaxing the great Carnegie series of studies in Canadian-American relations with his *North Atlantic Triangle* (Toronto, 1945), had found, strikingly enough, that his original plan to "set forth the interplay between Canada and the United States" had had to be extended to take in transatlantic influences stemming from Britain – and thus his significant title. His book was of double importance. Not only did it markedly reveal the transfer of forces and culture across the Atlantic lake and around the great triangle of Britain, the United States, and Canada; it also indicated that a massive set of studies on Canadian-American relations, whose very inception in the early thirties expressed the then-current concern with North American environmentalism, had ended in the forties in a new awareness of forces that reached far beyond the continental limits. Certainly a new approach to Canadian and North American historiography was taking shape.

29. See, as well as works of Professor Innis already cited, *Problems of Staple Production in Canada* (Toronto, 1933); *Settlement and the Mining Frontier* (Canadian Frontiers of Settlement, IX, part 2, Toronto, 1936); "Transportation as a Factor in Canadian Economic History," *Proceedings of the Canadian Political Science Association*, 1931; and "Significant Factors in Canadian Economic Development," *Canadian Historical Review*, XVIII, no. 4, 1937.

30. See note 25 above. Also, for a stimulating outline of the roles of Canadian metropolitan centres, Montreal, Toronto and Vancouver, and their competition for "hinterlands," see Professor Lower's essay, "Geographical Determinants in Canadian History," in *Essays Presented to G.M. Wrong*, 145-51. Indeed, he discerns in the whole pattern of Canadian economic development, "the characteristic expression of the staple trade, the metropolitan-hinterland relationship" (Two Ways of Life: The Primary Antithesis of Canadian History," *Canadian Historical Association Report*, 1943, 13).

31. Professor Masters here applies the concept of economic metropolitan dominance put forward by N.S.B. Gras in his *Introduction to Economic History* (New York, 1922) though he extends it as well to social and cultural fields. According to Gras, a city rises to metropolitan dominance over a hinterland region through four stages: first, it creates a well-organized marketing system for the whole area; second, manufacturing develops in the metropolis or the hinterland; third, there is an active programme of transportation development; and forth, a mature financial system is constructed to provide for the trade both with the hinterland and with the outside world (see preface to *The Rise of Toronto*, Toronto, 1947).

32. See C.A. Dawson and W.E. Gettys, *An Introduction to Sociology* (New York, 1948), 154-71.
33. See S.D. Clark, *Church and Sect in Canada* (Toronto, 1949), especially 90-173.
34. W.L. Morton, in his admirable recent study, *The Progressive Party in Canada* (Toronto, 1950), has written of the whole Progressive movement in strongly western environmental terms. Yet while interpreting Progressivism in the light of a frontier agrarian background, he has also showed awareness of the impact of metropolitan forces throughout. See also the foreword to this volume by S.D. Clark, noting that this western sectional protest ended by "becoming accommodated to the power structure of the metropolitan-federal system" (ix).
35. It has been said by J.B. Brebner that "the most substantial Canadian nationalism in time of peace has been economic nationalism" ("Canadianism," *Canadian Historical Association Report*, 1940, 8), and others, such as W.S. MacNutt, have echoed that view (see his letter to the editors of the *Canadian Historical Review*, XXXIV, no. 1, 1953, 108). Since economic nationalism is pre-eminently the result of metropolitan forces, it might appear that the way to the "national" heart of Canadian development, if that is a desirable goal, lies not through the frontiers of field and forest, where the environmentalist sought it, but rather through the metropolitan approach.

Saint John in the 1830s: river gateway to a New Brunswick hinterland.

Aspects of Metropolitanism in Atlantic Canada

METROPOLITANISM, THE PATTERN OF reciprocal relations whereby large urban communities focus broad areas on themselves, is intimately associated with regionalism. For regions usually centre on metropolitan communities, which largely organize them, focus their views, and deal with outside metropolitan forces on their behalf. Indeed, much of what is often called regionalism may be better expressed in terms of metropolitan relations and activities. In that belief, this discussion of metropolitanism in Atlantic Canada is offered. Because the subject is so large, it has been limited to the period from the mid-nineteenth to the early twentieth centuries, and to a selective consideration of the metropolitan roles of the three principal Atlantic cities, Saint John, Halifax, and St. John's during that period.

This time span is long enough to allow a considerable process of change to be examined, still highly significant today. Although its limits are inevitably imprecise, there is some validity in starting with the 1850s, after the end of the Navigation Acts and the old imperial system, and closing before the First World War brought striking new developments to the Maritimes and Newfoundland. As for the subject-matter, there seems no less validity in studying the three largest communities of the

Atlantic region in themselves: both as regional leaders, and because we might well pay more regard to urban history in Canada.

The fact is that, land of vast frontiers and wilderness or not, urban communities long have played a large part in Canadian development and this is no less true for the Atlantic region. Nor need the cities in question be huge and teeming by modern standards. It is far more the proportion of their population to the total in their regional community that has meaning. In 1861, for instance, Saint John had a population of 27,315 to 252,045 for all New Brunswick, or a proportion of close to 1 in 9; Halifax had 25,025 to 330,885 in Nova Scotia, or roughly 1 in 13; St. John's 30,475 to 122,635 in Newfoundland, or a remarkable proportion of almost 1 in 4. A century later, by the Canadian census of 1961, Saint John stood at something over 1 in 8, Halifax at about 1 in 8, St. John's around 1 in 9. Plainly then, even by present standards, each city has represented a decided concentration of population in its own provincial community, not to mention a concentration of capital and labour that would enable it to fulfil metropolitan functions.

These functions or attributes of metropolitan stature have broadly been held to comprise, first, the provision of commercial facilities for the import and export trade of the city's dependent region or hinterland (on which, of course, it in turn depends); second, the establishment of industries to process products of, or imports for, the hinterland; third, the development of transport services to channel traffic to and from the urban centre; and fourth, the creation of financial facilities for investment and development in the region. All these attributes can be seen in greater or less degree within the three cities under inquiry. But to these economic characteristics might also be added those of political power or military authority often centred in the metropolis; and, quite as frequently, the exercise of religious, educational, and intellectual leadership over its opinion.

Indeed, to a great extent a metropolitan system is inherently a system of communications, whether this carries goods, people or money, orders or ideas. As a result, it may be deeply affected by changes in technology; a point as true for the age that experienced the introduction of the steamship, railway, and telegraph as for that of automobility, jet transport, and television.

The effect of technological change on communications is notably clear in the case of Atlantic Canada. Although in assessing it, this general survey must to some extent put together material that is far from new, it is yet hoped that a restructuring in terms of metropolitan patterns and pulls will make the data more meaningful. And it is thought that a comparative analysis of the development of the three major Atlantic centres can promote new queries concerning their regional functions. The procedure will be to start with Saint John, then move out to sea, so to speak, in a properly Toronto-centred view of the globe.

II

In the mid-nineteenth century, Saint John held a prominent role in an Atlantic communications system extending to Liverpool and London in one direction, Boston and New York in another. It was the commercial metropolis for much of New Brunswick, exporting the timber wealth of the Saint John River from its position at the entrance to that long waterway, importing the British manufactures or American provisions needed for a hinterland heavily based on forest production. It was a focus of industry also, that utilized the chief product of its hinterland region in large-scale wooden shipbuilding. And through wealth acquired from the timber trade or the sale of Saint John ships in England, the city's business community was able to provide significant financial services, including by the later fifties three locally owned banks and four local marine, fire, or general insurance companies.

Yet Saint John's metropolitan stature had clear limits. First, although New Brunswick was past the frontier expansionist stage, the province was relatively poor and undiversified in depending on its forest staple. Second, since the whole region was largely composed of a series of separated river valleys, Saint John's sway over its own river and Bay of Fundy area by no means extended to the province's north shore. And third, since the city was not the seat of government, it could not enjoy the pervasive influence of a centre of political authority. Nor did it really exercise social or cultural headship, which remained with the genteel society of little Fredericton up-river.

Saint John's own leading elements composed a substantial, overlapping business élite of import merchants, timber traders, shipbuilders, and shipowners. The same individuals recurred in lists of the directors of banks, insurance firms, and other joint stock enterprises such as the Saint John Gas, Light, Electric, Telegraph, or South Bay Boom Companies: men such as William Parks, President of the Commercial Bank, or shipbuilders and shipowners such as Wright, DeVeber, and Zebedee Ring.[1] Nor did this Saint John business community lack strong political ties. Out of its background came such major political figures as R.L. Hazen and R.D. Wilmot, W.H. Steeves, a father of Confederation, G.E. King, provincial premier of the seventies – or Samuel Leonard Tilley himself, partner in the prominent firm of Peters and Tilley, merchants.

The business élite of Saint John was perhaps more limited in its outlook than its counterparts in either Halifax or St. John's. The New Brunswick port's outside connections largely ran to Portland as an intermediary for Boston, or else focussed on Liverpool; hardly a city of light. A scion of the mid-century élite (son of the president of the Bank of New Brunswick) recalled that Saint John businessmen would cross to Liverpool and Manchester twenty times "without ever going on to London."[2] Yet the sober, workaday masters of Saint John were lively and enterprising enough when it came to the city's main industrial activity, shipbuilding.

In the prosperous fifties, stimulated by the gold rush to Australia, Saint John yards turned out a splendid succession of large sailing vessels for Liverpool owners. There was James Smith's famed *Marco Polo,* hailed as the fastest ship in the world, after her 68-day voyage from Liverpool to Melbourne in 1852; or the *Morning Light,* of over 2,300 tons, launched by William and Richard Wright in 1855, which remained for twenty years the largest ship constructed in British North America. By 1858, of 100 major vessels over 1,200 tons sailing out of Liverpool, 32 had been built in Saint John, and the pace continued through the sixties.

Successful as it was in ocean transport, the city entered a whole new phase of problems when it looked to railways to improve its land communications in the prosperous mid-century years. Saint John interests were deeply involved in the scheme to build the European and North American Railway, which would link the Bay of Fundy port overland with the Atlantic shore at Shediac, and in the other direction with Portland,

Maine, there connecting with the rails to Boston and with the Atlantic and St. Lawrence to Montreal, open since 1852. Saint John was thus to become the focus of a great international overland route between coasts close to Europe, New England, and Canada. It was a bright vision, often more appealing than the alternative Intercolonial Railway project from Nova Scotia through New Brunswick to Quebec – though, conceivably (in the brightest moments of vision) both lines might be built, and tied together at Saint John. Of course, John A. Poor, the Portland capitalist who expressed his own city's metropolitan ambitions, had other hopes as to the final focal point of the railway scheme he was promoting. But in any case it did not succeed.

Neither Portland nor Saint John could organize the capital for so large a design, and construction problems had been underestimated. The European and North American was completed only between Saint John and Shediac by 1860, and then as a publicly owned road. Moreover, Saint John was not really well placed to dominate overland routes to the interior of the continent, a fact of growing ominous significance in the spreading railway age. When again in 1865, an attempt by a new company under William Parks failed to build the "Western Extension" from the city to Maine, many in Saint John viewed with disdain the coming of Confederation, and its concomitant bargain to build the Intercolonial, but via New Brunswick's distant shore. Indeed, they might sense that an oceanic metropolitan system in which their city had flourished was passing away to be replaced by new continental patterns with which they were less equipped to deal.

Yet Confederation was more coincident than causal in regard to changes that affected the whole functioning of Saint John as a metropolis. In fact, the changes did not plainly reveal themselves until after the depression of 1873 began. Most vital was the shift from wood to iron technology in transport. It was not the steamship that drastically affected Saint John's shipping industry, but the iron-built vessel. British yards had begun turning out cheap, capacious iron and steel steamships in quantities. They doomed Saint John's Liverpool sales and attacked the lucrative charter business of wooden sailing craft, secure while the steamship itself had been limited to fairly small wooden hulls, carrying fuel as well as cargo on a relatively few high-cost ocean runs. And while it had once been economic to build wooden ships in New Brunswick instead of England, now the great British iron and steel capacity made it increasingly uneconomic to do so. The effects came gradually. A peak year for Saint John yards was 1873, and as late as 1888, 2,000 men were still employed there.[3] But through the seventies and eighties, the city's major industry inexorably declined.

One should recall, of course, that the sweep of technological change also affected wealthier adjacent American centres. Thus New England's magnificent but costly clippers could not compete, and the region failed to build an iron ship industry. This in part was because Boston capital had turned from marine to railway investment, in efforts to organize and dominate continental routes west that proved only somewhat less abortive than Saint John's hopes of the European and North American. Portland declined. Boston itself was not so well placed to collect the traffic from the ever growing continental hinterland. It could be the chief regional metropolis of New England, but not a great deal beyond.[4] Railways, which had made inland western development so much more feasible and valuable, had shifted the emphasis from ports chiefly well located for the exchange of water-borne coastal and ocean traffic to those which also offered the most effective land access to broad continental territories.

All this was true for Saint John in the advancing railway age – itself another aspect of triumphant steel technology. Again the city was not in a position to benefit. Its own hinterland did not provide fuel or raw material for new heavy industry. And along with the relative down-grading of its timber resources went a decline in their quality, as the best pineries were cut over. Even in the 1860s it was becoming difficult to get good timber for large ships at Saint John yards.[5] Hence these underlying changes, affecting the commercial position, industrial enterprise, and even hinterland supply of the New Brunswick metropolis, were much more basic than any effects of Confederation, the National Policy of 1879, or the long depression of the later nineteenth century.

No doubt the lean depression years made the impact of change harder, especially for a city swept by the disastrous fire of 1877 that destroyed two-fifths of Saint John and $27,000,000 in property.[6] No doubt the protective tariff offered little to the business enterprises of a community largely geared to primary production, except for a declining industry tariffs could not protect. But world depression created none of Saint John's essential problems. And National Policy or not, the smaller business units of the Maritime centres would surely have faced powerful competition from much larger aggregations of capital and labour, once the age of overland communication by rail had tied them into major continental traffic systems. Here indeed lay the essential significance of the later nineteenth-century years for Saint John and its region; it was the difficult era when the old Atlantic system was failing and the New Brunswick metropolis had not yet adjusted to the new forces of continental dominance.

That adjustment came in the early twentieth century. It was, perhaps, only relatively successful, in that it could not restore all Saint John's vanished eminence, but it has largely endured to the present. Its effect was economic, yet it was achieved largely by political means for political reasons: not in spite of, but because of, the Atlantic region's membership in Canada. And it was built on the advantage the Atlantic region had to offer within that membership, year-round access to the ocean.

The Canadian federation had a political, national, need for winter ports of its own. In a sense, the process of developing them was a valid complement to the National Policy. For that programme, as Professor R.C. Brown has emphasized, must truly be seen as an expression of national aspirations, however much it might also enhance central Canadian metropolitan power.[7] If the federal state could pursue nation-building by tariffs, it could equally do so by railway and port development, by subsidies and preferential rail rates, to aid enterprises and areas disadvantaged by distance or tariffs. It was all a natural response to the problem of integrating regions within a Canadian continental entity.

The process of adjustment for Saint John really began when in 1887 business leaders in its Board of Trade opened a campaign to shift the winter terminus of the Dominion-subsidized mail steamers from Portland to the New Brunswick city. Then in 1890 the completion of the Canadian Pacific's Short Line from Montreal across Maine to Saint John meant that the Fundy port now had fairly direct access to central Canada, as well as by the more circuitous Intercolonial, intersected by the Saint John-Shediac line at Moncton. Now there indeed was hope that Canadian winter traffic still moving via Portland could be diverted to Saint John. Hence the city invested in building large ocean docks, to the extent of $1,000,000 by 1895.[8]

Late that year came the key political step. When city delegations repeatedly had failed to bring the federal government to grant a mail subsidy to a Saint John-based steamship line, the city's two MPs, J.D. Hazen and J.A. Cheslay, bluntly indicated they would resign their seats if nothing were done.[9] The Conservative cabinet, already in turmoil, and nearing highly doubtful elections, forthwith provided an annual subsidy of $25,000 to the Beaver Line for fortnightly service between Saint John and Liverpool. The Donaldson Line quickly followed in shifting its terminus from Portland; others soon did the same. Almost in months in 1896 Saint John emerged as a major winter port.

Thereafter, as the western Canadian boom developed, prairie grain flowed out of the port and imports for central Canada came in. Both the city and the CPR repeatedly enlarged the harbour facilities in a veritable race to keep up with cargoes. In 1910, the federal government entered directly into building ocean berths itself.[10] And though Saint John's old shipbuilding industry did not re-emerge, the city gathered repair yards, railway shops, sugar refineries and lumber mills. Finally, another technological change benefited it and its provincial hinterland. The development of wood-pulp mills gave a new significance to forest resources, especially those that had been inferior, such as spruce.

By 1914, accordingly, the New Brunswick city had moved far in adjusting to continental pulls, and had succeeded in making connections inward to share in western and central Canadian hinterlands. Its commercial future as a Canadian outlet and gateway would still largely depend on deliberate political policy, as in the provision of preferential railway rates. Industrial – and financial – pre-eminence had decisively moved to central Canadian metropolitan centres. Yet in the national continental system that had replaced the colonial and Atlantic one, Saint John clearly continued to play a metropolitan role within its own region.

III

Halifax and St. John's can be dealt with more briefly – not in any way as less significant, but as variations on a theme that has been established. The theme, of course, is the role of these communities in an Atlantic metropolitan system, and the effects technological change and continental pulls had upon them. However, there is more to say of Halifax during the period to be covered, since the changes in question affected St. John's later and more slowly.

The Nova Scotia city of the mid-nineteenth century did not have as full commercial control of an immediate hinterland area as did its New Brunswick neighbour. There was no long Saint John Valley to dominate; the open Atlantic coasts of the Nova Scotian peninsula enabled many lesser places to share in Halifax's importing or exporting functions, although at the same time no part of the province was wholly remote from its influence. Moreover, Halifax did not develop industry on the scale of Saint John: either wooden shipbuilding, or later enterprises. On the other hand, it was a notably larger focus of shipping interests and financial power. It was also political capital, intellectual centre – and perhaps social arbiter – as Saint John was not. Finally, Halifax, of course, was an imperial citadel and naval base: a transatlantic bastion of British metropolitan power that had strong ties to sustain and pounds sterling to spend. Still closely akin to Boston, despite the breach of the Revolution, the Haligonian descendants of Loyalist and pre-Loyalist New Englanders were happy to view London in their midst, in the fashionable society of the garrison.

As Saint John had grown with timber and the large shipbuilding it fostered, so Halifax had grown with the fishing staple and the schooners it required. The location of Halifax's superb harbour, at the corner of the continent adjacent to the main northwest Atlantic fishing grounds made it an excellent base for a fishing fleet. It was also well placed as a first mainland port of call for ships bringing imports on the great circle route from Europe to America; and for trading fish to the West Indies, in return for tropical products to be re-exported by coastal or transatlantic shipping. This extensive trading pattern, well settled by the mid-century, had made Halifax a major centre of shipping rather than shipbuilding, a commercial and financial emporium, and the wealthiest, most advanced metropolitan city in the British Atlantic provinces – focus of a fairly diversified regional society matured beyond the frontier phase.

The metropolitan stature of Halifax was evinced in the wealth and power of its merchants, notably its West Indies merchants, and in its banking institutions. In the 1850s and 1860s these included the long-established Halifax Banking Company, the Bank of Nova Scotia, the Union Bank and the Merchants Bank, begun in 1864, which would become the Royal Bank of Canada. Again their directors and those of Halifax insurance, gas, and water companies formed a business élite interwoven with wholesale merchants, shipping magnates, and steamship operators.[11] Men such as Enos Collins, Samuel Cunard, W.A. Black, and M.B. Almon were prominent. Their political pedigree was evident also. Although the old days of the Halifax oligarchy and the Council of Twelve had vanished, other potent names like Uniacke, Fairbanks, Kenney and Tobin also revealed the strong connections of the Halifax business world with Nova Scotian politics. As for wealth, Collins died in 1871 worth $6,500,000; Cunard in 1865 worth $5,000,000; and many others amassed sizeable fortunes.[12]

Cunard might have moved to England to direct his burgeoning steamship line, but the foundations of his fortune had been laid in Halifax. He had no less benefited his native city by establishing his "ocean ferry" (steamships running to schedule as sailing ships could not), and making it the first port of call in the regular steam service from Liverpool to Boston, begun in 1840. Boston was thoroughly grateful for the Cunard Line, with good reason; Halifax had reason also.[13] At the same time Halifax and Cunard could thank the British metropolitan concern for improved Atlantic communications that produced the vitally needed imperial mail contract and subsidy. Still further, Cunard might thank the imperial dockyard at Halifax for a lucrative coal contract to supply steam warships.[14] And all the Halifax merchants could appreciate the dockyard contracts for provisions, or the imperial expenditures on Halifax defences which exceeded £170,000 in the later sixties.[15] These investments in steam communications or improved facilities at Halifax were aspects of British metropolitan influence wholly beneficial to the Nova Scotia centre.

Yet the wooden paddlewheeler was the forerunner of the iron

screwsteamer, which in the seventies began to exert its effects on Halifax. No longer need the larger iron vessels call at the port for fuel after crossing the ocean; the tendency was to concentrate through runs at larger ports. Thus even in 1867 the main Cunard route ceased its stop at Halifax: an unfortunate coincidence with the inception of Confederation. And although Halifax had no major wooden ship industry to suffer, its functions as a wholesale centre did. For the ubiquitous iron tramp steamer could readily take cargoes direct to hinterland ports, instead of via Halifax warehouses. By the 1880s the ease of ordering goods direct by telegraph and the speed of steamship delivery was seriously affecting Halifax as an entrepôt.[16] Moreover, the decline in the West Indies sugar economy increasingly harmed Halifax shipping and fishing interests.

Nevertheless, the wealth and power of Halifax were such that it was a case of slowed growth rather than absolute decline. New industries were started, some aided by tariff protection: cotton mills, shoe factories, sugar refineries.[17] But the important response was as that of Saint John: to make the city an effective part of the Canadian continental system as a winter port. The work began as early as 1882, when indeed the Dominion government built a grain elevator at Halifax. But more important were the building of the big Halifax drydock in 1887-89, and the steady development of the Intercolonial Railway's deep water terminus, which by 1899 could handle twelve large ocean steamers at once.[18]

With first-class port facilities and improving rail connections, Halifax was now equipped to take its own considerable share of the Canadian boom of the early twentieth century. It prospered vigorously, able to hold its own with Saint John – and hold as well the Atlantic margins of New Brunswick, more susceptible to its own rail connections. In fact, it made little difference when in 1905 a long era ended for Halifax, and Britain, concentrating her naval forces, gave up the Halifax naval base. Formal transfer of the naval dockyard to a largely store-keeping Canadian régime came in 1910, to mark another aspect of advancing continental dominance. Still another sign of that advance came in the financial field. In 1900 the general manager's office of the Bank of Nova Scotia was transferred to Toronto, in 1907 that of the Royal Bank to Montreal, and in 1903 the august Halifax Banking Company became part of Toronto's Bank of Commerce as it invaded the Maritimes.[19]

Yet, if Halifax was thus being incorporated in the continent, it retained its essential strategic importance as a focal point for transatlantic communication. That was made abundantly plain only a few years thereafter, when the port was again called upon to prove its significance in naval war, as it had not been required to do since 1814. But that is another story.

IV

To conclude with St. John's: its metropolitan role might seem the least significant of the three Atlantic cities. Certainly its own hinterland was thinly populated and scarcely developed but for the fringe of fishing outports; it had virtually no industrial base apart from the cod and seal fisheries; and its financial services were limited by the backward state of the Newfoundland region in general. And yet, in other respects, St. John's had a decidedly powerful metropolitan role, as the commercial and shipping *entrepôt* of the great island. Its merchants and shipowners financed the fishing staple, marketed dried cod from the West Indies to the Mediterranean, imported and distributed foodstuffs and manufactures for the outports, and through the use and abuse of the credit system tied the fishing population closely to its business houses of Water Street. Here was a compact urban élite, notably internationally minded, whose social predominance was unrivalled. One cannot doubt the enduring influence of the dynasties of the St. John's business world, the Bowrings, Job Brothers, the Ayres, Newman and Company.[20] And one need scarcely assert the political ascendancy of St. John's figures like Charles Fox Bennett and Ambrose Shea, Robert Thorburn and Robert Bond, when all the class and religious friction of the province found its focus in politics at the capital.

The city, moreover, was well integrated in the old Atlantic nineteenth-century system, traditionally linked with Liverpool, London, and Bristol, increasingly with the Maritimes and Boston. Yet it was still remote from the continent, buying supplies rather than selling there, and little affected by continental forces – as the flat rejection of Confederation with Canada might show. The state of the fishing and sealing catches also affected it far more immediately than the world process of technological change. Indeed for much of the later nineteenth century St. John's was generally flourishing. It had four banks by the mid-seventies, direct steam service with England from 1869, the Atlantic cable since 1866, and regular steamship sailings to Halifax.[21] The eighties brought the beginning of railway building with the line to Harbour Grace and stimulated many small-scale industrial enterprises, of which Colonial Cordage survived.

But the well-being of St. John's continued to rest ultimately on the uncertain fortunes of the fisheries; its metropolitan ventures into industrial and transport development proved shaky and premature. After the Great Fire of 1892, that burned out most of the city's commercial firms and left 11,000 homeless, the whole strained, overextended financial system was in deep trouble.[22] The bank crash of 1894 that followed, the failure of renewed Confederation negotiations with Canada the next year, left the city in financial chaos and considerable bitterness over apparent Canadian indifference to the gravity of the problem. When recovery came, with prosperous world trade in the new century, and a Newfoundland boom based on railway building and the development of pulpwood and mineral resources, it seemed that St. John's had again decisively turned its back on Canadian continental connections.

But had it? With hindsight, one could say that the connections had only been delayed; or rather that they were, so far, premature for an island community which in its remoteness had not yet felt the full impact of technological change in its communications system. The decline of the old-style Newfoundland fishery in face of modern big-ship operations would not become fully apparent until the bad years between the two world wars. Commission government might then be regarded as a final, reluctant exercise of British metropolitanism; the establishment of American and Canadian bases on the island in the Second World War as a function of extending continental metropolitan dominance – to be consolidated politically in the Confederation settlement of 1949.

Furthermore, again with hindsight, one may note the growth of continental pulls upon St. John's even from the 1890s; above all, the fact that Canadian banks took over in the city after the collapse of its own financial institutions.[23] Also, the very Newfoundland railway boom was shaped, if not captured, by R.A. Reid, fresh from his building for the

CPR. And the pulpwood and iron-mining developments that began at last to diversify the Newfoundland region were largely in accord with Canadian continental interests. The real point is that St. John's, like its sister cities of the Atlantic region, was going to join the continent; each in varying ways, perhaps, but decisively – with changes in metropolitan patterns of communications which involved them all. What remain are questions. There is no intention here to put forward technological change as a kind of simplified economic determinism – but how far did it relate to the decision-making processes both of business and of government? How far was it the factor that made urban business élites in the Atlantic metropolitan centres aware of their own need to respond to change and make adjustments? How far did they utilize political influence to do so, and what were the reactions in their own regional communities? We need a great deal more study of the role of these urban élites, in the Atlantic region as elsewhere in Canada: more urban history, more business history, more study of the political and social interweavings of these entrepreneurial elements – which will inevitably carry us further into regional socio-cultural history as well. In sum, the restructuring of things we already know in this inevitably sketchy paper (that still leaves so much out), should only make us aware of how much we do not know, when we look at regionalism in terms of metropolitanism.

Endnotes

1. See *Saint John Business Directory and Almanac for 1857, et seq.* (Saint John 1857).
2. J.W. Millidge, "Reminiscences of Saint John from 1849 to 1860," *New Brunswick Historical Collections,* no. 10 (Saint John 1919), 135.
3. F.W. Wallace, *Wooden Ships and Iron Men* (London n.d.), 309.
4. A.P. Langtry, ed., *Metropolitan Boston* (New York 1929), 1067.
5. Millidge, *loc. cit.*, 131.
6. D.R. Jack, *Centennial Prize Essay on Saint John* (Saint John 1883), 151.
7. See R.C. Brown, "The Nationalism of the National Policy," in P. Russell, ed., *Nationalism in Canada* (Toronto 1966), 155-63.
8. F. W. Wallace and I. Sclanders, *The Romance of a Great Port* (Saint John 1935), 37.
9. *Ibid.*, 44.
10. *Ibid.*, 46.
11. See *Beecher's Farmers Almanack for 1850, et seq.* (Halifax 1850).
12. A.W.H. Eaton, *Chapters in the History of Halifax* (New York 1915), 839.
13. F.L. Babcock, *Spanning the Atlantic* (New York 1931), 48.
14. P.H. Watson, "The Two Hundredth Anniversary of the Halifax Dockyard," *Occasional Papers of the Maritime Museum* (Halifax 1959), 21.
15. *Ibid.*, 32.
16. P.R. Blakeley, *Glimpses of Halifax, 1867-1900* (Halifax 1949), 24.
17. *Ibid.*, 38-45.
18. *Ibid.*, 28.
19. See McApline's *Halifax City Directory for 1907-08* (Halifax 1907).
20. See *Year Book and Almanack of Newfoundland, 1913* (St. John's 1913); also C.R. Fay, *Life and Labour in Newfoundland* (Toronto 1956), 13-37.
21. P. Toque, *Newfoundland as it was and is* (London 1878), 76-87.
22. A.B. Perlin, "St. John's," *Atlantic Advocate* (June 1960), 47.
23. R.A. MacKay, ed., *Newfoundland* (Toronto 1946), 459.

The railways: Don Station on the Grand Trunk, Toronto 1860s. The land technology that spread metropolitan dominance.

Metropolis and Region: the Interplay Between City and Region in Canadian History Before 1914

FROM THE SIXTEENTH TO THE early twentieth century, from the opening of the Newfoundland fishery to the settlement of the western plains and Pacific slopes, Canada took shape primarily through the spreading of frontiers across the continent. Frontier areas, the forward zones of an expansive, acquisitive society, offered new supplies of natural resources to be put to commercial production. Generally, and increasingly, these raw areas of resource supply developed into populous, well structured regions with collective identities of their own. Yet the whole development of freshly opened frontier into firmly rooted region was linked throughout with the growth of the city, and especially with that of the largest, most powerful kind of city, the metropolis. In effect, frontiers themselves were the furthest hinterlands of cities, the trading territories dominated by urban centres. They were far-spread supply fields for urban places, emerging investment, market and service outlets; and, above all, enlarging spheres of influence for those most dominant urban places, the metropolitan cities. Behind the rise of frontier, hinterland or region in Canada lay the power of the metropolis, which ultimately disposed of their resource harvest, strongly fostered their expansion, and widely controlled their very existence.

At first glance, frontier and metropolis might mainly seem to represent contrasting or even antithetical states of human existence, the first connoting low population density, simple staple production and sketchy, fragmented social organization; the second, urban massing at a peak, advanced and highly specialized economic activities, and a complex social fabric. Yet they may also be seen as communities of settlement linked in the age-old, organic relationship which has persisted between country and town: between the dispersed society of the countryside and the concentrated urban populace, each of them supporting and serving the other. In this view, in the context of town-and-country relations displayed in Canada's past, 'frontier' may well be said to have represented country at its most countrified, the least developed sort of dispersed community at an early stage of growth, while 'metropolis' equally signified town society of an intensively developed kind. But however divergent they were, at either end of a scale of rural-urban interrelations, they remained integrally connected within one of the most basic and pervasive patterns of human history.

Between metropolis and frontier on this urban-rural scale would lie more mature countrysides of hinterland communities, each with towns and emergent cities of their own at various stages of growth, extending in series from the centres of metropolitan power. Still, the pattern of interconnection covered them all. Frontiers, too, could pass from being thinly held, scantily organized expanses into well integrated rural domains with villages and towns arising in their midst. Some of the latter centres might advance to cities, gain paramountcy over sizeable local hinterlands, and so in time acquire their own measure of regional metropolitan dominance under the greater sway from beyond. And this urban growth in general, from minor town to regional metropolis, went on hand in hand with that of the maturing countryside. Whatever the strains and discords that could occur in the process, town and country broadly grew up through interaction, in constant interplay.

The pattern and the process in Canada was by no means as neat and orderly as this schematic outline might indicate. Some frontier areas failed to develop far, or to become substantial, thriving rural hinterlands. Towns might be planted on a frontier itself; some to wither, a few eventually to attain metropolitan stature. But the key point remains that this great process of growth across both space and time did constitute a coherent whole. It produced systems of interdependent communities in town and country, not disparate sets of opposed elements linked only through the exploitation of the weaker by the stronger – though such exploitation most assuredly was present. In essence, as the regional character of Canadian life developed from frontier beginnings to transcontinental scope, so did the urban metropolitan network which focussed that life. The integral, reciprocal relationship of city and countryside was evident throughout.

Yet further, throughout the course of that development, the parts played by frontier and metropolis stand out with special clarity. The very extent of Canada's territory and the enduring emphasis on the exploitation of its natural resources long underscored the significance of frontiers – still patently present today in near-empty reaches of the North. But the role of the metropolis in developing the vast terrain has been no less apparent. Compared with the United States, Canada produced far fewer middle-sized cities and country towns. Its urban net did not become so thickly beaded and many-stranded; its country population remained much smaller and less broadly distributed. Hence the influence of a limited number of major cities was strongly, plainly, manifested across the Canadian landscape: cities which became notably large for Canada's total population, and were in no way inconsiderable within North America as a whole.

Rather more like Australia, Canada took form as a country with large metropolitan communities on one hand and large, sparsely occupied expanses on the other. The Canadian pattern was clear by the First World War, but it could be traced far back. In both cases, of course, it was in over-simple terms the result of environmental factors: the nature of the lands and resources that did not make for generally well diffused occupation, but did encourage sizeable population concentrations at major controlling points. In any event, within North America, Canada turned out to be significantly different from the United States in the degree to which metropolitan power could be exercised quite directly over great regional sweeps of the countryside, with much less mediation or internal competition along the way. Even a very general survey of Canadian urban-regional history gives repeated demonstrations of that power in decisive and far-reaching operation – both before and after the long years down to 1914 which constitute our present span of interest.

From the early days of European contacts in the sixteenth century, metropolitan forces thrusting across the Atlantic from France and England engendered and directed the spread of the initial Canadian fishing and fur-trading frontiers. They brought the beginnings of settlement, and the appearance of small colonial entrepôts and garrison centres, cities in embryo, such as St. John's and Halifax, Quebec and Montreal. Still, these urban outposts, like the colonial frontiers themselves, remained subject to the commercial, political and military control of the external transatlantic metropolises, to the final policies and purposes of the mercantile and government élites of Paris or London. The expansion of Montreal's St. Lawrence fur-trading hinterland to the western limits of the continent by the end of the eighteenth century, or the rapid rise thereafter of lumbering on great eastern rivers like the Saint John and the Ottawa, did not alter the fact that metropolitan markets and strategic interests in Great Britain effectively determined the course and fate of this frontier forward sweep.

In the earlier nineteenth century, farming as well as lumbering frontiers made increasing headway into the mid-continent to tap and occupy new resource areas. But their advance continued to take place under British external sway, and within a British-based metropolitan system of trade control, markets and investment. Along with spreading settlement – itself now largely fostered by immigration from metropolitan Britain – came advancing urban activities; and this in time promoted the rise not only of numerous local commercial towns, but also of incipient internal metropolitan centres, notably Montreal and Toronto. Yet in time as well, the outreaching British North American frontiers felt the powerful influence of other external metropolises, to be found in the burgeoning United States. Around the mid-century, when the old British imperial pattern of direct political and commercial regulation was fast disappearing, the colonial hinterlands instead were being increasingly tied southward by lines of trade and transport to an American metropolitan system that drew readily upon their resources, whether linking them to Boston and New York, or later to Chicago, St. Paul, and San Francisco.

Confederation in 1867 brought and expressed the efforts of an emerging central Canadian metropolitan system mainly based on Montreal and Toronto to organize the British North American hinterlands into a separate continental unit. The very opening of vast new western frontiers of farming and ranching displayed the workings of metropolitan forces, which politically were now directed from Ottawa. They were reflected in endeavours to counter American penetrations into the North West beyond the Great Lakes; in the federal control of land settlement and resources in the western plains; in the establishing of the North West Mounted Police as an instrument of metropolitan authority throughout the new domain. They were further exhibited in the building of the Canadian Pacific Railway to join the western regions to the central realms of rising Canadian metropolitan dominance, and in the erection of the protective tariff to develop and defend the east-west flow along a national traffic system.

In the Pacific West beyond the Rockies, the gold frontiers of the Fraser and Cariboo had produced the boom-town rise of Victoria in the 1860s, as a small-scale Vancouver Island metropolis that commanded the mining hinterland in the mainland British Columbian mountains. The waning of the gold fields turned a thinly-settled, financially strained British Columbia towards union with Canada; and the completion of the C.P.R. in 1885 finally sealed that union by effectively tying the Pacific province into the Canadian metropolitan structure. Victoria, a maritime commercial centre which had been linked by sea to San Francisco, the key American Pacific metropolis, and beyond that, to older connections with London, was soon displaced by the upstart rising power of Vancouver on the mainland, as the continental rail terminus that was destined to become a new metropolitan city dominating Canada's far western region. The growth of Pacific logging and fishing frontiers had much to do with Vancouver's advance, but more crucial were its through rail connections. And the fact that the trans-Canada track came at all to the city's commanding site on Burrard Inlet was essentially the result of central metropolitan purpose, enterprise, and investment.

In the great plains of the interior, the through railway similarly impelled the rise of Winnipeg as a regional metropolis. Around the turn of the twentieth century, when the western wheat frontiers were rapidly being occupied, the city at the gateway to the plains grew swiftly as the gathering point for grain transport eastward to the Lakehead and St. Lawrence, the main distributing point for goods flowing west to fan out by rail across the prairies. Beyond this regionally dominant centre, lesser but still fast-expanding cities like Regina, Calgary and Edmonton each gained sway over their own extensive hinterlands. All of them were fostered not only by the growth of their neighbouring agrarian frontiers, but also by the broad metropolitan system which linked them across the continent, and by the local metropolitan influence which they wielded over the economic, social or political interests of their own surrounding territories. By the First World War, the urban West had taken form no less than the rural West. If anything, it had advanced proportionately more rapidly and powerfully.

At the same time, the urban manufacturing East had clearly emerged. Through the later nineteenth and early twentieth centuries, factories spread in commercial towns and cities from Nova Scotia to western Ontario, encouraged by the protective tariff of 1879 and the widening markets along the national traffic system. Textile mills in the Saint John Valley and Eastern Townships, agricultural machinery works at Brantford or footwear factories at Quebec, heavy steel plants at Hamilton or Sydney – all marked a new era of increasingly specialized, industrialized urban concentration. But the greatest gainers were the leading metropolitan cities of Montreal and Toronto. In general, and in time, they accumulated a wider, more diversified pattern of industries, along with large-scale factory units and massed labour forces. Hence their influence as metropolises on a national scale became still more enhanced. Even industries which they did not control in neighbouring, competing centres they increasingly financed; or they profitted commercially by handling supplies and products for them. In sum, the national ascendancy of the financial and commercial interests of Montreal and Toronto was only strengthened further by the addition of an industrial component to the Canadian metropolitan system.

At 1914, Montreal still held a commanding lead, largely through its control of major railway lines and its greater industrial and banking power: the latter chiefly embodied in the wealthy, long established Bank of Montreal. Yet Toronto was a substantial second as a national metropolis, notably active in banking across the west, especially through its expanding Bank of Commerce. Indeed, the whole Canadian banking system was metropolitan in scope and consequence, since the existence of a set of large chartered banks with branches across the country focussed impressive financial authority in a few main urban centres.

Toronto, as well, acquired more wealth and metropolitan power through the development of new mining frontiers in the early twentieth century. The link between metropolis and frontier grew even more direct and manifest as the mining North arose. And Ontario's capital city became its main Canadian beneficiary. Mining frontiers, when they went beyond the superficial and transitory stages of gold rushes to the Cariboo or Klondike, involved heavy investment in deep-shaft mines, smelting technology and transport facilities. Essentially they were the domains of large urban-based companies whose local labour forces dwelled in compact town communities, even though these might well be set in thinly-populated surroundings. Such a pattern emerged in Albertan coalfields and in the metal mines of British Columbia's inland Kootenay area. But it became no less evident when the mineral resources of the huge Precambrian Shield were tapped in Ontario – in the great copper-nickel complex at Sudbury, the silver wealth of Cobalt, the hard-rock goldfields of the Porcupine District. City business power dominated them all. Behind it, the Toronto metropolis grew in size and outreach, as the main supply base for the new provincial frontier, the focus of its rail transport, and the seat of the provincial government that awarded mineral lands and regulated mining companies. Still farther behind this whole development stood the greater investing power of large American centres, particularly New York. But increasingly they operated northward through Toronto, as the focus of new mining promotions.

A similar picture could be drawn of metropolitan activity on northern forest frontiers by the early twentieth century. Mounting demands for newsprint to feed big city dailies spread pulp-mill towns into the Shield. They appeared from Newfoundland to eastern Quebec as well, and soon up the coasts of British Columbia. Again large-scale corporate business controlled: city-centred and city-financed. Moreover, the pulpwood frontier was closely linked to the development of hydro-electric power to operate the mills; and this, too, required substantial investment. The hard-living lumberman might still be a frontier archetype; but he was also the hinterland employee of an intensively organized and capitalized metropolitan business enterprise.

These latest frontier extensions, and the continuing development of settled hinterlands, by no means benefitted the major eastern centres in the same degree. Quebec; Saint John, New Brunswick; and Halifax were remote from the newer areas of growth westward or northward: their own hinterlands seemed to offer few more resource supplies to exploit. Changing technology on the oceans ended the once-great wooden shipbuilding industries of Quebec and Saint John by the late nineteenth century. The re-orientation of traffic to continental rail routes had undermined the former eminence of Halifax in shipping around the Atlantic coasts. As for St. John's in Newfoundland, it was even more remote from continental development, still vitally dependent on the great island's staple cod fishery and subject to the vagaries of the catch and distant market prices. In the early twentieth century, an era of general Canadian prosperity, these Atlantic places grew; but only slowly in comparison to cities from Montreal westward to Vancouver.

Nevertheless, the very conditions experienced by these eastern centres and their hinterlands again reflected the workings of metropolitan forces. It was the multiplying construction of iron ships in industrialized metropolitan Britain that had largely doomed the wooden wind ship on the high seas; the tying of the Maritimes by railway and tariff to the Central Canadian heartland that had opened them to the metropolitan dominance of large Montreal or Toronto businesses. St. John's, at least, did enjoy some metropolitan expansion of its own, when the new trans-Newfoundland railway tapped the interior of the island around 1900, and its pulpwood and mineral resources became productive. Moreover, Halifax and Saint John gained the position of winter ports in the Canadian continental traffic system; so that, when the St. Lawrence route was frozen, wheat areas as far west as Alberta effectively became part of their own hinterlands, as grain went out through national elevators at their harbours. Halifax, too, remained the Canadian northwest Atlantic naval base, just as it had been a British imperial bastion from its foundation in the mid-eighteenth century. Metropolitan influence quite plainly had political and military aspects as well as economic or social. The former attributes shaped Halifax strongly – and even more notably once the First World War broke out.

By that time, moreover, the metropolitan-urban network which still exists had taken form across Canada, in conjunction with the spread of fresh frontiers and the rise of maturing regions. Beyond the national metropolises of Montreal and Toronto, at the core of the urban hierarchy, the regional metropolises of Winnipeg and Vancouver, the lesser, or sub-metropolises of Regina, Edmonton, Calgary and Victoria, were linked to westward; and ties ran eastward to Quebec and the Atlantic centres. In the more intensively developed and thickly populated central regions, cities like Ottawa or Hamilton, London or Windsor, each held an influential role. And beneath all these major places, in their surrounding hinterlands, smaller cities and towns exercised their own subordinate territorial sway – often indeed competing and conflicting, but more broadly complementing one another throughout the Canadian pattern of urban-regional, town-and-country relationship.

Each of the leading metropolitan communities clearly had acquired a distinctive character and composition, closely related to the interests and activities of its particular region; but linked also to the ethnic make-up of its own inhabitants, their experiences, attitudes and circumstances, and to the ambitions and entrepreneurship of its own decision-makers. In fact, it is important here to underline the obvious – lest the foregoing survey may seem to have ignored it – that cities are made up of people, no less than the countryside communities. One does not really deal with impersonal forces or concepts in talking of city and region, metropolis and frontier, but with individuals and social groupings whose intentions or responses affect the whole course of town-and-country interplay. Only the need to exemplify the powerful effects of metropolitan influences on Canadian development in short space can justify paying such scant attention to the human factor. Regrettably, that situation must continue in the present paper, as we turn to consider the conceptual approach used in this general survey of urban-regional historic growth in closer detail.

II

The term 'metropolis' has had abundant currency; but as it has been applied here, it relates most directly to a classic statement of economic metropolitanism set forth over fifty years ago by the Canadian-born, American-based economic historian, N.S.B. Gras. Gras affirmed that major cities rose in wealth and power as the focal points of large areas – hinterlands – which they served, organized, and dominated economically. The outcome was a metropolitan economy: "the organization of producers and consumers mutually dependent for goods and services, wherever their wants are supplied by a system of exchange concentrated in a large city which is the focus of local trade and the centre through which normal economic relations with the outside are maintained." This metropolitan centre, in short not only channelled and commanded the commerce of its hinterland, but also largely controlled that between its own and other metropolitan areas.

The process whereby the metropolis attained such a position of domination went through four main stages, according to Gras. First, the city built up a marketing system for its territory, establishing warehouse, wholesale, and exchange facilities which became steadily more specialized. Second, sizeable manufacturing growth took place, either in city or hinterland, but increasingly directed by the former. Third, the transport system was actively improved; in part within the urban place itself, but more significantly without, to gain it better access to its hinterland and also to other metropolitan places. Finally, powerful financial institutions developed in the major city, to service both hinterland trade and that to the world beyond: banks, investment and insurance firms that mobilized and disseminated capital from the centre.

It may be queried whether these four stages in a city's rise to metropolitan status needed to take place in the specific sequence in which Gras depicted them – or whether all had to be fully realized before a city might properly be deemed a metropolis. Certainly in the Canadian case, transport development usually preceded noteworthy manufacturing growth; and at least down to 1914 some leading places that manifestly commanded large hinterlands still had only limited industrial activities of their own. In fact, Gras' presentation was more oriented to the mature industrial economies of western Europe than to the relatively new land like Canada, much closer to pioneer phases of existence. Nevertheless, if his four stages of metropolitan development are more broadly regarded as characteristic features of emerging metropolitanism, then each indeed can be associated with the rise of major Canadian urban centres to positions of economic dominance. Though the timing and degree of development might vary from city to city, their advance was clearly marked throughout by the key attributes of metropolitanism discerned by Gras: the commercial organization of a tributary market area, the fashioning of an effective transportation network focussed on the city, the provision of processing and manufacturing facilities for the hinterland and its centre, and the shaping of a financial system to furnish needed credit and investment – and thereby tie the hinterland still more strongly to the city by radiating lines of debt.

This, then, supplies a basic pattern for analyzing the ascent of the main Canadian cities to metropolitan roles during the nineteenth century, as in greater or lesser degrees they became commercial metropolises, transport metropolises, industrial or financial metropolises, with the most powerful and paramount among them displaying the fullest range of these functions. They could, however, exercise more than economic functions in dominating territories: from political direction to cultural headship. At root the metropolitan concept is plainly an economic or, better, a socio-economic formulation. Yet any broad-based analysis of the rise of Canadian metropolitan centres must no less plainly provide for other ramifications in their growth.

These could well include the truly decision-making power of a seat of government, the commanding grasp of a strategic military base, or the social control transmitted from a chief centre of religion and culture. Still further, cities might extend their sway through superior control over means of information; over the press and publishing in the nineteenth century, the cable, telegraph, and later the telephone systems; even over popular styles and standards in time to be merchandised through the mail order catalogue. In fact, one might venture to speak of an "attitudinal metropolitanism" beyond the economic or political varieties, though in part derived from them, whereby a particular city came to be accepted as a chief place of regard by a broad hinterland community: the place to which the main ways led and from which the main words came. It might assuredly be resented; but still it was watched as the prime focus of the countryside, where leadership lay and events of far more than local concern transpired – whatever else was occurring, much more dimly, in the distant world outside.

Consequently, metropolitanism should duly be considered as a many-sided phenomenon, although no doubt, its economic aspects remain primary. Yet however much metropolitan development may be grounded in economic facts and forces, it cannot fully be dealt with through measurable material data on trade flows, rates of investment, rail and water-borne tonnage and the like; even if the necessary mass of specific figures were available on urban-hinterland exchanges – which for the bulk of nineteenth-century Canada they are not. Moreover, though it is valid to trace the workings of metropolitan power through government and legislative policies or political processes, it is not sufficient either. There still remains the psycho-cultural domain of attitude and opinion: the influence of inertia in established patterns of communication, the force of change released by the very anticipations of change (as in railway promotion); the perceptions, aspirations and responses that again come down to the human factor, both individually and collectively.

In any event, the concept of metropolitanism that is here employed fits in readily with that of urban-regional interplay. The metropolitan-hinterland relationship is, in fact, just a particular and powerfully significant case of the general interconnections of town and country – or of city and frontier, when that is applicable. Metropolitan cities simply represent the top level of urban communities in interaction with their supporting regions. They may of course, have numbers of lesser cities and towns in their own broad hinterlands; but beneath the pre-eminent metropolitan centres these subordinate places have functioned within a similar pattern of relationships on a more limited and localized scale.

This whole urban-regional, metropolitan-hinterland pattern thus can organize countryside on town from bottom to top, from the mere village and its environs to the metropolis and great sweeps of territory. Naturally it is seldom nicely delimited, and there may be many shared, conflicting and fluctuating marginal areas of dominance. Yet certain consistencies in the pattern do stand out. For one thing, it again reflects the reciprocity of the urban-regional relationship noted at the outset: this remains a web of mutual support and dependence. For another, the greatest dynamic force clearly operates at the top, with the metropolis displaying the widest power to lead and mould. The hinterland may certainly react against that power, even producing protest movements to seek changes of its own; but this in the main still constitutes response to superior metropolitan dynamism and initiative.

This final point, however, re-affirms the fact that the metropolis also remains vitally affected by its interplay with hinterland or region. After all, it rose through its success in focussing that area, in dominating its supplies and services. The great city was made by its command of richly-yielding trading territory, even though, in the Canadian case, this might involve far distant operations or areas that were but thinly occupied and at rudimentary frontier stage of growth. Indeed, for that very reason the metropolitan-hinterland analysis seems especially applicable to the history of Canadian development in city and countryside; considerably more so, for example, than the central-place theory originated by the German geographer, Walter Christaller, in the 1930s which depict the structure of urban hierarchies and the role of top-level central cities in such a system.

The Christaller analysis largely turns on weighing the accumulation of retail trading activities at central places in the urban network of a thickly settled territory, theoretically conceived as a featureless plain without geographic barriers or diversities. It may thus be questioned whether such a model based on an old, close-knit central European society can come close enough in its assumptions and approach to past historical realities in the North American environment. This, at any rate, is an argument effectively presented by the American geographer, James E. Vance. His own work (in the 1960s) on the geography of wholesaling makes clear the importance of far-reaching wholesale trade in the expanses of pioneer America, the critical significance of the wholesale merchant as the prime agent in engendering and abstracting commerce from the open, dispersed settlements of a 'new' continent – and the pre-eminent role of the entrepôt city, the merchant's base of operation, from which the lines of trade spread inland, fostering further collecting and distributing entrepôts along their course, as trade enlarged in reach and volume.

To Vance, "cities grow in relation to their long distance ties, those which are carried on by abstraction and agency fully as much as by retail gravitation." He recognizes that the central-place model, which stresses the myriad face-to-face exchanges of retailing rather than the long-range abstract relations of wholesaler and market, could become more applicable as development continued in closely settled farming or manufacturing areas. Yet he maintains the primacy of his 'mercantile model', both explaining the historic growth of an America that began with the age of mercantilism, and as still being more widely relevant to the American setting today.

Vance's model has much to recommend it to the Canadian case as well. In fact, it obviously has close affinities with the metropolitan analysis: in emphasizing long-distance trading ties which initially spread overseas from European centres, in noting the leading role of an urban-based entrepreneurial élite, and in confirming that the resultant rise of cities stemmed largely from the successive organization and development of outthrust hinterlands. Nonetheless, his concept does not replace that of metropolitanism. In part, the two conform; in part, move to separate concerns of their own. In regard to the metropolitan analysis, the mercantile model, of course, pays only passing heed to non-economic aspects – even to non-commercial aspects. In some degree Vance's entrepôt city sounds a good deal like the commercial metropolis; but other features of advancing metropolitanism are less considered in his treatment.

Above all (and quite reasonably in the light of his purposes), Vance does not greatly examine the hinterland side of the urban-rural complex, concentrating as he does on city merchants and urban commercial growth. But we must go on further in the rural direction, to round out this broad consideration of concepts by amplifying those of region and frontier as they have herewith been employed.

It must already be quite apparent that nothing very esoteric is implied in the use of such well-tried terms, which broadly pertain to the world of the countryside, the hinterland, though as seen in differing aspects. In the case of region, this is indeed to be distinguished as a large and relatively mature hinterland, or, at any rate, as one in process of attaining such a level of maturity. That is, it is in course of developing fairly complex and ordered patterns of rural life and institutional organization, generally perceived and widely expressed 'regional' interests, and also a mounting degree of self-awareness as an enduring collectivity with its own identity. Still further, it will be acquiring its own substantial system of urban places, that may rise even to include a regional metropolis, or metropolises, beneath the greater national centres. It is probably unnecessary to add that while the region continues to form part – a large part – of the national unit as a whole, it too can be composed of a number of parts, sizeable sub-regions, all with identifiable features and sub-focusses of their own. But given the ever-changing process of history, it seems unwise to try to delimit these sub-regions too closely, or to produce a confining set of categories for them.

It does seem worth remarking, however, that a regional metropolis can greatly influence the evolution of a region's life and self-awareness by centring so much of its activities through the workings of metropolitanism. In short, as Quebec, Halifax, Winnipeg or Vancouver came to display regional metropolitan leadership across areas of Canada through exercising varied measures of political, economic or socio-cultural dominance of their hinterlands, they could also function as chief centres of regard in regional life, main focusses of regional opinion, and as major rallying-points for regional movements, especially in reaction to pressures or problems imposed from outside. In respect to internal regional concerns, on the other hand, there well might be more antipathetic responses from their local hinterlands. Thus Winnipeg business interests could be regionally well regarded in leading the way against the outside financial power of Toronto or Montreal; but rather less so when the more "inside" aims and ambitions of Brandon or Regina were involved – and less so again when western wheat farmers as a regional interest group weighed the power of Winnipeg grain merchants over their own crop prices and sales.

In any event, regions essentially persist: yet frontiers essentially pass away. The frontier is not only an outlying hinterland in a rudimentary stage of development, but one in a notably transitory state as well. Southern Ontario, for instance, may still be deemed a regional hinterland of Toronto; yet its predecessor, the Upper Canada agrarian frontier, has long since vanished. Impermanence, then, is a strongly characteristic mark of the frontier, and can apply whether it disappears with populous regional settlement or ends in scrub bush and deserted shanties. This transitory frontier hinterland may undoubtedly last widely different lengths of time. In a mountain gold rush it might rise and fall within a few years, exist for several decades on the western wheatlands, about half a century in Upper Canada, and much longer in the fur trading or Atlantic fishing realms before the nineteenth century. In fact, when one considers the size and long endurance of the northern fur frontier, in particular, he may admittedly be led to question the impermanence of frontiers, or be faced with the delicate business of trying to distinguish between short-term and long-run transitions.

No doubt Canadian historic experience does belie the older American frontierist assumption that all wildernesses are to be won; that frontiers advance steadily and as steadily are transformed into settled farms and booming cities. In great degree, Canadians instead live with a permanent frontier expanse to their northward: about as permanent as anything historically can be. Nonetheless, even in these vast hinterland areas frontiers come and go; and even the long-lived fur frontier has gone through many changes in time, shifts in location, and generally through many spatial retreats. Hence there has been transience here, too. But still further, the main Canadian frontiers of the nineteenth century, our prime concern, did pass away; did largely rise into enduringly organized regions from east to west across the land-mass. It is fair to add that quite minor northern wilderness frontiers that did emerge or exist within the same period – such as that of whaling in Arctic waters – have not been given attention here: basically because they did not greatly impinge on metropolitan development, or have a significant part in the overall growth of urban-rural interaction in Canada.

Again we return to the central theme of interplay. The frontier hinterlands dealt with were, throughout, closely linked with urban and metropolitan development. A frontier, new supplying territory that was largely entered under metropolitan initiatives, inherently developed its own urban places, as collecting, distributing and directing points for the metropolitan system that had extended to it. The frontier's first function in that system was to tap and transmit staple resources. But this required metropolitan investment in capital, man-power and organization for the area; not to mention providing the necessary technology to produce desired goods and get them to market. Hence one may view the essential economic pattern whereby a frontier came into being under metropolitan impetus as the tying of territorial raw resources to outside markets through the mediation of investment and technology. All four factors, resources, markets, investment and technology, must repeatedly come in to any appraisal of a frontier hinterland – or for that matter, a maturing regional hinterland as well. Particularly in the making of a frontier, however, the territorial fact that the nature of its resources involved relatively few men and limited investment as is the case in the fur trade, or as many people and much more infrastructure as on a farm frontier, would plainly be of consequence. Similarly, the temporal fact that the transport technology then available was that of the canoe or the railway, the sailing vessel or the steamboat, could greatly affect the rate of frontier expansion and transformation. So plainly could the fluctuations in market demands, and certainly the changing enterprise and power of investing metropolitan interests.

At any rate, it should be evident how fully the frontier fits into the metropolitan-hinterland relationship. It was virtually the furthest, newest territory dominated by the metropolis, and the most dependent and subservient in its rawness and weakness. But there were still varieties of frontiers; some assuredly less weak and directly subordinated than others, some with increasing degrees of local sufficiency and self-assertiveness as well. Moreover, the very growth of a frontier could naturally make it a market of value in itself. The metropolitan com-munity thus served as a source of supply as well as of demand. Once more the significance of this reciprocal connection would vary widely with the frontier. In the case of the fur trade, only a limited range of trade goods or supplies for the personnel of scattered posts was in demand. In the case of the sizeable populations on farming, lumbering and even mining frontiers, enlarging quantities of varied consumer and capital goods clearly were required, not to mention a growing range of services: commercial, financial, administrative, social and still more. Accordingly, many advancing frontiers could come to exert a substantial return influence on metropolitan communities themselves.

In a general way, the mixed varieties of Canadian frontiers may be grouped within ascending classes of complexity and development; though as always it must be kept in mind that such a rough typology is heavily subject to specific qualifications. On the first level, even so, there are the superficial extractive frontiers, mainly concerned with skimming off natural resources virtually as they are to be found, with relatively restricted investments in capital and labour and not much need to settle and re-shape a wilderness landscape. In this category largely belong the fur frontier, the original Atlantic fisheries carried on by summer-voyaging, transatlantic seamen, the eastern square-timber trade frontiers; and perhaps open-range ranching in the West and early placer gold-mining in the Pacific mountains.

The next level, the committed extractive frontiers, show far more engagement in terms of capital investment, enduring settlement and transformation of the natural environment, all necessary to secure the resource yields. The best examples here are certainly the broad agricultural frontiers of pioneer occupation, both eastern and western. Yet in many ways sawn-lumbering belongs: involving, as it developed, considerable investment in machine equipment and power supplies (especially on the later pulpwood or West Coast logging frontiers) and the growth of many a lumber-milling town besides. Other examples include the establishing of resident fisheries that spread outport settlements along the coasts, or the rise of closed-range cattle and sheep-raising; or, on mining frontiers, the increasing use of deep-shaft mining that required large and lasting commitments of both capital and labour.

At a further level, processing seems the indicative feature: on the agricultural frontier, connoting flour-milling, brewing and distilling, woollen-weaving, and many other enhancements of simple farm production; in lumbering, characterized by woodworking plants ranging from shingle, door and sash mills to wagon or furniture factories. Meat-packing similarly becomes associated with ranching, canning with fishing, and ore-milling or even smelting with mining: all to emerge within the respective hinterlands, but especially in their own fast rising urban places. At this stage, in fact, it could well be said that these very kinds of intensifying developments express the effective transition from frontier into maturely established region. Yet, recalling that none of these stages or categories are sharply determinate, but mark a continuing process, one may go still further, and trace the erstwhile frontier hinterland onward in either of two directions. It could at length become prosperously regenerative, or turn towards decline and even virtual abandonment. The former happier state implies that it gradually diversified its original staple dependence on a key resource supply: perhaps by developing sizeable manufacturing enterprises in its major towns, which did more than simply process local resources; and probably, as well, by acquiring profitable service industries – as was clearly the case in parts of central Canada well before 1914. In the second and sad direction, the ex-frontier area instead found no viable new base to substitute for a deteriorating initial resource supply: with results to be seen in impoverished or depopulating rural districts, ravaged woods and played-out mine towns, again plainly visible in different portions of the country long before 1914.

Throughout this whole pattern of frontier development the urban presence was apparent: not only at its higher levels or stages, of course, but from the outset. Certainly the committed extractive and the processing categories of frontiers displayed proliferating urban places that advanced in size and rank, from agricultural villages to milling towns, from lumber ports to commercial cities. Yet urban communities were inherently linked even with the superficial extractive frontiers – and not merely in the sense that metropolitan forces virtually brought them into being in the first place. It has certainly been noted that urban outposts of the metropolis appeared within the frontier itself, to collect its products for transmission, to distribute necessary goods and supplies, to focus organization or maintain direction and control.

In truth, the urban outpost often marked the very inception of a frontier, since from here trade, control, and settlement was projected outward into the landscape. Town and country interplay then went on increasingly creating the multi-facetted urban and regional systems of modern-day Canada. But always in this long historic interplay the roles of metropolis and frontier have stood out – seeming opposites but actual conjuncts in a process that has shaped so much of basic Canadian development.

The Canadian National Exhibition in Toronto in the early twentieth century.

The View from Ontario: Further Thoughts on Metropolitanism in Canada

AS THE GOLDEN SUNSET FADES away, I refuse to. There is still more to be said about metropolitanism as I see it, taking a reflective look out my Ontario window, a look that also does a little glancing forward. In this regard, an Ontario metropolitan perspective ought mainly to elicit wider views and contentions concerning Canada over all, yet Ontario instances could well be used – to cite the classic wording of the British North America Act – "for greater certainty, but not so as to restrict the generality of the foregoing". That is the sense in which I turn to the metropolitan approach in Canadian history once again. Of course, one conceivably might think that such an approach has had its day by now. Certainly, and very naturally over the space of three decades, it has encountered questions and charges levelled by critics. Some of their indictments have marked metropolitanism down as centralist myth, insufficiently explanatory and passé with its period. Others have deemed it too determinately geographic or too vaguely indeterminate; too restrictively ecological or too airily impressionistic; and worst of all, too liberal and élitist: in short, not at all the kind of thing the scholar of today should be doing. It seems the hounds of time are on my track. It would be wise to take to cover, and watch as the cortège sweeps past to other quests; counting myself lucky just to be preserved in historiography, as one critic has generously suggested.[1]

That happened to earlier advocates of the frontier thesis in North American development, so why not to an exponent of a replacing, contrariwise, metropolitan thesis? There are at least two reasons why not. First, the frontier and the metropolitan themes were not all that separately successive or antithetical, and considered together, still have much to offer. Second, the metropolitan approach (in my mind) was just that – not a thesis, but a viewpoint on some major historical patterns which can still be revealing. It was, and is, a way of perceiving and integrating some broad elements in past experience, not a comprehensive design for history, such as Marxist doctrine. For North America and other lands of fairly recent settlement particularly, it was a means of looking at and bringing together the historic occupation of great territorial sweeps by extensive frontier growth, and the intensive development of dominating urban centres both inside and outside these territories. Each process was observed as widely evident. They were further seen as related and interacting. Hence if that be gravely ecological, the plea is "guilty."

No doubt, such a view of interplay, drawing on *both* frontierist history and urbanist history, did underline environmental, geographic contexts. But then people live in space, as well as in class, ethnic and family frames, or those of gender and generation; and they structure space and relate to it, as well as to the other great societal factors. In the spatial dimension, operating conjointly with that of time, dispersed peripheral communities (or varied kinds of countrysides) were vitally linked with concentrated core-communities (or various levels of urban places). If this pervasive net of rural-urban linkages appears by nature geographic, so be it. In terms of frontierism and metropolitanism, however, it essentially connotes that frontiers, the thinnest-spread, most rudimentary versions of countryside, were themselves outlying hinterlands of cities, and subject to far-reaching impulses and controls from the largest, most dominating sort of city, the metropolis. And if that seems indeterminate, or just impressionistic, I still think it can be amply substantiated in history by the ties that stretched across distance to join metropolis and hinterland, whether the latter constituted an opening frontier, a developing region or a well established, mature countryside.

The nexus persisted over space and time, even though specific exemplifications of metropolis and hinterland could demonstrate many changes throughout.

This matter of demonstration raises the question as to whether a metropolitan approach can in any case provide adequate explanations. Urbanists may contend that it does not pin down *why* cities grew, one of the many great issues that social science is always going to settle. Yet I was once instructed that history inherently deals with hows, not whys and have behaved accordingly. God, Marxian teachings, sociological or psychoanthropological models well may hold the keys to generic causation. But I simply carry on in my experiential, particularist mode, ordering this point with that, to verify how such-and-such a change occurred – how a city or metropolis rose or fell in functions and regard, and how frontiers or regions were associated with such a course – without hoping to settle the fundamental urban "why;" for I lack the ultimate wisdom, science or faith to do so. To repeat, what I seek is merely to apply an *approach*, one that can illuminate continual town-country interactions: something as old as civilized society.

That is certainly not to say that more comprehensive explanations for urban (or rural) development cannot be realized. Only that the metropolitan step on the way remains useful, and should be worked in. Moreover, it often now appears that practitioners of urban studies strive to find their grail of unifying general theory either within urban organizational complexes left insufficiently related to countrysides, or within class patterns not adequately conditioned by ever-present facts of space. Yet even a multinational corporation of today is a spatial grouping, with its own structure across distance and its own urban-country links. Even a proletariat lives somewhere, in defining locales, and élites have their territorial nets and urban decision-centres, whether under American capitalism or Soviet communism. Metropolitanism – whose operations have obviously changed greatly between Greek city-state and modern megalopolis – still provides a skein of interpretation, of explanation, as one very essential part of understanding the city and its experience.

I should, however, leave these highly general assertions and get down to Canadian cases, first taking up a keen contention regarding centralist "myth". This was most directly put in a succinct article by L.D.

McCann in the *Urban History Review* of February 1981, "The Myth of the Metropolis: the Role of the City in Canadian Regionalism". It effectively traced the course of city-regional development in Canada to the present, concluding that "the rise of the western cities has created a challenge to the myth of metropolitan domination by Toronto and by Montreal".[2] In large amount I agree. In fact, it is hard to take issue with the content of this article, which seems admirably sound to me: only with the assumption (in its form) that the term metropolis was somehow to be limited to a central-Canadian Toronto or Montreal – in a kind of national category of disrepute – but did not apply to Vancouver, Winnipeg, Quebec, Halifax or other cities.

In my own assessment, a lot more Canadian places than those two big nasties acquired metropolitan features and functions. Indeed, McCann's article itself referred to "regional metropolitan development" and to the "hinterland's rising metropolitan centres".[3] So why were only Montreal or Toronto to be seen as conveying "the myth of the metropolis"? Because they might have some claim to national ascendancy? It seems an unnecessary distinction between a national metropolis and a regional (non-)metropolis. Besides, Toronto, and to some extent Montreal, could act as regional metropolises no less than national ones. Regionalism was not solely a phenomenon confined to the Plains and Pacific Wests or to the Maritimes and Atlantic. It was alive and hearty in Ontario; in Quebec it has become embodied in full-blown separatism. And in both these central domains it found regional metropolitan focusses, as it did to west and east beyond.

Furthermore, few historians would claim that Montreal or Toronto were destined to dominate all Canada forever, any more than London or New York – so what was mythical about their own phase of national dominance? Professor McCann's article allowed that this period did reach from about Confederation to after the Second World War. I might extend it further in either direction; but in any event, this would leave the "myth" admitted fact for around a century. Naturally, the process of change goes on – there is no time-freeze – and new metropolitan centres arise in Canada to contend with old, to share or take over some of the latter's scope of dominance. In that regard, "the gradient of metropolitanism has been altered" (to quote McCann) without any question.[4] But that does not make the whole pattern mythical; its reapportioning in fact continues.

Still further, the author himself recognized that, for all the rise of some new Western contenders, the Atlantic region and the North continued under well established metropolitan sway[5]; leaving his "myth" an enduring reality for great areas of the country, which reasonably included Quebec and Ontario as well. It is important to add that McCann went on in the pioneering *Heartland and Hinterland: a Canadian Geography* (1982) to acknowledge the far from mythical force of the metropolis; although he saw this largely in terms of staple theory and the workings of industrialism: both somewhat time-bound frames themselves. With specific regard to the Atlantic area (as evidenced in his report of 1983, "Metropolitanism and Branch Businesses in the Maritimes, 1881-1931"), he stated emphatically that "the sting of the metropolis" was felt throughout the region, "from the smallest village to the largest city".[6] Moreover, "the locus of metropolitan dominance . . . now . . . rests in central Canada."[7] In other words, he himself came to treat the "myth" as fact – perhaps as unwelcome fact, but fact nonetheless.

As for the main Atlantic cities themselves, one could deem it fairly manifest in history that they did arise as regionally leading places, to exercise considerable degrees of ascendancy over wide locales and carry on discernibly commanding functions for sizeable lengths of time. If they failed to make the National League, history is not just a success story. It would be hard to deny in any case the persisting, and still changing, real significance of a Halifax, Saint John or St. John's. Their roles have surely been as regional, or sub-regional metropolises, centring a great deal of hinterland activity and regard upon themselves, even if no one of them became solely pre-eminent or able to withstand more powerful metropolitan invasions from without. Again in my reading, nothing restricts the functioning of metropolitanism in Canada merely to a couple of nationally ascendant central cities – yesterday or today. Assuredly, it does not in Ontario, where Ottawa, Hamilton, London, Kingston and more, have all notably, if diversely, displayed historic metropolitan features, whether national, regional or sub-regional in scope.

Nevertheless, it is a rooted Canadian habit to equate metropolitanism with centralism; to view it as denoting the invidious rule of "Upper

Canada" or "The East", depending on where you stand, in opposition to all that is good, honest and local in our broad expanses. In that respect, distance does not lend enchantment as much as foster disenchanting symbols or traditions of dislike. Another kind of gradient, one of repugnance, operates across space, wherein Nova Scotians may carp at Halifax but line up with it against Toronto's machinations, whereby Calgarians will fume at Edmonton but make it an ally in denouncing the central greed of Ottawa. In this sense there is assuredly a wide historic awareness of centralism – too readily labelled metropolitanism – that is strongly shaped by the long-enduring impact of central Canadian ascendancy. To W.L. Morton, metropolitan studies integrally expressed "centrality" while minimizing "regionality", the realm of the hinterland. I took this up in a journal article over a decade ago, and perhaps might quote a relevant passage of my response:

> Metropolitanism by no means has to be identified with a centralist or Laurentian view. It is as regional (and as metropolitan) as St. John's is in relation to Newfoundland . . . Winnipeg to a prairie hinterland, Halifax to a Maritime – along with all their further series of connections existing within or without the original space that may thus be delineated.

So much for the printed word, or my word. Despite it, one still hears of the "dichotomy" of metropolis and hinterland, although they represent a joint association, not a mutual exclusivity. We equally hear of the pernicious rule of central metropolitan might and the exploited impotence of the hinterlands – as if (for only one thing) offsetting political commands did not exist within the regions themselves – see the western provinces and long years of federal oil deals, or the mass of provincial measures meant to protect regional industries and jobs. Admittedly the actual powers exercised might vary greatly from B.C. or Alberta to Quebec and on east, but they do operate. Political offsets to regional dependence function along with that very dependence, whether they are exhibited by public protest stances or in-house deals and trade-offs, by sheltering provincial regulations, or special policies to promote regional equalization. The last may be inadequate, unfair in many ways, or only enlarge dependence. Yet the fact remains that all the major regions get special treatment, some more so than others! Historic federalism in Canada obviously evinces regionalism and centralism both, while metropolitanism runs through each of them. Especially in Ontario.

Let me, however, enlarge on my stand that metropolitanism can include, but does not only comprise, far-reaching central hegemonies. It can equally focus and structure regional spheres in Canada, whether in Atlantic or St. Lawrence areas, Great Lakes or Western territories; even though geography and history have worked somewhat differently in each region so as to make each big example different and distinctive. Throughout written Canadian history – and beginning with wholly external, transatlantic metropolises – metropolitan forces have drawn on, organized and developed hinterland domains: over time extending networks of power and interest from newer, emerging internal places which would both complement and compete with the links back to older established centres of dominance. Without question, many centripetal forces thus entered into play; but the result was not just some all-engulfing centralism. Instead there were multiplying complexities of relationships and power transfers.

In sum, the process produced various territorial ranges of connective urban systems and levels of metropolitan domination, based on effective routes of access, on advantageous resource supplies and geographic features, increments in labour, technology and capital, as well as on influential political responses and human enterprise. Along with all this went factors of perception or regard: leading places and regional entities do to a significant extent develop as they are regarded and felt to be such – an important matter of attitude. And nothing in this complex, many-facetted metropolitanism has tied it historically just to one or two central Canadian cities; though it did express pervasive aspects of urban headship from St. John's right through to Victoria. If, then, that be centralist myth – make the most of it.

With respect to Ontario, and its forebear, Upper Canada, incipient metropolitan patterning came in the earlier nineteenth century to centre on York/Toronto, a backwoods seat of government with an initial headstart in authority and prestige as an imperial garrison-base, not to mention its own fast advancing commercial activities. No doubt, that little capital's economic reach was still at first considerably qualified, given its various port-rivals along Lake Ontario, the hold of other towns on Upper Canadian districts more remote, and above all, the dominance of much bigger Montreal over the key St. Lawrence route to the sea. No doubt, too, the hopes of young Toronto's official and mercantile élites were recurrently found to exceed their grasp. The fact that they tried and quite often succeeded, proved far from inconsequential, however. They built on the perception they shared concerning the focal importance of a rising Toronto – and which others in the town's expanding hinterland increasingly felt also. Thus came regional integrating thrusts which were expressed in highway building and railway projects, in Toronto's own outreaching banks and wholesale houses. Not everything was due here to geography, impersonal economic forces or the capital's political advantages: much as well stemmed from human attitude, interest, and decision. Altogether, they paid off in a burgeoning regional metropolis, able by the late century to dominate most of Ontario itself and to deal effectively with the outside powers of Montreal or New York, while connected into both their greater metropolitan systems. And so metropolitanism in this Ontario case was quite plainly engaged in region-building – whatever nation-building it may have carried on besides.

Much the same could be said regarding other Ontario centres that attained at least sub-regional metropolitan stature over the nineteenth century. Ottawa was a special case (though indeed each was in its own way), a frontier mill-town which rose into a national political metropolis, yet at the same time held its own northeastern regional hinterland of lumbering. The inevitable pulls of two very different sets of metropolitan perceptions (and realizations) tell much about Ottawa's consequent historic experiences. As for Hamilton, it of course, outlived being largely superseded by Toronto as a trade and transport centre in the southern central districts, to become a main Ontario embodiment of industrial metropolitanism, a hub of steam and iron technology for both the province and nation. Kingston, the almost-metropolis of early Upper Canada, did not overcome its own besting by Toronto, but kept its own local domain still, where lake and St. Lawrence met. And London gained headship in the farming southwest; a city affluent, assertive and conservatively confident, like so much of the rich hinterland it commanded – traits that are often ascribed to the Ontario region in general, although they are not as pertinent to such harsher, more subordinated hinterland areas as the northern wilds of "New" Ontario. But in any case, the metropolitan aspects that are fully displayed in Ontario's past do plainly bear upon its continuing "regionality" and not just on its "centrality", as earlier criticism would have contended.

From here on, however, I propose to reflect on more recent criticisms raised against my metropolitan approach, most incisively expressed in an article by Professor Donald F. Davis of Ottawa, that was published in the *Urban History Review* in October, 1985, though delivered in an earlier form to the Canadian Historical Association at Vancouver in 1983.[9] The author kindly sent me copies of both renditions; we had an amiable correspondence on the original version which led him to make some revisions touching on my work for his final product. Along with his critique, he offered some appreciated compliments. Thus I am left as happy as I might be; but feel no doubt in any case that his well-considered article, "The 'Metropolitan Thesis' and the Writing of Canadian Urban History", presents a comprehensive, instructive analysis of forms in which metropolitanism has been applied, both by myself and others. Although I will endeavour now to take it to task it remains a salutary, thought-provoking assessment – and as such I deal with it.

The weight of Professor Davis' critique of my own body of writing is strongly (though by no means entirely) placed upon its alleged omission of the "human equation" and its neglect of "the study of power as wielded by élites."[10] As a known, card-carrying élitist I might well object; yet it is evidently a matter of how you handle élites; which is to say, not just by "spatial urban networks," but by "social networks" such as those of "kinship, amity and clientage."[11] In fact, Dr. Davis contends that "spatially biassed concepts like metropolitanism should be regarded as being at most 'limited generalizations' applicable to but one stage of urban development."[12] That is, to the bygone nineteenth century, when capitalism was more "sedentary," more identified with urban home bases, before the time "in which corporations and governments have become the arbiters of urban growth and decline."[13] They have since shrunk the significance of "the spatial distribution" of power. What matters now, it appears, is a *socially-based* distribution.

There is merit in this view, which I will get to later. For the moment, I am the more struck by the inference that world-striding, "footloose" corporations of today may no longer have very significant spatial locations in urban centres; or that their allied counterparts, national state authorities, may no longer be found located in sedentary abodes, fixed there by a weighty apparatus of politicians and bureaucrats, whether set within Washington's Beltway, in Canadian government capitals, or in great cities elsewhere. Considering the massive investments now involved in built environment, people and equipment, such a depiction of free-ranging, modern corporate and government gypsies does not seem thoroughly convincing. Undoubtedly, if needs and costs appear commensurate, plant operations, management units and bodies of workers can be shifted – to other centres, where they immediately get into telex and computer touch with headquarters. Yet a comparable state of mobility runs back through centuries: I give you the very development of North America. Similarly, some government offices may also move; a whole new capital like Brasilia may even be erected – but as another definitely located urban base. The latter-day changes, in my opinion, still involve spatial redistributions of power; that remains inherent. In fact, what is called for now is not a limited verdict that metropolitanism has lost its "sedentary" or spatial attributes, but a recognition of its wider power thrusts through giant international corporations or swelling super-governments. They themselves, indeed, can constitute metropolitan instruments in action.

And what of the "social distribution" of power? Surely that is not new, but bound up with the course of metropolitanism in Canada throughout – at least since a ruling royal bureaucracy in Paris took charge of developing New France, or a London mercantile élite founded the Hudson's Bay Company. Besides, as Canadian societies took shape, their own rising élite groups were centred closely within physical bounds in dominating urban places. Granted, élite elements today are considerably *more* mobile in membership, and numbers of their personnel may migrate from Vancouver to Toronto, Dallas to Calgary, or back. Granted also that ties of kinship, amity and clientage do reach over space (they usually have) and that horizontal lines of class can be as compelling as vertical bonds of place, ethnicity, or sometimes still, religion. Nonetheless, it would be excessive to consider that urban élite members no longer identify with the city communities in which they are resident for any sizeable length of time. And while individual figures, their families and companies may come and go, the resident élite cores remain – for new in-migrants to enter as participants. These newcomers, indeed, may soon associate themselves almost fervently with their changed abode – as I know from listening to ex-Torontonians in Halifax or Edmonton denounce the centralized CBC, praise their far less avaricious local lifestyle, or deplore the smug narrowness of their former city. Thus they evidently absorb the perceptions of their new setting, and take on its own colouration! Be that as it may, however; it does seem true that while business corporations and governments may repeatedly shift in their various staff components, an identification with the resident urban place remains quite functional and renewing among metropolitan élite groups – and not just a job-bound adherence to some extra-urban, arbiter organization.[14]

Nor is it very different on other levels in the urban community, which display their own neighbourhood, behavioural, and institutional associations with their particular city; although it may clearly take longer for many immigrant elements from abroad to adapt to the local urban conditioning. In general, the constituency of a metropolitan urban society largely maintains a distinct, localized identity, whatever class lines or flows of transience may cut across it. If anything, that entity now looks rather more distinct from the hinterlands beyond it, in spite of the spread of urbanization far past city limits, and in spite of much improved communications – which can actually confirm differentiating recog-nitions of space instead of ministering to some shared global-village ethos. Does Brockville or Goderich, any more than Antigonish or Abbotsford, deem itself an outlying segment of some "village" Toronto or New York? Clearly, small local communities hold their own limited identities; to a large extent delimited and defined in spatial terms. And in the contrasting big-city world, climbing central business districts, mounting traffic congestion and soaring municipal budgets set only a few graphic perceptions of the distinctive, continuing metropolis. It would be most ironic if "metropolitan" became a non-word for the urban historian today, when the wealth, governance and human problems of the metropolis attract so much attention.

But it is certainly possible to agree that social networks which conjoin in allocating power within metropolitan spatial layouts need more examining themselves. The upper-level mercantile associations, from boards of trade to business federations, the industrial, banking and financial coteries, the speculators' and developers' webs (forgive the word), the linking urban echelons of transport, advertising, clerical services and media, all merit study of their social make-ups, affinities and behaviour. So do those of professional sectors, whose own nets can span the country but equally contain major metropolitan concentrations. So does working-class organization, centred in the masses of chief cities, but attaining country-wide proportions. Hinterland societies, too, have interrelated organizations to consider: the social, yet spatial, networks of farming, fishing and resource pursuits; those of regional business, manufacturing and support services, plus more besides. Even where social power may not look notably present, further nets can be distinguished; for instance, those of immigrant collectivities, heavily derived from metropolitan pulls themselves, and linked internationally as well as locally across realms of space.

Of course, it is apparent that a great deal of work already goes in all these multiple fields. Not enough of it, however, is presented in terms of metropolitanism or makes use of that approach – as it assuredly could do. This is said despite Professor Davis' claim that the metropolitan-hinterland paradigm was a "rather sterile hybrid", one which "proved of only limited usefulness in guiding research."[15] Mule-like in progeny or not, it has turned up pretty widely in scholarly writing across Canada (as the critic himself suggests by somewhat regretting the fact)[16], and it surely has a large, important agenda still to deal with.

As for aspects of that agenda regarding Ontario to 1914, and after, much of what has just been generally prescribed should still apply. Yet further than that, there are naturally quite particular features to observe. For but one example, there is the unique trans-regional and international system of water communication by way of the Upper St. Lawrence and Great Lakes which fronts most of the province. A lot of history has taken shape along that linking system, along which, too, port-towns on the "front" grew to major cities, as their reach penetrated inland. Then, as well, there is the special base-area of "Old" Ontario, the fertile river-and-interlake lands below the Shield which acquired a sizeable population in farms and towns, and across which land lines were run by trail and nineteenth-century rail to web the interior right from lake-front city to remote northern resource post. These obviously spatial nets may much involve economic factors, capital, technology, enterprise and policy; but they can also comprehend social relations, collective and individual, along with immaterial matters of regard or cultural perceptions. And all of these may be instructively treated in terms of metropolitan-hinterland interaction – despite other approaches that without doubt might be applied as well. A New Ontario mining frontier, like that of the Cobalt silver strike, accessible overnight by sleeping car from the Toronto metropolis, is interestingly distinct from a Klondike gold-rush field. The industrial "Soo", bridging between New Ontario and Old, might lie in a bleak and rugged hinterland, yet it significantly lay as well on the Lakes' main traffic line, and under a metropolitan complex of business power. Such topics as these may certainly be illuminated by the metropolitan approach. Considering those of another sort, one additionally could look for more localized, intra-regional study of a city's workings with its own adjacent surroundings; and this may well include places of varied components in different locales, whether they be Peterborough or Brantford, Belleville or Windsor; since the metropolitan kind of association can still be discerned for numerous lesser centres that have orbiting districts beyond them. Nor do such places have to rise ever higher in size and sweep to merit consideration.

They may halt or decline instead, after whatever period of noteworthy local ascendance. I have already remarked that metropolitan history, like history *in toto*, is not simply a celebration of making good. That went out with mediaeval hagiography. Thus once very active Great Lakes shipping centres, from Cobourg to Collingwood, fit within this aspect; and some valuable work has already been done thereon. The same goes for the promotional efforts of Old Ontario's many boards of trade and newspapers, for mercantile, transport and industrial entrepreneurship in the growing, aspiring towns; for workers' unions, protest movements, and a host of regional social networks, including those of religion, education and welfare. One yet could add the social, human interlinkages of Ontario farming, lumbering, mining or local manufacturing communities. All can fit instructively into the metropolitan scheme. Their span of success is not the only measure. Their emergence, growth, decline or adaptation together count for more.

Returning to the important critique by Professor Davis, however, the question of "the human equation" which he raised persists in broader terms. He has argued that the metropolitan approach "has difficulty in fitting the human factor into the history of urban development", and this is witnessed by "a fundamental evasion" in ascribing "'metropolitan ambitions' to cities rather than to the individuals to whom they properly belong."[17] That does look a bit hypercritical to me. In history, one may often, very commonly, speak of Britain's imperial ambitions, of the resentments of the Canadian West, or the glowing hopes held by mining boom-towns, well knowing that each depicted entity really contained a lot of different-thinking individuals – yet easily accepting the short-hand for the aggregates within the context used.

It is similarly permissible to talk of élites, social networks and power distributions, as meaningful collectives composed of individual human beings – just as we accept "city", "region" or "nation-state". Nevertheless, the levied charge continues: "Ambitions, like dominance and power, are attributes of élites, *not* cities. Nor do cities exercise economic control: entrepreneurs and business corporations do."[18] Agreed; one might even welcome this healthy reminder of factual particulars, but the personal agents of power and control were still *in* cities and *of* cities. If the comprehending collective framework is left out here, it is analogous to saying that no army as such ever won a battle, only its commanders; that revolutions are not class and communal upheavals but happenstance medleys of individual leaders and followers; that there is no urban history but only urban historians. And yet, in any event, no one need think that a city's dominance was not exercised by actual people who built it up; or that its aspirations did not reflect its citizens' desires, which were by no means confined to the élite component only. My own approach does not evade the "human factor".

But does it consider it adequately? The charge is made that when I got too close to people in my work, as in studies of later nineteenth century commercial élites in Winnipeg and Victoria, I ignored [my] own thesis".[19] This no less ignores the weary point that it was not envisaged as a prescriptive theory but as an approach, a way of looking at related aspects of experience, not a model pattern of prerequisites which were alone to be applied. Such chiefly internal studies as my papers on Winnipeg and Victoria, set within localized business frames, accordingly required few references to broader metropolitan perspectives – although some were still invoked, and they surely did not stand in conflict. No more did similar writings of mine involving the aims and responses of business *persona* from St. John's and Saint John to Edmonton and Vancouver.[20] They were implicitly consistent with the metropolitan approach, which certainly came in where it was called for; and all of these short selective articles helped me develop thoughts about it further. I did, however, find the need to deal with metropolitanism much more explicitly throughout a longer and more comprehensive survey of Toronto to 1918, an urban biography organized essentially in metropolitan terms.[21] Thereupon, one reviewer of this book, published in 1984, found it dealt altogether too much with the élite constituency that wielded metropolitan power![22] It is admittedly hard to please everybody – though that need not keep historians awake too many nights.

Rallying boldly still, to meet these problems, I continue to affirm that my version of metropolitanism can and does comprise human responses throughout, and is not depersonalized. Dr. Davis has averred, instead, that my "ecological" emphasis on metropolitan-hinterland agencies in interaction gives rein to only impersonal forces, and indeed has "generally exhibited a strong technological determinism."[23] To stressing the significance of transport technology amid the vast Canadian space I would submit another (smaller) plea of guilty. Nonetheless, I would assuredly hold that living persons promoted, constructed and ran the new railway lines, or that crucial sailing-ship technology turned on shipwrights, builders, seamen and port merchants. The proper point is that people, not faceless forces, applied particular technologies within natural and human-contrived environments. If that sounds gravely ecological – and I have already admitted an ecological bent, derived as it was not from outmoded Chicago sociologists but from an early personal engagement with mediaeval historical studies[24] – I still would definitely contend that individuals and bodies of individuals, local societies and linked ones far afield, are all contained in metropolitan-hinterland relations, which in no way have to be envisaged as merely impersonal workings. Human beings shaped them, and are essential in the resulting equations. Personal ideology and enterprise, self-seeking or altruistic interest, are just as much engaged as any "forces" – in fact, animate their content.[25]

Yet the real crux of this critic's wide arraignment of my approach is that it stands "accused . . . of deliberately avoiding the problem of dealing with the internal social structure of the city, except as it related to economic decision-making."[26] In other words, my view is superficially external, as well as being but limitedly economic. He has found me out: I am not a complete urban historian. And within his own perspectives of interest he is quite right. Metropolitanism, by very nature, is not completely concerned with the city, but with the relationships *between* city and country. Its field is neither the total history of the former nor the total history of the latter. Instead it covers the *impingements* of one upon the other, which affect each to a striking extent, whether in areas closely contiguous or distantly outreaching. Nor are these impingements only to be seen in matters of economic decision. They may be displayed in political patterning, administrative and military structures, social forms or cultural trends. Their influences both penetrate the hinterland countrysides and impact on major urban communities – with much more than superficial consequence for city social life and context, for ambience and built environment. In brief, this mode of approach may "avoid" dealing fully with all the urban attributes, but it very deliberately considers a broad range of them. I have said it before, but here goes again: metropolitanism is less and more than urban history; and can be less, or more, than regional or national history also. The accusation falls, therefore, as inappropriate and immaterial.

These varied contentions, illustrations and reflections have necessarily ranged beyond Ontario, while yet dealing with it. In that respect, Professor Allan Artibise of Winnipeg perhaps got nearer to pinning down my own metropolitan case, when he surmised that it was "an important approach to the study of Canadian history generally", though "not really a theory that explains Canadian urban development."[27] From this Dr. Davis has inferred that "it had, therefore, little relevance to urban historians".[28] I accept the initial surmise – but not the subsequent inference. While never meant to be a full-fledged urban theory, my metropolitan rendition can throw light on a lot of urban Canadian history, as on much of Ontario regional, or national development as well. And in that placid opinion, I keep plugging away with it. Meanwhile, my friend Donald Davis might have to demonstrate by delivery that the application of his brand of social rather than spatial power-distribution can clean up root questions of urban growth. He was good enough to name me the godfather of Canadian urban/metropolitan historians.[29] In that capacity, I make him an offer he cannot refuse.

Endnotes

1. Donald F. Davis, "The 'Metropolitan Thesis' and the Writing of Canadian Urban History", *Urban History Review* 14 (2) October 1985, 109.
2. L.D. McCann, "The Myth of the Metropolis", *Urban History Review* 9 (3) February 1981, 57.
3. *Ibid.*, 54, 55.
4. *Ibid.*, 57.
5. *Ibid.*, 53.
6. L.D. McCann, "Metropolitanism and Branch Business in the Maritimes, 1881-1931", *Acadiensis* 13 (1) Autumn 1983, 112.
7. *Ibid.*
8. W.L. Morton, "Some Thoughts on Understanding Canadian History", *Acadiensis* 2 (2) Spring 1973, 106; J.M.S. Careless, "Metropolitan Reflections on 'Great Britain's Woodyard'", *Acadiensis* 3 (1) Autumn 1973, 106.
9. Davis.
10. *Ibid.*, 103.
11. *Ibid.*, 108.
12. *Ibid.*
13. *Ibid.*
14. See John Taylor, "Urban Autonomy in Canada: Its Evolution and Decline", in *The Canadian City: Essays in Urban and Social History*, eds. G.A. Stelter and A.F.J. Artibise (Ottawa 1984), 493-94.
15. Davis, 102.
16. Davis, 108: ". . . an extraordinary amount of time and energy has been spent in dissecting the relationship between metropolis and hinterland. . ."
17. *Ibid.*, 103, 108.
18. *Ibid.*, 108.
19. *Ibid.*, 103.
20. I do not detail these various studies here since they are duly cited in Davis' footnotes.
21. That organization is most basically displayed by the book's series of chapter-themes: after "Government Village", "Commercial Port-Town", "Railway and Regional Hub", "Industrializing City", and "Nearly National Metropolis" (that is, financial).

22. Meyer Brownstone, *Urban History Review* 14 (1) June 1985, 74-76.
23. Davis, 103.
24. As I wrote in my letter to Davis, 11 July 1983: "In then taking [N.S.B.] Gras (first via [D.C.] Masters) to inform a metropolitan concept, I was also considerably influenced by my own background in mediaeval English and French social history, the former with Wilkinson at Toronto, the latter with Taylor at Harvard, on mediaeval French regionalism. . . . In fact, I only probed into the Chicago School later, working back from studies on metropolitanism, and found their ecology pretty arid. . . ."
25. Davis largely lays the problem of "natural forces" on me, by reasoning that seems to run in this wise: You are an ecologist. Therefore you must deal in natural forces (non-personal, non-individual). You must in doctrine uphold "the ecological complex", four-square, of social organization, population, technology, and environment. These (by definition?) are non-personalizing; and of them organization, anyway, "seems at base to be merely a by-product of innovations in technology and changes in the overall environment that are largely beyond the power of local communities to control" (Davis, 103). Who says so – other than he? Suppose I don't accept that it must come out this way, by the sheer compulsion of his formulation? Suppose my work considerably brings in persons and constituent groups, enterprisers and competitors or opponents? Aha!, says Davis, You have ignored your own "thesis". Except that I didn't think I had one to begin with – in the sense of his restrictive line of argument – and so, 'round we go again.
26. Davis, 108.
27. *Ibid.*, 103.
28. *Ibid.*
29. *Ibid.*, 96.

PART THREE

Cities and Regions

Introduction

IT WOULD HARDLY BE SURPRISING if this particular section overlapped with the preceding one. Still, I present it here as a separate subject area because not all my urban and regional investigations have been that explicitly directed to metropolitanism, and because – obviously – it is altogether possible to deal with urban or regional developments without tying them always to some mastering metropolitan theme. Conceivably in my instance, metropolitanism may have remained underlying, none the less; but I consider that I have written enough on cities and regions *per se* to furnish the next section in itself.

The opening piece below, "Somewhat Narrow Horizons", declared my position on the significance of Canadian urban history in 1968, when that history was not greatly practiced; by no means as it was increasingly to be in the two decades thereafter. This "declaration" came as my Presidential Address to the Canadian Historical Association then meeting at Calgary, and was printed in the C.H.A. *Report* for 1968. I dare to think that it had some effect as a stimulus at that time; though no doubt I was in part responding to an urbanist wave already on the rise.

The second section reflects my own mounting attention not just influential urban communities, but to Canada's Pacific region; for there, beginning in 1966, I spent a series of summers and also a full year very happily teaching at the University of Victoria. One published result, among a number of articles, chapters and reviews pertaining to British Columbia, was this product of 1972: "The Business Community in the Early Development of Victoria", which was first written for *Canadian Business History: Selected Studies, 1497–1971*, edited by David S. Macmillan.

The third item in this section also expressed my enlarging perceptions of the West, the great plains as well as the mountains and coast.

Those perceptions were to be notably enhanced when I sat as a member (and subsequently chairman) of the Historic Sites and Monuments Board of Canada from 1972 to 1985. This expert advisory federal body worked through researches, discussions, and site inspections which over time took me from northern Newfoundland to northern B.C. and the Yukon; thereby adding strongly to my awareness of Canada's historic regions. But the specific paper submitted here as illustration, on "Urban Life in the West, 1870–1914", was simply an analysis of certain prominent attributes in the growth of four burgeoning western cities before 1914; namely, Winnipeg, Edmonton, Calgary and Vancouver. Yet if it covered only a little, it connoted a whole lot more in my gazing westward. And delivered in Calgary in 1971, it was published the next year in *Prairie Perspectives II: Selected Papers of the Western Canadian Studies Conferences, 1970, 1971,* edited by A.W. Rasporich and H.C. Klassen.

The fourth study in this theme area returns to my regional home grounds: "Some Aspects of Urbanization in Nineteenth-Century Ontario". It was composed as a chapter for the book produced in 1974 under the editorship of F.H. Armstrong, H.J. Stevenson and J.D. Wilson, *Aspects of Nineteenth-Century Ontario: Essays in Honour of James J. Talman.* An old and admired friend, Jim Talman had retired as Chief Librarian of the University of Western Ontario, but continued to be an active senior historian – and still does at this date of writing, as a highly regarded member of the Board of Trustees of the Ontario Historical Studies Series, which I chair. My own essay for the *festschrift* offered in his tribute gave me a chance to go into the major social process of urbanization, using the Ontario region and its cities as the special case in point.

Montreal, the chief Canadian metropolis in the 1860s.

Somewhat Narrow Horizons

IN RISING TO SPEAK, I am all too conscious I am not rising to the occasion. Here is a glittering academic audience ready for my profound disclosures. Beyond, the wire services, radio and television are waiting to rush them to the country (I think). But what have I got to say? I heard earnest counsel on this, from men of knowledge and concern, who urged me to speak on one or another of the grave issues confronting this country and our age. I fully share their concern and I appreciate their confidence. But what do you do when you find you have little new to add in a historical context to your expressed views of urgent Canadian problems – or find that others are saying what you believe about current questions better and more fully? The answer is, do something else. Perhaps tell funny stories; or, on the eve of a critical national election, instruct everyone to go out and vote for the party of his choice. I tried to be a simple historian. I looked up the addresses of my predecessors as Presidents of the Canadian Historical Association for possible source materials.

I naturally found considerable variety. Some were general, on the "where stands History now" basis; some were quite particular, expressing a specialized research interest of the address-giver. Many were eloquent;

many had messages of strong significance; all tended to increase my own consciousness of inadequacy. But I especially liked a sort of unfinished trilogy of the earlier 1950s: "Broad Horizons" by Professor A.L. Burt, and "Wider Horizons" by Professor G.E. Wilson.[1] No one, apparently, has had the nerve to complete the series with "Widest Possible Horizons." Nor have I. Instead I have been stirred to move the other way, to "Somewhat Narrow Horizons," in order to express an interest in a history of rather limited, localized Canadian dimensions, well down from international, national or even provincial levels. Its field is Canadian urban development, or better, the city in Canadian history. If I do have a message, then tonight it will lie here.

The city in Canadian history: that sounds an obvious parish adaptation of Lewis Mumford's all-encompassing theme, *The City in History*. But while Mumford's omnibus volume not inconceivably misses Canada, it seems remarkable that Canadian scholarship has not paid more attention to the history of the city in this country. It is true that geographers, political and social scientists and serried ranks of planners are notably involved in urban studies in Canada, and some of their work has significantly contributed to aspects of our urban history. Yet the number of historians who have themselves contributed is scant indeed. Aside from a few books or articles, the writing of anything that may broadly be termed Canadian urban history has been left to authors of "popular" accounts of the glory that was Montreal or the grandeur that is Toronto.[2] And though some of these may have insight as well as enthusiasm, evidence as well as anecdote, the usual product is still that of the journalist or chronicler: worthy people for their purposes, but not generally held as substantial scholars in other fields of history.

It might be said that, considering the glory of Montreal and the grandeur of Toronto, not much more is required of Canadian urban history. But that is no more sensible than to disdain to look at general Canadian history and politics on the grounds that they are as dull as, or full of, ditchwater. Either for Canadian cities or politics, one may at least fall back on the defence of "A poor thing, but mine own." Still, the fact is, that as men have formed governments and factions, grown crops or reared families, so they have for a long time lived in cities – even in Canada, land of all outdoors. Cities have had an integral part in Canadian historic experience, and deserve attention as considerable phenomena in the life and growth of the country – whether or not they be judged by some imperiously qualitative standard as good, bad or indifferent *vis à vis* the world outside.

In other countries, certainly in Britain and Europe and in the United States, the growth of the city is well recognized in historical inquiry. It would be strange if in Canada there should be no similar need for investigation, because here, somehow, the urban cultural background of Europe failed to apply, or the North American conditions that saw "cities in the wilderness"[3] emerge almost from the start of European settlement did not operate north of the forty-ninth parallel. In reality, of course, work is proceeding in Canadian urban history at the level of thesis research, which in due time will add to publication. In fact, I am not very far in the van in making a contention few would really reject, that urban history can and should be a growing field in Canadian historical study. What I seek to do, therefore, is less to substantiate that contention than to illustrate it: to point out various particular considerations in the history of cities as found in the Canadian context.

The broadest, most evident consideration is the social process of urbanization in Canada. We may be a small people clinging to the margins of an intractable, near-empty land-mass; we may be deeply and constantly conditioned by the fact of terrain; yet we are equally a highly urbanized people, over seventy per cent urbanized; and more than half our population now lives in metropolitan areas, the smallest of which are conglomerations of some 100,000 each. If only to subscribe to the dictum that each age need ask its own questions of the past, we have reason to inquire into the development of our urbanized social life.

Certainly, on the most "applied" level, any study of pressing problems of urban concentrations today (or their counterpart, depressed rural areas) inevitably leads back into the course of history. But further, if earlier Canadian generations sought to learn about the occupation of primeval land-space, closer then to their own society, we surely should inquire into the occupation of urban living-space, which began in Canada with the founding of Quebec or Montreal. It may seem mere local anecdotage to note that both towns soon suffered from traffic congestion, or that early Halifax or York soon had to face questions of the unavailing poor, public disorder and crime. Yet these conditions obviously do not just emerge in large-scale modern cities, whether urban communities generate or simply concentrate social problems. We need to trace those problems through, in the towns that chiefly experienced them; and so far we have only made beginnings.

Furthermore, one should note that so-called "rapid" urbanization is not simply a feature of the present era in Canada. Our urban population which now nears eighty per cent of the total (it was less than twenty in 1871) did increase by 7.1 per cent between 1951 and 1961, and 8.5 per cent in the preceding decade. Yet in the largely depression years of 1881 to 1891 it grew by almost seven per cent, and by 8 per cent in the boom decade of 1901 to 1911.[4] These earlier years, in short, all but equalled our recent rates of urban increase, and even the seventies and nineties had higher rates than more "modern" times from 1911 to 1941. All this may invite conjecture about the impact of trade cycles and National Policy where cities and towns were concerned. Or one may see the same potent combination of steam-and-steel technology and potent continental resources working to develop urban accretions in Canada just as in the contemporary United States. At any rate, steam-age Montreal, Toronto and Hamilton deserve particular examination, no less than New York of the trusts, railroad Chicago or Carnegie's Pittsburgh.

Still further, urbanization can go hand in hand with the settlement of major land frontiers. This is scarcely surprising, since towns rise concurrently with newly productive regions as market, service or processing centres; in fact, a town nucleus may well precede farm settlement. But the process of creating new western urban centres has been paid less attention in Canadian history than in American, where indeed the point has been made that frontier expansion is a function of urban expansion.[5] We tend to view the era before the First World War as that which above all produced the agrarian West. Yet it also saw Winnipeg jump from 42,000 to 130,000 between 1901 and 1911 and Vancouver from 29,000 to 120,000, tripling and quadrupling themselves.[6] The same decade saw Edmonton multiply seven times over, and Calgary ten – far faster than Alberta in general.[7] All this may be known and noted. But should not the startling rise of the urban as well as the farming West be given full analysis?

Nor is this story of impressive urban development only a matter of post-Confederation Canada. Between 1815 and 1834, Toronto, for example, grew thirteen-fold, rising with the settling of another farm frontier from a mere governing village to a city at the point of economic take-off as a regional metropolis.[8] Moreover, in agricultural Upper Canada from the census of 1861 farming townships began showing evidence of rural depopulation, of a growing movement off the land.[9] This may be regarded as an initial symptom of decay, the start of our sad decline from happy, healthy buggydom to the morbid morass of urbanism. But if that is so, roll up the map and close the books: they will not be needed for some years to come. In any case, the agrarian myth of North America, whose folk heroes cleared dark forest into smiling farmland, has only limited possible application to Canada, where a good deal of forest is better left standing, and much cleared land will not smile.

The plain point is that Canada in history has been much more broadly a land of commercial than of farming frontiers. And on the former, the urban centre has held clear dominance from the days of the fur trade on, even though the wilds might persist around the key economic activity: whether trapping, lumbering, mining or tapping energy resources. Accordingly, from the early stages of Canadian history forward, urban development has had a characteristically important role to play. For this was pre-eminently a land of "cities in the wilderness" – to transfer Carl Bridenbaugh's apt phrase.

Hence significant urban communities could emerge not primarily dependent on a farming hinterland around them, each with a comparatively large concentration of the territorial population. Thus the governing, garrison, and fur trade towns of Montreal and Quebec together disposed of close to twenty-five percent of the population of mid-eighteenth century New France,[10] and had other concerns than the realm of seigneurial agriculture. Thus in the earlier nineteenth century Halifax grew as a wealthy Atlantic shipping entrepôt with little relation to Nova Scotia rural settlement; and the busy shipbuilding port of Saint John developed a remarkably extensive and effective unionism among its ship labourers while most of New Brunswick was still a forest frontier.[11] St. John's, moreover, where the sea was the true wilderness hinterland, held nearly a quarter of Newfoundland's population by the mid-century,[12] dominating the fishing outports from its great houses on Water Street. Similarly from Quebec William Price ruled over the timber kingdom of the Saguenay,[13] while Bytown controlled the vast Ottawa timber empire – often uneasily, because of its turbulent shantymen, a veritable proletariat in the wilderness.

But there is no need to go on multiplying examples. In brief, the city had a potent and distinctive role in Canada long before there was the present state called Canada, and whether agrarian settlement had widely occurred or not. It seems better now to turn to other considerations regarding the Canadian city – one of which will not be metropolitanism. I leave that out only because I have held forth on it before, and will do so again elsewhere. Certainly there is no doubt in my mind that the relationship of dominant cities to their hinterlands (to which there have been passing references here) is a fruitful subject in Canadian history, as it is the relationship of metropolitanism to regionalism, or of Canadian metropolitan centres to still bigger centres outside the country; in each case in political, social and cultural terms as well as economic.

Metropolitan relations, however, particularly involve systems of communications that link the urban centre with its hinterland region; and the topic of cities and communications deserves some comment here. Whether the city be analyzed in essence as temple, court, armed camp, storehouse or marketplace, it cannot function in any or all these regards except as a focus of communications also. Without them, it does not influence, command, supply or serve; it withers inside its own limits. All depends on the ability to transmit goods, men and information (and so wealth and power) either to or from the urban centre. Urbanization, in fact, is not just the bringing of people from the country into the city. It is also the bringing of the city to the country through effective communications, so that more and more of the population acquire urban standards, wants and interests. This kind of urbanization, now fostered by mass media, is incidentally quite consistent with the decentralization of industries or cities in our increasingly electronic age.

In Canada as elsewhere, the city has functioned as a focus of communications. It has exercised power because it is a focus, operating as a decision-making centre where élite groups concentrate, from compacts to corporation managements. And to a high degree a city has gained or lost power over areas outside it as technological change in communications systems has worked to its benefit or disadvantage. These may be airy generalizations or only statements of the obvious. But they can also serve as guides for further inquiry into the city's role in Canadian history.

For example, one could study the rising western towns of the 1900s in terms of the communications they focussed and led back to the East – Winnipeg, Regina, Calgary and many more. Not only the influence of the railway line, stockyard or elevator, but the prairie press and the mail order catalogue besides, are bound up in explaining the rapid emergence of an urban-oriented twentieth-century society out of pioneer existence on the plains. Almost instant civilization, thanks to city-centred communication. Just add people and stir.

As for urban élites and decision-making, there is so much we need to know about the merchants, financiers, entrepreneurs and promoters whose developmental schemes reached far beyond their city's confines, and by success, failure or political involvement repeatedly affected Canadian growth for good and ill. But Professor Alan Wilson touched admirably on this subject in a paper given before this association two years ago.[14] And though it might be thought that I am simply reciprocating a kind mention he gave me there, I will make this specific reference and add little more than one point to it.

By Montreal's harbour, towered over by the great port facilities he did much to make possible, stands a statue of the Honourable John Young. But who knows him as other than a minor political figure or a free-trade advocate of the mid-nineteenth century? Who knows his work with the Montreal Harbour Commission – that significant group whose efforts to develop the river berths and downstream channel was instrumental in bringing Montreal ascendancy over Quebec as a deep-water ocean port? There are many sequels to be written on Montreal's St. Lawrence empire and the men who shaped it, just as there are on urban-imperial projects and builders from one side of the country to the other.

As for the effects of technological change, there is the impact of the iron steamship and the railway on the oceanic system of communications in which the Maritime port cities had thrived. Of course this is referred to in works concerning the regional economy of the Maritimes, or their provincial discontents after Confederation. But where are the studies of the attempts of Halifax or Saint John to cope with their changed situation, or the accommodations they partially achieved as continental winter ports? We have nothing like Edward Kirkland's *Men, Cities and Transportation*, treating similar changes as they affected New England, and particularly Boston's response to them.

Why not such a work, indeed, on Toronto's notably successful attempts to take advantage of the new means of rail communication? Books on railways as such, however useful, are not sufficient in themselves to bring out the work of the Capreols, Cumberlands and Gzowskis in their own city milieu. Similarly, the story of the Canadian Pacific is not exactly adequate to express Vancouver's drive to use rail and road to enlarge its hinterland eastward – nor to include the beneficent effect of the Panama Canal on the city's communications, enabling it to enter rich Atlantic markets when Pacific ones had proved limited. Finally, what of a study of Edmonton's role as "gateway to the North," when with the rise of bush flying after the First World War it found itself in touch with northern reaches on a scale never possible before? True, some of these things have been partly done – or thinly, in popular studies – but seldom in terms of the city where the men, the designs and the means to technological decision came together in significant complexes well worth the historian's attention.

There is one last area for consideration here: the city in the cultural growth of Canada. Once more it is plain that Montreal is not Paris, nor Toronto Florence (Naples possibly?). Yet it is no less plain that the cultural developments we have experienced have been inevitably urban-centred. That may be only a world-wide truism. The arts, like money, concentrate in towns – and need the money too. Nevertheless, the fact that Canada has not known a landed aristocracy has meant that the essential clientele for the arts have been the wealthier ranks of the city burghers. And unlike the United States, of course, we have had few princely-capitalistic patrons. Lacking either the great country houses or the Newport estates, cultural development in Canada has been intimately associated with the well-to-do of the urban community. Nor has the growth of state expenditure and the spread of what I might call "cultural democracy" greatly altered that association.

This might seem to reduce artistic endeavour to the question of who will pay for it and where, ignoring the individual creative spirit of the artist, drawn as his muse listeth. Still, even though the artist may seek Precambrian or psychedelic immensities, there must be something in the fact that he dwells in, studies in, and usually gets his "school" label in, some particular urban setting. It may be that the Canadian artist in various fields can be better comprehended through studying the quality and style of his urban surroundings – in a country which has neither a landed aristocratic nor a rooted peasant culture, apart from dwindling elements in French Canada. At any rate, it can be argued that the history of literature, music, architecture and other arts in Canada would all be illumined by studying them in conjunction with the history of the cities where they so largely grew and found their public.

If the city has been inseparably linked with the development of the arts in Canada, so it has been with education. Again this can seem obvious. Most of our universities, and the biggest ones, are in large population centres. The most complicated and expensive machinery of the public school systems are naturally to be found there. And yet there is more to be discerned. First, except for the Maritimes, Canada has followed a historic pattern of developing largely urban universities; there have been relatively few rural "college towns" on the widespread American model. The battle over urban university centralization was perhaps decided for English Canada in the 1860s, when denominational colleges in Canada West failed to break the hold of Toronto University on the provincial endowment, and not long thereafter there began the move to federation at Toronto as the only way to meet growing educational costs. Certainly it is clear that western provinces, and Quebec, adopted similar patterns of urban centralization. Now that new demands have brought the proliferation of universities (still city-centred) there seems only more reason to assess the university and its teaching as a product of Canadian urban culture – not forgetting the church in this respect, so long and so closely linked with higher education.

Second, there is a considerable assumption that mass public education, in English Canada at least, has stemmed from rural democracy and the backwoods log cabin school. But the investigation now proceeding shows far more convincingly that school needs in developing urban centres shaped the effective state school system established in the Province of Canada during the 1840s and 1850s; the earlier, inept local schools had little to do with the Ryersonian bureaucracy and centrally directed educational machinery set up at Toronto.[15] The problems of city numbers and the illiterate, imputedly dangerous, poor focussed issues of state support, property and personal rights, and of free and compulsory schooling. And improvements in state education, as in state social welfare and control measures, took form increasingly in urban areas – to be spread outside from there – precisely because it was there that needs led to innovations. Here again is a theme worthy of development in Canadian urban history: the city as an educational, and social, workshop, producing changes of regional or national significance in the whole fabric of Canadian cultural life.

But has the history of the city anything to say on Canada's most insistent problem, the relations of French- and English-speaking cultures? At all events, cities have been deeply involved in the strains between the two. One need only point to Montreal's links with the Lower Canadian rebellion of 1837, the election violence in the city in the 1840s, the furore over the Rebellion Losses Bill. More interesting is the special experience in urban history Montreal and Quebec provide as cities of two cultures: different in nature from other major Canadian cities, where there may be an ethnic mosaic within an English-speaking cultural dominance, or recent immigrants in ghetto communities; but where there is no such rooted bi-cultural division. Hence one could profitably study the political, social and economic evidence of the workings of dual cultures in these two urban entities, each with its own long tradition and its considerably different record of Anglo-French relations – perhaps because the English have never really posed a threat to the French of Quebec city, not at least, since the 1760s.

Much more could be said on the significance of urbanism in French-English relations in regard to heading up and polarizing conflict, in regard to making "hot" information all too available, and in regard to adding the general tensions and problems of urban living to the sensitive areas of cultural divergence. But it is time to call a halt. In so doing, I am conscious none the less of all I did not say of Canadian urban history: on themes such as class, ethnic, and religious relations in the city;

on labour, immigration, unemployment and relief; on social problems and policies; the roles of families, children, women and men in urban settings; alcoholism and the temperance movement; industrial and financial development, wholesaling and retailing; not to mention the press, the professions, the crafts, and the amusements. There is besides the whole question of the city's role in national and regional politics and its own municipal political life. There is the history of its internal services, transport and utilities; its planning and speculation, its buildings, its general ambiance. And still the list could be extended to cover its people in individual and collective personalities, the "urban biography" of their whole community.

It is sufficient to say, surely, that this is no small subject, either for Canada now, or for the Canada of yesterday. Without in any way excluding other approaches to a country such as this, the urban society and culture that has emerged requires an urban history. And urban history, after all, has both intra-national and supra-national connotations. Cities form part of an urban network that spreads far beyond Canadian boundaries. In only one regard, as agencies that focus information flow, they are centres for the breeding and exchange of ideas, units in an emerging world pattern, not of the global village, but of the global megalopolis. Beyond "Somewhat Narrow Horizons," therefore, broad vistas may open indeed.

Endnotes

1. See *Canadian Historical Association Annual Report*, 1950 and 1951.
2. Studies in Canadian urban history include *The Rise of Toronto, 1850-1890*, by D.C. Masters (Toronto, 1947); "Metropolitanism and Toronto Re-examined," by F.H. Armstrong, C.H.A.A.R., 1966; and writings by J.I. Cooper on Montreal and E.G. Firth on York. There is material also of significance for urban history in such volumes as *Manitoba, A History*, by W.L. Morton (Toronto, 1957); *British Columbia, A History*, by M.A. Ormsby (Toronto, 1958); *Histoire Economique et Sociale du Québec, 1760-1850*, by F. Ouellet (Montreal, 1966); and *New Brunswick, A History, 1784-1967*, by W.S. MacNutt (Toronto, 1963). Among more recent popular works are *Montreal*, by K. Jenkins (New York, 1966); *Halifax, Warden of the North*, by T.H. Raddall (Toronto, 1948); *Vancouver, from Milltown to Metropolis*, by A. Morley (Vancouver, 1961); and *Edmonton, A History*, by J.G. MacGregor (Edmonton, 1967).
3. Carl Bridenbaugh, *Cities in the Wilderness* (New York, 1955).
4. Figures are derived from the retrospective statistics on population increase in the *Census of Canada* for 1931, Vol. I, supplemented by the *Census* for 1961.
5. C.N. Glaab and A.T. Brown, *A History of Urban America* (New York, 1967), p. 51. See also RC. Wade, *The Urban Frontier, the Rise of Western Cities*, 1790-1830 (Cambridge, 1960).
6. See note 4.
7. *Ibid.*
8. E.G. Firth, *The Town of York, 1815-1834* (Toronto, 1966), p. lxxx; F.H. Armstrong, *loc. cit.*, p.40.
9. See A.R.M. Lower, *Canadians in the Making* (Toronto, 1962), p. 260.
10. Guy Frégault, *La civilisation de la Nouvelle-France* (Montréal, 1944), p. 217.
11. Richard E. Rice, "The Growth of Trade Unionism in Saint John," unpublished M.A. thesis for University of New Brunswick, 1968.
12. St. John's had over 30,000 inhabitants in 1855 to Newfoundland's total of 122,638. See *Census of Canada*, 1931, I, p. 150-151.

13. See Louise Dechêne, "Les Entreprises de William Price," *Histoire Sociale* (Université d'Ottawa), avril 1968.
14. A.G. Wilson, "Forgotten Men of Canadian History", *C.H.A.A.R.*, 1965, pp. 73, 79-80. See also his *John Northway, A Blue Serge Canadian* (Toronto, 1965), and F.H. Armstrong, "Approaches to Business History in Canada: The Historian's Approach," *Proceedings of the Fourteenth Annual Meeting of the Business History Conference*, University of Western Ontario (London, 1967).
15. Susan Houston, "The Vagrant Child in Upper Canada: A Social Issue in Education, 1850-1865," seminar paper, University of Toronto, !968, stemming from doctoral research in progress.

Victoria product of gold rushes: Government Street in the 1860s.

The Business Community in the Early Development of Victoria

THE RISE OF VICTORIA FROM the Hudson's Bay fort of the 1850s to the substantial commercial city of the later nineteenth century may be readily associated with striking events like the Fraser and Cariboo gold rushes, the political course of able Governor Douglas and the somewhat colourful officialdom about him – or the still more colourful doings of Amor de Cosmos, a kind of dedicated opportunist in politics, working toward the crucial decision of federal union with Canada. Far less likely is Victoria's growth to be associated with the more prosaic, lower-keyed activities of the city's businessmen. None the less, their quieter, continuing operations played an essential part in making the Vancouver Island community the chief entrepôt of young British Columbia. Nor was the process lacking in colour or in noteworthy figures of its own. To trace that process, the development of the business community in conjunction with Victoria itself, is thus the object of the present study.[1]

Before 1858, and the onset of the gold rush to the Fraser on the neighbouring mainland, Victoria was a tranquil little hamlet of some three hundred inhabitants clustered about a fur trade depot. Fort Victoria, founded in 1843, did have the distinction, of course, of being the Hudson's Bay headquarters on the coast, as well as seat of government for the colony of Vancouver Island that had been erected in 1849, still in the keeping of the fur trade company. As a part of a great British commercial and imperial enterprise, and on the open Pacific within the world reach of British sea-power, Victoria was by no means wholly isolated or unchanging. Parties of colonists had arrived from the United Kingdom to settle among the Company's officers and employees; the mild climate and fertile soil of the adjacent districts gave them good crops. The Company had opened valuable coal mines up the coast at Nanaimo in the early fifties, and the timber wealth of the Island's heavy forests was initially being tapped. Finally, there was an increasing trade southward in coal, lumber, and sometimes fish or potatoes to San Francisco, the bustling Californian gold metropolis, from where most of the colony's necessary imports were derived.

Nevertheless, Victoria had remained an outpost community of small endeavours and limited opportunities. It was not one to invite much business enterprise when the fur company dominated the major economic activities – not to mention political – and when markets were either local and scanty or far off and uncertain. True, the Hudson's Bay interests had worked at developing farms, mines or sawmills, and had diversified their trading operations on the coast well beyond the traffic in furs. Yet problems of access to market and to sufficient shipping plagued them too, while the established, hierarchical ways of the old fur monopoly inevitably made new adjustments harder. Outside of the quasi-bureaucratic world of the Bay Company, moreover, there scarcely was a business community, other than well-to-do tavern keepers like James Yates (a former Company employee), some artisans, and a few independent settlers engaged in trade.

John Muir, formerly a Company coal-miner, sent spars, piles and lumber to Victoria from his small mill at Sooke, for shipment to the California market. Captain William Brotchie had pioneered in opening the spar trade, but found it hard to get adequate transport, and subsequently became Victoria's Harbourmaster. And Captain James Cooper, who had commanded Hudson's Bay supply vessels, had set up as an independent trader, bringing the little iron schooner, *Alice*, out from England in sections, then shipping cargoes like coal, cranberries and spars to San Francisco and the Hawaiian Islands. The role of sea captains in early business development on Vancouver Island was notable, in fact. But shipmasters then had long been roving businessmen, used to trading where they could, seeking cargoes, and commissions in their own or other's service. They were particularly prominent in early lumbering on the Island. Of fourteen subscribers to the Vancouver Steam Saw Mill Company five were ship captains, the rest Hudson's Bay officials or associates.[2] The Company itself introduced the first steam saw mill machinery to Victoria in 1853, but the venture failed from lack of sufficient capital, and the mill did little before it was destroyed by fire in 1859.

This, then, was the restrictive climate for business enterprise in early Victoria: lack of funds outside the Company for any but the smallest scale of operations, and lack of stimulating demands generally. The San Francisco market itself was far from satisfactory, when the products of Washington or Oregon were competitive and closer, and also did not face duties there. During the California boom that reached a peak in 1853, demands had been high enough to make the Vancouver Island lumber trade important; and of the nineteen lumber ships that left Victoria that year eighteen were bound for San Francisco.[3] When the boom faded, however, so did much of the Island's wood trade. Coal did better, earning a place in the California market as good steamer fuel; but again it could suffer from price fluctuations and the competition of coal from Britain, Australia or the eastern United States. In short, down to 1858, Victoria had not yet found a trade pattern that could encourage much business growth. Then came gold, to change the picture almost overnight.

In the spring of 1858, news of gold strikes in British territory along the lower Thompson and Fraser valleys reached San Francisco. The mass hysteria that makes gold rushes surged within the city, and thousands prepared to leave for a new El Dorado. Some might make their way to Puget Sound or by rough overland trails up through the mountainous interior, but most chose the quickest, surest route by sea, the four-day passage to Victoria. For here was a port of entry to the British far western domains, the one place of transhipment for the river journey up the treacherous Fraser, unnavigable by large ocean-going vessels. The importance of already existing patterns of transport in focussing this flow of traffic is fully evident here. The mass of shipping that was now swept into highly profitable runs to Victoria was simply following a recognized lane to an established harbour that lay beside the entrance to the Gulf of Georgia, from where the fur trade had long maintained contact with the mainland posts of the interior by way of the Fraser route.

For Victoria, however, the flow of ships brought golden inundation by waves of eager miners, who needed food and shelter, transport to the interior, supplies beyond what they had carried with them, and had money to spend for it all. The first four hundred and fifty arrived in April on the American steamer *Commodore.* They came in ever-mounting numbers through the summer, until, it was estimated, the town's population had climbed to seven thousand.[4] Most of the newcomers soon had to be housed under canvas; Victoria became a veritable tent city. But construction proceeded rapidly, brick as well as wooden buildings going up, while land values soared – rising for choice lots from an initial fifty dollars to three thousand dollars and more.[5] For with the miners had come entrepreneurs with capital, store and hotel keepers, commission merchants and real estate buyers, who were ready to invest in the business which they envisaged would accrue to Victoria from its services to the gold fields.

Some, of course, were essentially speculators, planning to grab a quick return and move on. Others were agents of established San Francisco firms, seeking new branches, and still others were more vaguely attracted by the thought of commercial opportunities in another California-like boom. Many would leave, especially after the initial enthusiasm of the rush ran out in disillusionment by the winter, and contraction and depression followed. But enough of the new commercial element remained, along with miners in the hinterland, to bring an enduring change to Victoria. And when the next year sufficient finds further up the Fraser kept the mining frontier going, then its main outlet continued to grow also as a town. Though Victoria's population had fallen back under three thousand by 1860,[6] it had indeed become an urban centre with a trading pattern of its own, supplying a considerable market on the mainland and exporting quantities of gold to San Francisco.

The pattern was strengthened in 1860, when Governor Douglas declared the town a free port. New Westminster, established near the mouth of the Fraser in 1858 as capital of the new mainland province of

British Columbia, faced the burden of custom duties as well as the problems of Fraser navigation. It became little more than a river-steamboat halt, while Victoria remained the terminus for ocean shipping. The Vancouver Island town, indeed, had the best of both worlds: free external contact with an international, maritime traffic system, customs and licences on the mainland to check encroachments on its inland trade from over the American border. Accordingly, although Victoria's business life, like its population, ebbed and flowed with the fortunes of gold mining, it nevertheless acquired substance and solidity as an entrepôt, building a merchant group alongside the older Hudson's Bay and official elements that would steadily gain in stature.

Its business community grew particularly with the new rush to the Cariboo goldfields in 1862. Over the next two years, as Barkerville and other mining towns emerged far in the interior, as the Cariboo Road was opened to serve the fields, and as their deeper-driven mines increasingly needed capital and a greater volume of supplies, Victoria once more rose apace. But this time its business operations were necessarily on a bigger scale, in provisioning, transporting and financing for the larger enterprises of the Cariboo – where, moreover, farming and ranching were soon widening the bases of hinterland activities. It was good evidence of growth when Victoria was incorporated as a city in 1862, and its Chamber of Commerce was organized in 1863. That year, indeed, *The British Columbian and Victoria Guide and Directory* could say of the new city, "Her true position as the center and headquarters of commerce north of the Columbia has been placed beyond a doubt."[7]

In these early years of growth, Victoria's business community of several hundred had acquired some significant characteristics, as well as many individuals worthy of note. One frequently remarked feature was the high proportion of Americans in the rising merchant group; another, its strongly marked cosmopolitan flavour as well. The former was to be expected from the commercial ties that made Victoria an outpost of San Francisco. The latter reflected the multi-national nature of gold rush society, whether among miners or those who would mine the miners, and whether in California or the British possessions to the north. But if Victoria had become "in effect, San Francisco in miniature,"[8] it none the less had features of its own. There were the continuing elements of the older settler society and the Hudson's Bay-official élite. Some of their members did quite well by the Victoria boom, in hotels, stores and real estate; James Yates, for instance, piling up sufficient fortune to retire. Besides, other businessmen of British or British North American background arrived to share in the town's expansion, and later more generally stayed on, when Americans tended to withdraw. Finally, some of the "American" business migrants were better included in the multi-national category, since a number of them had earlier been immigrants to the United States; and, having moved on temporarily to San Francisco, had now moved on again.

In this regard, it has been noted that of the first 450 newcomers who arrived in 1858 aboard the *Commodore* from San Francisco, only about 120 were either British or Americans (about equally divided), the rest being mainly German, French or Italian.[9] There was also a notable Jewish admixture in the cosmopolitan influx of the gold-rush era, not to mention a significant contingent of American Negroes, and additional numbers of Slavs, Hawaiians and Chinese. The commercial community that took shape in Victoria was more Anglo-American in its upper ranks, more varied on the level of small shopkeepers or skilled tradesmen. Yet French, German and Jewish names figured prominently on the higher levels, while two Negroes, Mifflin Gibbs and Peter Lester, set up the first large general store to compete effectively with that of the Hudson's Bay Company.[10]

Adolph Sutro, a cultivated German Jew, arrived in 1858 to extend the wholesale and retail tobacco business he and his brothers had established in San Francisco. The Sutro warehouse in Victoria continued under brothers Gustav and Emil, although Adolph shortly afterward returned to San Francisco, to make a fortune in the Comstock Lode and become one of the Californian city's most lavish benefactors.[11] In similar fashion David and Isaac Oppenheimer, also German Jews, arrived from California to develop a wholesale dry goods business in Victoria. After flourishing for years, they were to move to the newly founded town of Vancouver, where they became two of its wealthiest citizens and David a celebrated mayor.[12]

And in the days of the rising Victoria business community there were, besides Sutros and Oppenheimers, men like Selim and Lumley

Franklin, English-born Jews, who again came in the early wave from San Francisco. They were two of Victoria's first auctioneers, prospered in real estate and as commission agents, promoted shipping and cattle sales. Selim, moreover, sat for Victoria in the Vancouver Island legislature from 1860 to 1866, while Lumley was mayor of the city in 1865.[13] Still further, there were names like Ghiradelli and Antonovich, commission merchants, Jacob Sehl, furniture dealer from Coblentz, and P. Manciet, who kept the Hotel de France (a leading establishment in the sixties), all to demonstrate the variety of this new little urban business world.[14]

As for Americans, almost the most significant for the future was William Parsons Sayward, of New England origin. In 1858 he came up from a lumber business in San Francisco to found a similar one in Victoria. His wharf and yards grew over the years; but, more important, he went into sawmilling at Mill Bay in 1861, and ultimately became one of the chief figures in lumbering on the North Pacific coast.[15] Then, there was C. C. Pendergast who opened an office for Wells Fargo in Victoria in 1858. From the start, Wells Fargo played a major part in banking, in exporting gold to San Francisco, and for some time in handling mail for the business community: all of which made "Colonel" Pendergast a man of wide regard.[16] Equally well regarded was T.N. Hibben, a South Carolinian whose stationery and bookselling firm, begun in 1858, would have a long existence in Victoria. Still others prominent in the American segment of the community were Edgar Marvin, hardware and farm machinery importer (an 1862 arrival who became United States consul), and J.A. McCrea and P.M. Backus, both auctioneers.[17] Theirs was an important occupation at the time, when so many cargoes as well as properties inland were disposed of through auction sales.

There were also agents of San Francisco shipping lines, wholesalers and forwarding houses in the Victoria trade; for example, Samuel Price and Company, Dickson, De Wolf and Company, or Green Brothers. Sometimes their local representatives were Americans, but often instead they were Victorians of British background, serving as local partners in their firm – which itself might reach back far beyond San Francisco in a chain of interlocking partnerships to New York, Liverpool and London. Dickson De Wolf, for example (locally Dickson and Campbell), was based on H.N. Dickson's of London, and also had houses or correspondents in Liverpool, Boston and Halifax.[18] Yet from the time of the Fraser gold rush, a good deal of Victoria's expanding wholesale trade was handled by local commission agents and general merchants, who of course had San Francisco correspondents. And in this field it seems evident that the British segment of the business community became particularly important.

The relative prominence of British wholesale merchants in the basic import trades no doubt related to the fact of operating in British territory, and the likelihood of securing better contacts with colonial authorities or the still influential Hudson's Bay Company – not to mention the possibility of their having useful business ties back to Great Britain herself, where some of them returned to visit. A good illustration is that of J.J. Southgate, an Englishman who had been a commission merchant and ship-handler in San Francisco, but moved to Victoria in 1858 with a letter of introduction to Governor Douglas. Southgate soon prospered there, gaining, for example, a contract to provision His Majesty's warships lying in nearby Esquimalt harbour.[19] He built a fine brick store (still standing), with financial backing from Commander H.D. Lascelles, R.N., dealt in real estate, took the lead in organizing a Masonic Lodge, and was elected to the legislature in 1860.[20] Another example is that of the Lowe brothers, Thomas and James, two Scots commission merchants in San Francisco, who similarly transferred their business to Victoria in 1861-2. Thomas was an old Hudson's Bay man who had close links with the Company trading network along the coast, and in the fifties had pioneered in selling coal from the Company's Vancouver Island mines in the San Francisco market.[21] It was notable, incidentally, that the Lowe firm wrote the letter of introduction that Southgate carried to Douglas.[22] Subsequently the brothers took over the latter's wholesale business when he was absent in England; and James Lowe became President of the Chamber of Commerce in 1866, though he failed to win election to parliament in 1869.

Among many other leading early British businessmen one may mention R.C. Janion, with Liverpool and Honolulu connections, J. Robertson Stewart, Robert Burnaby and G.M. Sproat, President of the local St. Andrew's Society in 1863. Born in Kirkcudbrightshire, Gilbert Sproat had come to Vancouver Island in 1860 in the service of Anderson and Company, a big London firm of shipowners and shipbrokers who were developing a large steam sawmill at Alberni on the west coast of the Island. He became manager of the mill himself when its initiator, Captain Edward Stamp, resigned; but he also built up his own importing and insurance business in Victoria.[23] Another Anderson employee was to become Sproat's partner, Andrew Welch, an Englishman with a distinguished business career ahead of him. And Thomas Harris, also from England, Victoria's first butcher, grew to be a well-to-do provisioner and the city's mayor in 1862.

The British element was also found in banking, for the wealthy London-based and chartered Bank of British North America had opened a Victoria branch in 1859. A few months previous, however, the town's first private bank had already been established by Alexander Macdonald, an enterprising Scotsman who had come up from California with the gold rush in hopes of living by it. He did well at first, making advances in gold dust for sale in San Francisco. But in 1864 his bank was burgled (through the roof) of well over $25,000, which ruined him, and sent him fleeing back to California.[24] The Bank of British Columbia, again London-based with a royal charter of 1862, proved more substantial and reliable, helping to finance wholesale operations, and soon, indeed, the government itself.

"British" at this period quite properly could cover subjects of the Queen who came to Victoria from the eastern colonies of British North America. It is of interest to note that there was some (prospective) Canadian content in contemporary Victoria business and professional circles, as evidenced by Thomas Earle, wholesale grocer and later member of parliament, an Upper Canadian who arrived in 1862.[25] Gradually more eastern British Americans did appear, usually still by way of California; but one of the earliest significant indications of their coming was in journalism. The first newspaper, the *Victoria Gazette*, established in June, 1858, may have been an extension of American press enterprise, but it is worth observing that its publisher, James W. Towne of California, was born in Nova Scotia.[26] And the far more important David Higgins, who arrived in 1860 and subsequently would edit Victoria's enduring *Colonist* for many years, was similarly of Nova Scotian birth, if American upbringing.[27] Above all, there was the founder and first editor of the *British Colonist* (begun late in 1858), Amor de Cosmos, also a native Nova Scotian, who also came via California. His vehement and erratic career in press and politics may not suggest too close an analogy with Joseph Howe; but at least there was some Nova Scotian ingredient added to early Victoria, through this transplanting of Bluenoses from one coast to another.

The character of this business community, strongly associated with the American Pacific metropolis but also with the older British metropolis of the Atlantic, did not greatly change for years the stamp it received in the gold boom era of the early 1860s. New men were to come forward, additional interests to develop; but the men largely emerged out of older firms and partnerships, and the broader economic developments did not alter Victoria's basic role as a maritime commercial entrepôt serving a simple extractive hinterland. Of course, declining gold production from the mid-sixties onward, the coming of Confederation with Canada in 1871, and the mounting influence of Canadian metropolitan power thereafter – signalized by the National Policy of 1878 and the building of the Canadian Pacific in the next decade – all brought significant changes that inevitably affected Victoria business more and more. Yet well into the 1880s, and perhaps even to the nineties, the patterns of Victorian commercial society set between 1858 and 1864 continued as a basis; even while American or continental European elements within it decreased or were assimilated, and British and Canadian elements were enlarged. This, then, is the general framework for the next two decades. It remains to discuss the newer activities and the newer men that did emerge inside it.

The falling output of the gold mines after 1864, and the failure to find rich, easily workable new fields, did not seriously harm Victoria at first, still living on the momentum, so to speak, of the expectations of more finds, and with some stimulus to trade derived from the American Civil War. Falling gold revenues and heavy colonial debt burdens, however, did lead in 1866 to the union of Vancouver Island and British Columbia as an urgent move of retrenchment. And this union sharply affected Victoria by removing its privileges as a free port. It was almost the hand-writing on the wall; continental costs of development and need for customs duties had defeated the interests of maritime free trade. At the public proclamation in Victoria of the new united province of British Columbia, so the *Colonist* noted, members of the crowd variously informed the sheriff that he was reading his death-warrant, warned a red-nosed bystander that port was no longer duty-free, and urged "a seedy-looking individual" to hurry up Government Street to buy a suit while he could still save fifteen per cent.[28] At least there was the consolation that Victoria remained provincial capital – to New Westminster's chagrin.

Activity in lumbering had offset in some degree the lessening role of gold. At Alberni, Gilbert Sproat's steam saw mill had reached a splendid peak in 1863, producing over eleven million feet of lumber, until the rapid exhaustion of timber close to water, accessible to the hand or ox-logging of those days, forced its closing by 1865.[29] However, the saw mill that W.P. Sayward had opened in 1863 up the Island's east coast near Cowichan thrived on a more accessible timber supply. In 1864 his mill alone brought two million feet to Victoria, and by the close of the decade put him into the export trade.[30] At the time of the union of 1866, moreover, there were six Vancouver Island saw mills in operation, much of their produce being marketed by way of Victoria. Furthermore, during the depression of the later sixties, they and the Burrard Inlet mills, that had now appeared on the mainland at Moodyville and Hastings, ended the former dominance of American Puget Sound mills over the import market.[31] While for some years following, Island lumbering failed to grow markedly, an important productive basis had been laid for future development, in which the Sayward milling and lumbering interests would play full part.

Then there was coal. In 1858 the Hudson's Bay Company had returned control of Vancouver Island to the Crown, and by the next year its trading rights on the mainland had ended. Thereafter the Company had sought to concentrate on its original concern, the fur trade, divesting itself of other complicating ventures, such as its coal mines in the Nanaimo area. Thus in 1862 it sold these holdings to the Vancouver Island Coal Mining and Land Company, which was based in England and backed by British capital. (It also seems to have had an oddly literary connection, since T.C. Haliburton was its first chairman and among its investors were Agnes Strickland and the father of John Galsworthy).[32] In Victoria, the thriving firm of Dickson, Campbell and Company served as its agents, George Campbell being made a director. Much of the Vancouver Coal Company's output went directly from Nanaimo to market, to San Francisco or the Royal Navy based at Esquimalt. But some as well went via Victoria, where Charles Wallace, also of Dickson and Campbell, managed the two ships that the Company bought for its trade in 1864.[33] The next year coal production rose to 32,000 tons; and to 44,000 in 1868.[34] But by 1870 it seemed to have reached a plateau, and in the following decade the Company ran into trouble, owing to lack of further capital to develop new mines, and competition not only in the American market but within Vancouver Island itself.

The latter competition came from Robert Dunsmuir, the son of a Scottish coal master, who had first been employed at Nanaimo in the Hudson's Bay Company mines, but had been engaged in his own independent workings there since 1855. In 1864 another English coal mining venture, the Harewood Company, was launched, backed by the Hon. H.D. Lascelles, commanding H.M.S. *Forward*, and Dunsmuir became its resident manager.[35] Though he drove his miners rigorously (which did not stop them entertaining him to a public tea that year),[36] he could not overcome the fact that the Harewood Mine, after starting well, began to peter out. Dunsmuir withdrew. In 1869, however, he discovered the truly rich Wellington Mine, and set up a company to work it, with financial aid from another naval officer, Lieutenant W.N. Diggle of the *Grappler*.[37] The Dunsmuir Company soon flourished, having one of the best coal seams on the coast and thus well able to stand the competition in the San Francisco market. Moreover, it undertook dock and railway developments at Nanaimo that ministered to that town's growth. And some of the benefit would redound to Victoria, since it kept much of the supply trade of the area. Hence, by the seventies, at least, growth in this coal hinterland could help balance decline in the older one of gold.

And then there was shipping. During the 1860s Victoria became the centre of shipping and shipbuilding interests of its own. It started, of course, with the rush of mining traffic to the Fraser. At the outset the Hudson's Bay Company had commanded the transport service; its pioneer steamers, the *Beaver* and *Otter*, would long be famous around the coasts and up the lower reaches of the river. But because of the demands for transport during the gold rush, Governor Douglas had recognized the need to allow American steamboat captains to enter the river navigation. A number of veterans of Puget Sound or Columbia River steamboating thus came in, and largely found it practicable to make Victoria their base of operations, as the main terminus of the Fraser trade. Captain William Irving became the most prominent and enduring of them – but here again the description of "American" is misleading, since he was a Scot, with much seagoing experience behind him before he pioneered with the first steamboat in Oregon.[38]

Irving joined with another Scottish steamboat pioneer from the Columbia, Alexander Murray, to build the stern-wheeler *Governor Douglas* at Victoria in 1858, her engine being brought from San Francisco.[39] This "first steamer built in the province for the inland trade" was soon joined by a sister ship, the *Colonel Moody*.[40] The previously mentioned merchants, Thomas and James Lowe, invested in the vessels; James for a time was an agent for the line, as were the also-mentioned Samuel Price and Company.[41] Irving built still more ships at Frahey's yard in Victoria, the *Reliance* in 1862 and the *Onward* in 1865.[42] The Hudson's Bay Company also acquired new craft to meet their competition and that from American steamboats. But the fall in gold-mining activity after 1864 led American captains to leave the Fraser, so that for the rest of the decade Irving's and the Bay Company's ships between them controlled the river.[43] Indeed, this situation virtually continued until Captain Irving's death in 1872, and afterwards his son, John Irving, built a still larger shipping domain.

Joseph Spratt was significant also, because the Albion Iron Works, the foundry and marine machinery works he established in Victoria in 1862, became central to the subsequent growth of the city's shipping activities. After having had some training as a marine engineer in England, Spratt had gone to San Francisco, where he had opened a foundry and reputedly built the first steam locomotive on the Pacific coast.[44] As well as running his iron works, he went into shipbuilding, later salmon-canning and whaling, and organized a shipping line up the island's east coast. In any case, by the end of the 1860s he had added the beginnings of industrial enterprise to Victoria. And by that time, too, nine of the seventeen steamers trading to British Columbia and eighteen of the twenty-eight schooners were Victoria-built.[45]

As the sixties drew to a close, however, the city was in a state of depression. The newer activities in lumber, coal or shipbuilding had not yet hit full stride, and what was still far more apparent was the passing of the gold frontier, with its consequent effects on the wholesale trade, real estate and financial interests of the Victoria entrepôt. Business in the city in 1869 was so slow, in fact, that thistles grew in the gutters along Government Street, while the population was falling back again to little more than three thousand.[46] In this condition, it is not surprising that the business community was considerably despondent, or that, in the midst of continuing discussions on joining the new and far-off Canadian Confederation, some of its members might look to the simpler, sharper release of annexation to the United States. At any rate, the Annexation Petition of 1869 appeared in Victoria in November, signed with 104 names in all.

It is true that this was a limited number; that many of the signers were small men, not leading merchants; and that they included a large element of foreign born who had no strong political positions, either anti-British or pro-American, but voiced what was indeed "primarily an expression of economic discontent."[47] It is also true that the essential issue in Victoria was union with Canada or no union; that annexation was never a real alternative. Yet it is possible, besides, that doubts and fears expressed in anti-unionism among Victorians found a sharper focus in some of those businessmen who did subscribe to annexation: a matter of choosing the devil you knew at San Francisco to the distant unknown one at Ottawa, especially when the former so obviously commanded power and fortune. And certainly one might see concern for the wholesale trade or property values in such substantial signatories as Isaac Oppenheimer and David Shirpser, dry goods merchants, W.H. Oliver and W. Farron, heavy investors in Victoria real estate, or Emil Sutro, tobacco merchant, and T.N. Hibben, the prominent stationer.[48]

At all events, the flurry passed with little consequence; and within a few months Confederation was settled policy. By the time it took place in July, 1871, a brighter Victoria was ready to welcome it, hopeful indeed of the terms that had been agreed upon, including a railway to link East and West. For it well might be expected that a Pacific railway would have its terminus in or near Victoria, crossing to Vancouver Island over the narrows at its northern tip. Certainly the fact that a survey party for the projected Canadian Pacific were present in Victoria for the celebrations that accompanied the proclamation of British Columbia's entry into Confederation did not lessen the festivity.[49] And Victoria's businessmen could thus anticipate that change would also mean improvement for their community.

As the 1870s opened, it was a good thing that Victorians did have expectations from Confederation, for times continued slow in many respects: their city's population only passed 4,600 by 1874.[50] However, they could look to some federal relief from the provincial debt burden, some aid from a broader union in meeting the high costs of developing transport in the rugged hinterland. And there was the prospect of the railway, which raised new visions of Victoria as the San Francisco of the North, with its own transcontinental rail link like the newly opened Union Pacific, and its own Pacific oceanic empire of trade. Politically, at least, the city had been connected into a new continental system. Now it looked for the necessary communication network to be constructed also, to put it on the highroads of world development.

Gradually, moreover, its basic hinterland trades improved. Gold production, after reaching a low point in 1870, went up in 1871, and up still further in 1874-5, although it never came near the scale of the early sixties.[51] Coal output also began a steady climb from 1873 to 1879, though bigger years of growth would come in the next decade.[52] And if lumbering on the Island experienced no great advance yet, a new hinterland enterprise of considerable export potential made its appearance: salmon-canning. The salmon-canning industry had reached the American Pacific coast in the 1860s, from earlier beginnings in Maine and New Brunswick; but it was first established on the lower Fraser in 1870, independent of any American connection.[53] Victoria commission merchants effectively financed the Fraser river canneries and acted as agents in exporting their product directly to Great Britain.[54] For the canning process offered a means of overcoming the barrier of distance between a rich North Pacific food resource and a hungry industrial market. Furthermore, it produced a valuable trade that did not face the impediment of ever-rising American tariff barriers.

British Columbian salmon-canning grew slowly at first in the seventies, faster in the eighties, by which time the industry had spread northward to the Skeena (in 1877) and to the Nass and beyond. Victoria businessmen continued to play a major role in the enterprise: J.H. Todd provides a good example. Born in Brampton, Upper Canada, he had gone to Barkerville in 1863, speculated in mines and operated a successful merchandising business before moving to Victoria in 1872 to undertake another. Through profits from mining properties, and through acting as agent for canners on the Fraser, the Todd wholesaling firm was able to acquire two canneries there and another at Esquimalt. Subsequently it added a much larger one on the Skeena obtained from another prominent Victoria house of the day, Turner, Beeton and Company. Todd and Sons, in fact, continued to operate from Victoria as late as 1954, its fishing interests ultimately going to B.C. Packers.[55]

Furthermore, the redoubtable Joseph Spratt of the Albion Iron Works early entered the business. He developed the oilery (for pressing out herring oil) that he had opened on Burrard Inlet in 1868, at the site of the present city of Vancouver, into a floating salmon cannery.[56] Popularly termed "Spratt's Ark," it was a pioneer in the area's canning industry. More important in the long run, however, was R.P. Rithet, a Victoria wholesale merchant of widespread interests and enterprises. After acting as an agent for local Fraser river canners, he organized a number of them into the Victoria Canning Company in 1891, to meet the competition of two British-backed companies, British Columbia Canning and Anglo-British Columbia Packing, who had acquired virtually all the other canneries on the river.[57] That story, however, runs beyond this study, and is more important here to examine the advancing career of Robert Paterson Rithet as an exemplification of Victoria business in itself.

Born in Scotland in 1844, he was in the Cariboo in 1862; but after a few years came to Victoria, still in his early twenties, to find employment in the wholesale trade. In 1868 he was working for Sproat and Company; indeed, was running its Victoria office, since Gilbert Sproat, a man of many parts – merchant, insurance agent, sawmill manager, lobbyist, author and ethnologist – was then mainly in London, directing the Committee on the Affairs of British Columbia that he had organized.[58] The next year Rithet moved to San Francisco, to deal with the firm's interests there; evidently a promotion, for Sproat had sent him "kind words of confidence" by letter.[59] And here he came in close contact with Sproat's San Francisco partner, Andrew Welch. Welch, who had begun as a bookkeeper from England and worked with Sproat in the Alberni sawmill before entering into partnership in his wholesale business, was already emerging as a wealthy and prominent member of the San Francisco commercial élite. Before his death in 1889 he was to become a millionaire several times over, do much to develop the shipping trade between Victoria and that city, gain control of the Burrard Inlet mills at Moodyville, and thus build up a large-scale lumber export business.[60] Rithet could hardly have made a better connection. It resulted, eventually, in his own partnership with Welch.

Before that transpired, he returned to Victoria, still in Sproat's service; and there in 1870 had a stiff little encounter with a Mrs. Sutton, who did not approve of his attentions to her daughter. In fact, he broke his engagement to Miss Sutton by formal note to her mama – a Victorian touch in the wider sense of the term.[61] That year, moreover, Rithet left Sproat's firm to join that of J. Robertson Stewart, one of the old original British merchants in Victoria, who carried on insurance business for Bri-tish and American companies, and helped direct the British Columbian Investment and Loan Society, as well as operating a large wholesale warehouse.[62] In May of 1871, Rithet was "at present managing his business" because of Stewart's illness.[63] The latter soon decided to dispose of his interests and retire to Scotland. Andrew Welch bought him out, with Rithet's cordial approval.[64] In fact, that August a new firm was announced in the press, Welch, Rithet and Company, successors to J. Robertson Stewart. "We began," wrote Rithet, "under very favorable auspices, when the colony seems to be about to enter an era of improvement and progress. . . . with houses in San Francisco and Liverpool we should be able to make a business, and our outside connections are also tip-top."[65]

Thereafter through the seventies, and on into the eighties, Rithet's interests continued to grow: in wholesaling, shipping, insurance, lumbering, canning, grocery importing, and generally financial investment in a wide range of enterprises. With Welch, he became engaged in the sugar trade of the Hawaiian Islands; they acquired control of plantations there.[66] He invested in the mills at Moodyville, the Albion Iron Works, in sealing, whaling and in farming. He became president of the Board of Trade and a justice of the peace in the 1870s, mayor of Victoria in 1885, then was elected to the legislature in the 1890s.[67] And on Welch's death he took over as head of both Welch and Company, San Francisco, and R.P. Rithet and Company, Victoria.[68] There is no space to deal with his later ventures in the mining and railway development of the British Columbia interior, nor in the building of deepwater dock facilities at Victoria through his Victoria Warf and Warehouse Company. All that can be noted is his connection with the continued growth of the city's shipping interests through the founding of the Canadian Pacific Navigation Company in 1883. And this brings in another of the leading Victorian entrepreneurs of the era, John Irving.

Irving had assumed control of his father's steamship company in 1872, although only eighteen years of age. Gold discoveries in the Stikeen and Cassiar districts in the seventies revived the coastal shipping trade, and Irving moved vigorously into competition, adding new boats to his fleet. At the same time growing settlement on the mainland and its expanding needs produced more traffic to the Fraser, while soon plans for the Pacific railway's construction brought a further stimulus. In 1878 Irving obtained a contract to carry the first shipment of rails from Esquimalt to Yale, and from then on increasingly left all rivals behind.[69] His chief competitor was still the Hudson's Bay Company's fleet. In 1883 he successfully arranged to merge it with his own.

It might not be without significance that a year earlier John Irving had married the daughter of Alexander Munro, Chief Factor of the Company in Victoria – nor that two of the bride's brothers worked for R.P. Rithet, who himself had married one of the Munro girls in 1875.[70] At any rate, the Canadian Pacific Navigation Company that now emerged to combine the lines under his management had Rithet as one of its directors and chief shareholders, along with Munro and that other noted business figure, Robert Dunsmuir of colliery fame.[71] Understandably, one of the line's fast ships was the *R.P. Rithet.* Irving's shipping empire (a far cry from Captain Cooper's little schooner, *Alice*) took over minor companies at the end of the eighties, and increasingly went into inland navigation on the lakes of the interior. It was ultimately bought out by the Canadian Pacific Railway as its coastal service in 1900. That, in itself, marked the passing of Victoria's as well as Irving's steamboat hegemony; but it had been a very good run indeed.

Meanwhile Robert Dunsmuir's coal operations had grown steadily. In 1873 his one mine, the Wellington, had turned out 16,000 tons (just entering full production) to 45,000 for all those of the Vancouver Island Coal Company's.[72] In 1880, his holdings alone produced 189,000 tons, and three years later he bought out his partner for $600,000.[73] He was well on his way to being the province's outstanding industrialist capitalist, with a fleet of cargo vessels, a mine railway and a large part of the Albion Iron Works besides.[74] As if to fit the classic picture of the nineteenth-century capitalist, he had a hard reputation with labour. He faced strikes at the mines in 1877 and 1883, brought in strikebreakers, and on the former violent occasion, a gunboat and the militia also. Apart from this, Dunsmuir now settled in Victoria, was also moving into railway promotions and construction. In 1883, the Esquimalt Railway Company of which he was president (it included the powerful figures, Leland Stanford and Charles Crocker of San Francisco, and C.P. Huntington of New York) obtained a contract from the federal government to build the Esquimalt and Nanaimo line, on terms that included a lavish grant of land.[75] Begun in 1884 under Dunsmuir's direction, it was finished in 1886, for the first time giving Victoria overland access to the coal hinterland.

Yet the seventy-mile Esquimalt and Nanaimo was a rather small consolation prize for Victoria not securing the Canadian Pacific – which was essentially what it turned out to be. Through much of the seventies the city had envisioned and urged the transcontinental line by way of Bute Inlet and Seymour Narrows to Vancouver Island, and hotly protested proposals for a Fraser valley route to tidewater instead. In 1874 the railway on the Island was at least promised anew by the Mackenzie federal government, but the bill for it was defeated in the Senate, leaving Victoria bitterly disappointed, and much angry talk of secession in political and business circles. But though the dispute rose and fell in the ensuing years, with recurrent swells of separatism again, the fact was that the capital or the Island did not necessarily speak for the province as a whole; and the British Columbian mainland communities saw far more benefit to be gained from a Fraser valley rail route. Here was, indeed, still further indication that the island community of Victoria had been brought into a continental system, and now had little weight to bear against the whole thrust of Canadian metropolitan designs. The best that could be done was to look for consolation prizes.

The Esquimalt dry dock and the E. and N. itself were two of these. And by the time that Dunsmuir undertook to build the latter (seeking truly magnificent consolation for himself and friends in terms of subsidies, coal fields and lands), Victoria interests were ready to make the best of the inevitable. Hence, in 1884, when the C.P.R. was already well advanced in its building, both up the Fraser and into the Rockies from the east, a final settlement of terms was harmoniously achieved. Victoria still had a sizeable and prosperous maritime trading domain; its population stood at twelve thousand that year,[76] and the city was thriving and hopeful. For at least it would have its own Island railway now.

Not only was the Island railway opened in 1886, but the C.P.R. that year also carried its first through trains to the Pacific – to Burrard Inlet. And this really marked the ending of an era for Victoria, for now Vancouver's meteoric rise was under way, as the true beneficiary of the transcontinental railway, the National Policy and the forces of Canadian metropolitanism in general. The little lumber settlement on the Inlet had been launched into its role as Canada's chief western outlet and Pacific port of entry. Not till 1898 did the import trade of the upstart city pass that of Victoria's; yet the trend was there before that was to make Vancouver the new British Columbian entrepôt and distributing centre.[77] In the later eighties and nineties Victoria would further develop its coal, salmon and lumber trades, along with new growth in deep-sea fishing, sealing and also in grain exports. But a reorientation of commercial patterns from sea to land was in process, in which Victoria could not hope to dominate great new hinterlands of deep-rock mining in the interior ranges or of agriculture on the prairies. A phase was over for the maritime city; and the completion of the transcontinental railway signalized it better than anything else.

There had not been want of energy or initiative in the Victorian business community. Men like Rithet, Dunsmuir and Irving demonstrated that fact, as did W.P. Sayward, who had built a large new lumber mill at Victoria in 1878 – which by 1890, was cutting nearly eleven million feet a year itself, while Sayward's logging camps were scattered up the Island, feeding his large-scale export trade.[78] Others, perhaps, in the community had showed less enterprise, being more content with things as they were, in a pleasantly civilized little world readily open to greater worlds in San Francisco or London, but remote from the harder cruder surroundings of the continental interior. Yet it would be difficult to prove such a point; and in any case it was not so much lack of enterprise as lack of situation and economic leverage that had placed it beyond the power of Victoria's businessmen to deal with changing patterns of trade. They had responded successfully to various favourable factors in the climate of enterprise; there was not much that could be done when the unfavourable overtook them.

There are many other names that could be singled out in the period of the seventies and eighties that would show the general stability and substance of this business community. Many firms from gold rush days continued in being, carrying on names like Southgate, Hibben, Dickson and Campbell, Sehl, Pendergast, Heisterman and others. Some early merchants indeed had died, retired or left, the Lowes going, one to Scotland, one to San Francisco, in the seventies; David Oppenheimer shrewdly moving to Vancouver in 1886, to become "the father of Vancouver's jobbing trade."[79] Yet there were still others who had known Victoria's earlier days actively on hand, like William Ward, manager of the Bank of British Columbia since 1867 and clerk before that, or A.H. Green of Garesche and Green, whose large private bank had taken over from Wells Fargo in 1873 but who had worked for that agency previously.[80] A notable feature of the Victoria commercial community, in short, was still its continuity; new leaders largely rose from within its own ranks. But no doubt this was the result of there having been no spectacular advances since the gold rush to bring new groups of entrepreneurs. Victoria was already an "old," settled, quietly-growing town, after less than three decades of urban existence.

Its ties with San Francisco and Britain remained fully evident. In 1886, the bulk of its external trade was still directed to the former, though British goods continued to be of much significance as imports, and exports of salmon to Britain (and eastern Canada) were fast rising.

Offsetting San Francisco influence, of course, was British influence through politics, capital investment, business personnel, and the very dealings with major firms in San Francisco that were themselves part of a London-Liverpool and Glasgow metropolitan network; like Welch and Company, Dickson, De Wolf, Falkner Bell, and several others.[81] Noticeable, too, was the growth of eastern Canadian agencies and imports in Victoria by this time, behind the national tariff wall; but nothing comparable to the change effected in a few years through the C.P.R. – to which one might ascribe the fact that advertisements for Canadian firms and products clearly began to displace those of San Francisco in Victoria directories by about 1890.

And thus, in a sense, passed the San Francisco of the North, gradually to be replaced with today's centre of tourism and retirement enterprises, and of that truly big modern growth-industry, provincial government. Yet the businessmen who had seen Victoria rise from a fort or a gold rush tent town to a flourishing port city in well under thirty years, had no cause to minimize the comfortable affluence they had acquired, and done much to give to their adopted home.

What had the business community done for Victoria? In the first place – without forgetting other factors, the role of politicians and bureaucrats, of the labour force, or simply, the citizenry of consumers – they had essentially shaped its economic functions, furnished the bulk of jobs and services that made it an operative centre of urban population. In the second place, they had considerably influenced its political, social and cultural life, businessmen having widely entered into provincial and municipal politics, benevolent and religious societies, educational movements, literary, musical organizations and the like. To deal with this would be to write another chapter. All that can be said here is that the record of early Victoria's business community in participating in primarily non-economic activities in their society seems as good as, or better than, the record of similar groups in comparable Canadian cities at similar stages of development. And this, again, is not to see this very human collectivity of fallible, self-interested individuals as peerless visionaries and altruists. It may have been more a result of Victoria's relative isolation, insularity and small size, whereby the entrepreneurial element readily came to know, and feel committed to a fairly compact local society that did not soon become heterogeneous and amorphous through continued rapid growth.

In the third place, the business community marked Victoria's character in the broadest sense: in its identity, to use a not-unheard of term. The city's affiliations with California that still exist surely relate not just to sea and sunshine (unlike the humidity of Vancouver and the northwest American coast) but to the historic communications and exchange that its merchants sustained with San Francisco. Victoria's oft-noted "British" attributes, also, may well be derived less from an obsolete Bay Company officialdom or a small emigrant English gentry than from the strongly British element in the dominant wholesale trades, which easily maintained the outlook and of the old gentry élite as it rose in wealth and social position. And finally, even the faint continuing touch of cosmopolitanism in an otherwise provincial city – which seems to give it a more mature ambiance than many an older Canadian town – assuredly may come from the original non-British, non-American component of the business community that largely persisted through Victoria's first formative decades. There is, then, much more in the early development of Victoria than the affairs of provincial governments or the vicissitudes of public men.

Endnotes

1. On the general significance of this theme, see D.T. Gallagher, "Bureaucrats or Businessmen? Historians and the problem of leadership in Colonial British Columbia," *Syesis*, Vol. 3, 1970, pp. 173-186.
2. W.K. Lamb, "Early Lumbering on Vancouver Island," I, *British Columbia Historical Quarterly*, January, 1938, p. 43.
3. *Ibid.*, p. 46.
4. *Gazette* (Victoria), December 25, 1858.
5. Alfred Waddington, *The Fraser Mines Vindicated* (Victoria, 1858), p. 19.
6. *British Colonist* (Victoria), June 12, 1860.
7. *The British Columbian and Victoria Guide and Directory for 1863* (Victoria, 1863), p. 49.
8. W. Ireland, "British Columbia's American Heritage," *Canadian Historical Association Annual Report for 1948*, p. 68.
9. *Ibid.*, p. 69.
10. M. Ormsby, *British Columbia: A History* (Toronto, 1958), p. 141.
11. R.E. and M.F. Stewart, *Adolph Sutro* (Berkeley, 1962), *passim.*
12. "The Oppenheimers of Vancouver," typescript, British Columbia Archives (hereafter BCA).
13. British Columbia Archives, Vertical Files (hereafter, BCAVF).
14. Edgar Fawcett, *Some Reminiscences of Old Victoria* (Toronto, 1912) p. 60; British Columbia Miscellany, Bancroft Library, Berkeley.
15. W.K. Lamb, *op. cit., II, British Columbia Historical Quarterly*, April 1938, p. 114.
16. Fawcett, *op. cit.*, p. 64.
17. BCAVF.
18. *Prices Current* (San Francisco). See advertisements from 1853 onward; also E. Mallandaine, *First Victoria Directory* (Victoria 1860), p. 42. For Samuel Price, *Gazette*, January 25, 1858-J.N. Thain was the local representative.
19. *Colonist*, February 2, 1865.
20. Fawcett, *op. cit.*, p. 62; *British Columbian and Victoria Guide*, p. 137.
21. On the Lowes, see J.M.S. Careless, "The Lowe Brothers, 1852-70: A Study in Business Relations on the North Pacific Coast, " *B.C. Studies*, No. 2, 1968-69, pp. 1-18.

22. *Ibid.*, p. 10.
23. I.M. Richard, "Gilbert Norman Sproat," *British Colonial History Quarterly*, January, 1937, pp. 22-3.
24. BCAVF.
25. British Columbia Miscellany, Bancroft.
26. BCAVF.
27. *Ibid.*
28. *Colonist*, November 20, 1866.
29. W. K. Lamb, *loc. cit.*, II, p. 105.
30. *Ibid.*, p. 114.
31. *Ibid.*, p. 121.
32. BCAVF.
33. P.A. Phillips, "Confederation and the Economy of British Columbia," W.G. Shelton, ed., *British Columbia and Confederation* (Victoria, 1967), p. 51, BCAVF.
34. Phillips, *loc. cit.*, p. 51.
35. Ormsby, *op. cit.*, p. 215.
36. J. Audain, *From Coal Mine to Castle* (New York, 1955), p. 36.
37. *Ibid.*, p. 51.
38. M.A. Cox, *Saga of a Seafarer* (New Westminster, 1966), p. 8.
39. E.W. Wright, ed., *Marine History of the Pacific North West* by Lewis and Dryden (New York, 1961), p. 81.
40. *Ibid.*
41. Careless, *loc. cit.*, p. 10. Lowe Papers, BCA, T. Lowe to A.C. Anderson, July 2, 1859.
42. Lewis and Dryden, *op. cit.*, p. 140.
43. *Ibid.*, p. 82.
44. BCAVF.
45. Phillips, *loc. cit.*, p. 57.
46. S. Higgins, "British Columbia and the Confederation Era," *British Columbia and Confederation*, p. 28.
47. Ireland, *loc. cit.*, p. 71.
48. BCAVF.
49. *British Colonist*, July 20, 1871.
50. *City of Victoria Directory for 1890* (Victoria, 1890), p. 122.
51. *Annual Report of the Minister of Mines* (Victoria, 1900), chart, n.p.
52. *Ibid.*
53. Phillips, *op. cit.*, p.55.
54. K. Ralston, "Patterns of Trade and Investment on the Pacific Coast, 1867-1892: the Case of the British Columbia Salmon Canning Industry," *B.C. Studies*, No. 1, 1968-9, p. 42.
55. BCAVF.

56. J.M. Grant, "British Columbia in Early Times," *British Columbia Magazine,* June, 1911, p. 494.
57. Ralston, *loc. cit.*, pp. 42-3.
58. Richard, *loc. cit.*, pp. 22-9.
59. BCA, *R.P. Rithet Letterbook,* I, Rithet to G. Sproat, December 11, 1868.
60. BCAVF.
61. *Rithet Letterbook,* Rithet to Mrs. Sutton, April 16, 1870.
62. *British Colonist,* November 11, 1869.
63. *Rithet Letterbook,* Rithet to R.P.D. Duff, May 9, 1871.
64. *Ibid.*, Rithet to A. Welch, August 24, 1871.
65. *Ibid.*, August 25, 1871.
66. *Colonist,* July 26, 1889.
67. BCAVF. See also *Victoria Illustrated* (Victoria, 1891)pp. 77-8.
68. *Ibid.*
69. BCAVF.
70. *Colonist,* April 17, 1889.
71. Lewis and Dryden, *op. cit.*, p.303.
72. Audain, *op. cit.*, p. 52.
73. *Ibid.*, pp. 65, 73.
74. *Colonist,* April 13, 1889.
75. Audain, *op. cit.*, p. 79.
76. *City of Victoria Directory for 1890*, p. 122.
77. *Annual Reports of the British Columbia Board of Trade,* 1887–1900 (Victoria, 1900), tables, n.p.
78. *Victoria Illustrated,* p. 50.
79. L. Makovski, "Rise of the Merchant Princes," *British Columbia Magazine,* June, 1911, p. 57.
80. BCAVF. Francis Garesche was drowned in 1874, but the firm continued in both names.
81. See directory and newspaper advertisements of period for indications of operations of these firms. On all three, for example, see *San Francisco Directory for 1873,* M.G. Langley (San Francisco, 1873), and on Falkner, Bell specifically, W.T. Jackson, *The Enterprising Scot* (Edinburgh, 1968), pp. 222, 374, *passim.* Falkner, Bell also appear in the Lowe and Rithet letters – and Jackson's work notes that the Scottish American Investment Company, for and with which they dealt, bought extensive California ranch property on the recommendation of John Clay (who had been George Brown's estate manager in Ontario), as well as involving Thomas Nelson, the leading Edinburgh publisher in its investments. Nelson was Brown's brother-in-law, who with Clay succeeded in restoring Brown's Bow Park estate to financial health after the latter's death. One can see many ramifications here worth tracing out!

The developing urban west: Edmonton in the early twentieth century.

Urban Life in the West, 1870–1914

THIS IS A TALE OF four cities – Winnipeg, Edmonton, Calgary and Vancouver – or rather, a comparative treatment of some features in their life and growth down to the First World War. It is obviously a pretty selective treatment, in leaving out major centres like Regina and Victoria, not to mention a host of emergent urban places in the West from Brandon to Nanaimo. The limit of space in a paper is one good reason for thus restricting the selection. Another, even better, is that the author has a good deal more yet to learn. But the choice does take in the two largest western cities, along with two rising smaller ones in the period, and represents a broad regional distribution. Hence it should still be possible to say something in general about the life of the urban West, in its initial, formative era.

It bears affirming at the outset that the urban West was decidedly a fact of life before 1914, however much more fully it was to develop in later periods. The settlement of the plains agricultural frontier, the rise of mining frontiers in the western mountains or lumber frontiers in river valleys and on the coast, must not obscure the basic fact that with them, integrally related to them, went continued and important urban growth. By 1901, half the population of British Columbia was urban (50.48 percent). Although the relative lack of farming land in the Pacific province, and the concentrating tendency of mines and sawmills, can of course explain this comparatively high degree of urbanization, it is notable that even on the prairies over a quarter of Manitoba's population then was urban (26.89 percent), and well over a third (37.88 percent) of the future Alberta. Moreover, by 1911 the urban segment of the population had risen to 51.9 percent in British Columbia, 38.07 percent in Alberta and 43.43 percent in Manitoba, suggesting that during the great western boom urbanization in these provinces was actually proceeding a bit faster than rural settlement – and markedly so in the older community of Manitoba, which exhibited an urban increase of over 16 percent, double the national average for the decade.

In short, in these large jurisdictions the town grew more than the country in the classic era of the rise of the West, although the rate of urban growth naturally was tied to the ups and downs of the general process of land settlement. In particular, Winnipeg, Edmonton, Calgary and Vancouver rose to become economically affluent, technologically advanced, and socially fast-maturing urban units. Calgary and Edmonton, especially, might not yet compare in size to leading eastern Canadian cities; but then neither did the latter to giant American or European centres: what was more meaningful in every case was the relation of each place to its own surrounding community. Here again the four western cities stood out significantly. Vancouver in 1911 had a population of 121,000 to 392,000 for British Columbia, Winnipeg 136,000 to Manitoba's 461,000, and Calgary and Edmonton 43,000 and 31,000 respectively to 374,000 in Alberta (giving Edmonton, incidentally, a far higher proportion of its province's total population than Toronto had had in reference to Ontario at the time of Confederation). But simple demographic quantities give only part of the story. Qualitatively speaking the four cities also displayed much power over communications, trade patterns and development processes in their regions, exercised growing social and cultural influence, and two of them of course also enjoyed political dominance as provincial capitals.

Clearly, then, the urban factor strongly represented by western cities should enter into any broad assessment of western development before 1914; and their origins and characteristics should be traced back further than just the era of manifestly rapid urban growth in the early twentieth century. That effort might well extend, in any full analysis of western urban history, to the very beginnings of town-style life in fur trade posts or mining camps. But for our purpose here it should at least go back to the 1870s for Winnipeg's emergence as a city, to the 1880s for the others. This I propose to attempt by picking out certain aspects of western urban life in the period that seem particularly to invite comment, though many others might certainly be chosen also. On any of them I can do little more than offer generalizations or reflections. Yet this paper can only be a "probe" (to use Marshall McLuhan's favorite expression for a fast way out) into a field that needs a great deal of investigation: investigation that is under way in graduate theses, but has not issued in much scholarly publication so far.

II

The first aspect for consideration derives from the pre-eminent importance of nineteenth-century industrial technology in the rise of the western Canadian cities. Though they emerged on far-spread frontiers, virtually from the start they were involved in the steam-and-steel technology of transport, which alone, then, could overcome continental distance and swiftly end frontier isolation. In this experience they were indeed like similarly evolving American cities of the railway age; but our concern here is with their evolution in Canada. And if it be a truism to assert the vital importance of the technology of transport to their growth, then this, like many truisms, is still worth examining.

All four cities were to a critical degree creations of the railway, a fact that marks them off in a significant way from the older main urban communities of eastern Canada. It goes without saying that Halifax and Saint John, Quebec and Montreal, had emerged in an age of basic water transport as nodes on oceanic or riverine traffic systems. So did Victoria at the other side of the continental land-mass, while Toronto was already a well-established urban entity and wholesale entrepôt before the coming of the railway, whatever consequences the new means of transport would have for the lake city. Similarly, Montreal industry took off in the day of canals and water power, before the impact of steam in factories and on rails – great as that was to be. In general, in the eastern cities, the patterns set by water continued to have great weight, even as the railway age developed, whereas in the West their role by comparison was minor, indeed.

True, Vancouver was an ocean port and grew with the waterborn commerce that came to its spacious harbour on Burrard Inlet. Yet spacious harbours alone have seldom made great cities, without good access inland to valuable hinterland trades or without good reason to break bulk and tranship cargos for distribution into other areas. And Fraser River navigation offered only difficult and limited access to the interior, while coastal shipping could carry on only a restricted kind of exchange along the rugged British Columbian shorelines. It was the railway, of course, which made Vancouver. The new technology of land transport – though it assuredly needed the Fraser Valley for access – joined the interior to the little sawmill community on Burrard Inlet and made it the terminus of a continental traffic system. Land lines gave value to sea lanes for Vancouver. That fact was clearly evidenced by its rapid urban development after the C.P.R. had reached to its waterfront in 1886-7, as compared with the relative stagnation of New Westminster, the river port, and Victoria, the older island centre of maritime trade.

Within four years a modern city of brick and stone emerged from slash and forest at Vancouver. Through rates on the C.P.R. awarded it regional dominance as a distributing point. Though development slowed drastically in the depressed nineties, mining in the West Kootenays and the Klondike rush brought new stimulus, and in the prosperous new century growth shot up in a fast ascending spiral. More stimulus was added as the Great Northern, Canadian Northern, and Grand Trunk Pacific all made plans for entry into the city. Real estate values exploded in the trade and population boom. By 1911 land office business showed a gain of 4100 percent over 1891. No wonder the advice then given on how to get rich in Vancouver was, "Take a map of the Lower Peninsula, shut your eyes, stick your finger anywhere and sit tight."[1] And though deflation might come by 1914, nothing changed the fundamental fact that railways had brought a new Pacific metropolis into being.

As for Winnipeg, while York boats and waterways had first shaped the transport pattern for the little settlement on the Red to northward as, later, cart brigades and river steamboats did southward, its urban development was commanded by the railway. R.C. Bellan puts it effectively in a discussion of Winnipeg's contest with Selkirk for the Canadian Pacific's "Rails across the Red." He notes that as far as geographic site was concerned, Winnipeg should have been located twenty miles further north: its riverside location might have mattered in the days of fur trading and pioneer settlement, but for its growth as a major distributing centre for a commercial agricultural community, location on the railway main line was crucial. It was the bending of the C.P.R. southward to the town that enabled it to grow as a wholesale entrepôt, leaving Selkirk, not Winnipeg as the hamlet of unrequited hopes.[2]

Actually, the railway had already set its mark on Winnipeg's development before this great victory (by negotiation) in 1881. Steamboats on the Red in the 1860s had been ancillaries to Minnesota rail connections, and they in turn were supplemented in 1878 by the Pembina Branch line south to American tracks at the border. The emergence of Winnipeg as a city in the seventies was thus greatly stimulated by railway contact and railway expectations, climaxing in the frantic land boom of the early eighties, well before the line from the East was complete. But then, it has been well recognized that the effects of railways on cities lie not only in their construction or operation but in their projection as well. Certainly Winnipeg was powerfully affected by the image and prospect of rail transport. And whether its offers of bonuses for bridges and branch lines were well considered, or its bargain with the C.P.R. in lands and tax exemptions, the city did become the focus of a rail network that tied an expanding farm hinterland into the transcontinental traffic route. Thus it grew with the prairie West as its foremost gathering and distributing point – thanks to the technology of railways.

Again, Calgary's and Edmonton's locations on the long Saskatchewan River system had small consequence for their rise as urban places. If early Edmonton did see steamboats like the dauntless *Sir Stafford Northcote*, the difficulties of the waterway, with its shallows, currents and shifting sand bars, made overland trails fully necessary in the pre-railway era, as more than supplements to water traffic. The coming of the railway, indeed, profoundly altered the traffic potentials of both places. In Calgary's case, the C.P.R.'s choice of the southern, Kicking Horse Pass route, and its arrival at the Elbow River in 1883, so clearly and so quickly changed a Mounted Police post into a flourishing cattle-freighting and lumber-milling town that no elaboration is required here. In the case of Edmonton, the impact was less immediate and direct – precisely because that village did not initially find itself on the Pacific railway as had been expected from the Sandford Fleming survey before its change to the southern route. But the opening of the Calgary and Edmonton C.P.R. branch in 1891 undoubtedly facilitated development in the Edmonton area, leading to the incorporation of the town of Edmonton the following year, despite the fact that the C.P.R. track, which stopped on the south side of the river at what became Strathcona, proved both a hindrance and a sore point. Thus the acclaim for the grandly named Edmonton, Yukon and Pacific (all four thousand yards of it), which by 1902 crossed the Low Level Bridge to the north side of the Saskatchewan, bringing in rail connections with the south. The whole situation was much improved when in 1913 the C.P.R. itself at last came directly into town over the new High Level Bridge.

But meanwhile the Canadian Northern had arrived by way of the north bank in 1905, providing direct through service to Winnipeg. And the Grand Trunk Pacific was also on its way, to give Edmonton access to still another transcontinental, as well as having the link south to the C.P.R.! One evident result was the rise of the well-served city's wholesale trade. There were two wholesale firms in 1906; by 1911 the number had risen to nearly fifty. "Edmonton's future is absolutely assured as the great metropolis of Western Canada,"[3] it was proclaimed, as railways and expectations from railways sparked a roaring boom through 1912 – 14. The amalgamation of Strathcona with Edmonton in 1914 was virtual recognition of the fact that they had been bound by steel into one urban entity, with fresh ambitions of its own to dominate still more hinterland by branch lines north and west.

As for Calgary, it had risen to commercial dominance in southern Alberta through its position on the Canadian Pacific main line and as the rail gateway to Edmonton and the north after 1890. The opening of the Canadian Northern route to Edmonton might lessen the latter role at a time, too, when Calgary was deeply rankling over the northern town becoming capital of the new province of Alberta. Yet meanwhile the additional building of the Crow's Nest Pass line had linked Kootenay mining development to Calgary's supply trade. Indeed, a promotional supplement to the Calgary *Herald* in 1910 could grandly declare, "For 150 miles to the north, south, east and west of us lies a large section of land all of which is absolutely tributary to us, rich in agriculture, in minerals, forests and natural resources, and probably without parallel in the Dominion in the possibilities of growth and development."[4] Rosily promotional indeed; but anticipations of such possibilities brought on the great Calgary boom of 1910–12. And while much of it was the mass hysteria of real estate speculation in paper fortunes, underlying the concurrent growth in urban concentration was also the focusing, dominating potential of rail transport – Calgary's prime cause for existence.

One consequence of the strategic importance of transport technology to western urban life was a celebrated love-hate relationship with railways. City-dwellers as well as farmers wanted the railway, then deplored its pervasive power. City journalists extolled the wealth and progress it would bring to their community, then attacked its unjust rate structure, its selfish, greedy, heartless tyranny. In Winnipeg in the eighties the Board of Trade took a vigorous lead in protesting the Canadian Pacific's monopoly privileges and "suicidal" rates policy to Ottawa.[5] An Edmontonian, commenting in print on Calgary in the early 1900s found it "C.P.R. everything; the coffee you got was C.P.R. and the very hens laid C.P.R. eggs," although in his own town, the same line had now "reluctantly loosed the shackles, snarling at every encroachment on the vindictive privileges granted this blood-sucking corporation."[6]

In Vancouver, a writer in the *British Columbia Magazine* of 1911 began his discussion of Vancouver and the Railways with, "once upon a time a city gave itself away in order that a great railway might be induced to establish its terminus there" – a somewhat fast epitomizing of the complex real estate deals that had accompanied the extension of the C.P.R.[7] However, he concluded happily, while once Vancouver was on its knees to railways, now they could not stay away. But it was Bob Edwards in the *Calgary Eye Opener* who duly had a last, best western word. In his enjoyable feud with that rising politician and C.P.R. solicitor, R.B. Bennett, Edwards climaxed the photographs of the various accidents on the railway which he had been running with one of Bennett himself, under the simple caption, "Another C.P.R. Wreck."[8]

Now it is true that easterners had their own discontents with railways, from the temporary frustration in mid-century Montreal with the Grand Trunk's indifference to the city's interests to the vehement attacks of George Brown, the Toronto *Globe* and the Clear Grits on that railway "octopus." But for the sheer enduring care and concern, one would have to give the decision to the westerners. Whereas the East had had, and to some extent still had, alternatives by water or American through routes to keep railway power in check, the West was far more exposed to transport monopoly enhanced by distance, tariffs, and its narrower economic base – and what is more, it could readily see its dependence and subordination.

Still further, main-line railways were obviously embodiments of outside metropolitan forces; something Montreal had once felt regarding the London-based Grand Trunk, or Toronto had sensed in respect to the same line, seeing it instead as enhancing Montreal's domination of Upper Canadian traffic. As for western cities, they might view local lines that served their own regional metropolitan interests as "good" (as Winnipeg did MacKenzie and Mann's rail complex in Manitoba). But the main lines were all too often "bad" exemplifications of outside control. Here was, in fact, a characteristic response to the metropolitanism inherent in the industrial technology of transport that was both shaping and mastering the development of the West. Hence the broad significance of the reaction in the young western cities to railways, which had made them yet continually threatened to unmake them again.

III

Much more could be said of attitudinal responses in the rising urban West to questions of transport, beyond the specific material concerns of economic interest groups. But it is necessary to turn to another area, this time to the kind of institutional pattern in which urban life was organized in western communities. The primary institutional pattern was obviously that of municipal government. Here one might expect a political structure not too different from the mayors and councils of the older eastern cities. Yet one might also expect a different spirit to inform it: a greater manifestation of popular democracy in towns so recently sprung from the frontier, unlike the established élitist ways of older eastern centres. If so, one might be rather quickly disappointed.

It is true that a kind of open camaraderie persisted in western cities that had grown so quickly from pioneer villages, and where – for years after 1914 – there were many who well remembered the original huddle of houses and shanties on the open prairie or among the stump fields. Nevertheless, the sense of common achievement in city-building often displayed at civic celebrations and community social occasions, did not go far enough to sustain a lively common interest or participation in municipal political affairs. In general, government in the cities was soon left in the hands of an élite in-group. This municipal élite had links with wealthy business interests, and often contained prominent mercantile figures; but it was more widely drawn from lawyers and lesser entrepreneurs who made a fairly regular profession (or business livelihood) out of directing government for a citizenry that normally preferred to be left alone. On occasion, however, there might be challenges from the latter body, often stimulated by the business community seeking to lower costs and taxes, as when in Winnipeg, in 1884, the Board of Trade sucessfully pushed a "citizen's ticket," which was elected to expel interests that had presumably fostered extravagance and speculation in the late-lamented Winnipeg land boom.

At times, too, there were more clamorous scandals; for instance, the Calgary "land grab" of 1904, when city fathers had apparently arranged a quiet sale of real estate for friends, until irate taxpayers forced the sale to be revoked and several heads to roll at City Hall. On the whole, however, élitist urban government seemed broadly acceptable and sufficiently effective. And in particular, it did make the municipal régime a satisfactory vehicle for community sentiment and aspirations, guarding city interests against outside forces, embodying civic pride and encouraging local development. This point is aptly made, again regarding Calgary, in a recent study by Mr. M.L. Foran, but it seems to me broadly true of municipal authority in the other cities under consideration.[9]

As for the relative failure of a western frontier environment to produce more than a brief initial democratic activity in town government,

W.L. Morton has observed that the frontier scarcely existed as a conditioning process to instill democracy or individualism in the American West after 1870.[10] Railway technology (once more) had brought frontiers within a few days reach of older regions: democracy and Americanization in the West would thenceforth be the product of a total American environment, not of a separate frontier world. Hence in the Canadian West – where, indeed, the railway instrument of eastern metropolitanism and industrialism often preceded the settlement of land frontiers – society would be especially likely to exhibit not only the forms but also much of the content of eastern institutions, including the municipal. Of course there were differences. But they were less the result of frontier influences *per se* (however these are to be read) than of the fact that this assuredly was a different region: with different terrain, climate and resource patterns, and with distinctive problems of distance, development and population needs.

One might add that, when strong democratic surges did subsequently manifest themselves in Western urban life, they were as likely to stem from Winnipeg's North End or the Vancouver docks as from the frontier; but that largely takes us past our period. Returning to it, the western urban élites generally continued to maintain themselves throughout with little difficulty, despite some efforts to reform civic administration towards the end of that time.

In Vancouver at the start, the election of Mayor MacLean in the first civic contest in 1886 in some degree marked the defeat of the original pioneer "aristocracy" of sawmill operators by an energetic newcomer group of real estate entrepreneurs, contractors and wholesalers, heavily involved in developing their extensive Vancouver properties. Thereafter, leadership largely remained in a relatively small, development-oriented circle; though at times this produced notable figures like David Oppenheimer, mayor from 1888 to 1892. One of the city's first and most powerful wholesale merchants, Oppenheimer held land all over Vancouver, along with electric light and street railway interests and drainage and improvement companies. Under him the city acquired municipal waterworks and sewerage facilities – together with Stanley Park – and at his death in 1897 he was eulogized by the Vancouver *World* as "one of the Fathers of Vancouver."[11] In any case, Vancouver grew so fast that it was hard to integrate new elements into social leadership, as H.C. Klassen's study has indicated, so that its class structure perhaps remained more rigid than that of other large Canadian cities.[12]

The civic élite in Winnipeg also had its outstanding figures; for instance, J.H. Ashdown, reputed the largest hardware dealer in the West, who was alderman on the first council after the town's incorporation in 1873 and mayor of the city in 1901–8. A pioneer inhabitant of Winnipeg since the early sixties, Ashdown had led in seeking incorporation, in negotiations to bring the railway there in the seventies; and, in the eighties, as President of the Board of Trade, carrying Winnipeg's protests against the railway monopoly to Ottawa. Other typical representatives of the city's political leadership were its first mayor, F.E. Cornish (a London, Ontario, lawyer), later successors Mayors Waugh and Evans (insurance and real estate) and John Arbuthnot (a lumber dealer) who had three terms of office in the early twentieth century.

It was also typical when the Winnipeg *Commercial* observed, in 1893, that the city council of that year consisted of five lawyers, three real estate and insurance agents, two wholesale merchants, one contractor, and one member "with no particular profession" – an unfortunate situation when "Winnipeg is almost solely a commercial city . . . whose existence depends so completely on its distributing trade."[13]

Generally, Winnipeg's principal businessmen seemed to prefer participation in the Board of Trade to activity in civic government, as an institution better calculated to promote the city's basic economic interests. Certainly the Board of Trade, established in 1879, was remarkably effective in asserting Winnipeg's growing impulses to regional metropolitan dominance. Not only did it energetically take on Ottawa and the C.P.R., but also won a significant victory by getting the right to set western wheat grades transferred from eastern cities to western boards of trade; and it gained control itself of Manitoba wheat-grading. Then, as a concomitant of Winnipeg's advancing control of the grain trade, it fostered the establishment of the Grain Exchange in 1887. Boards of Trade similarly emerged in Vancouver, Edmonton and Calgary as another institutional expression of western urban life. Yet the Winnipeg Board was clearly the most powerfully developed: perhaps an indication of the greater maturity of that city's business interests. The Calgary Board, on the other hand, began and died three times in the town's early years, before it finally took hold.

Calgary, as Foran has pointed out, had its own in-group of continuing municipal politicians; men like the hard-working Wesley Orr, journalist and real estate dealer, councillor from 1888 to 1893 and mayor in 1894-5; a man whose very life became civic politics. But major businessmen like A.E. Cross, the brewer and ranch owner, Pat Burns, the meat packer, and the leading lawyer (Senator) J.A. Lougheed, left municipal affairs to a lesser entrepreneurial circle, while they took the decisions outside that might do much more to shape the growth of Calgary. And so the "Big Four" cattlemen, Cross, Burns, George Lane and A.J. McLean, themselves put up $100,000 to launch the first Stampede in 1912; it was hardly a municipal product.

Edmonton, similarly, although the smallest and closest to the frontier of the four cities, also showed élitist tendencies. Indeed, it was its Board of Trade, founded in 1889 as the first west of Winnipeg, which decided to seek the town's incorporation. The civic régime begun in 1892 again took on the characteristic pattern of government by an in-group of community leaders, such as the pioneer settler, Matt McCauley, chairman of the first regular school board, mayor from 1892 to 1894, legislative member and later warden of the federal penitentiary; or John McDougall, the wealthy general merchant and financier, and mayor in 1897 and 1908. Yet in any case, provincial politicians could often do more for Edmonton than municipal worthies, such as confirming it as capital in 1906 or giving it the provincial university in 1907. And then there was Frank Oliver of the *Edmonton Bulletin*, the city's federal member. As Laurier's Minister of the Interior, he was a highly influential figure – but none of this really redounded to strengthen an Edmonton municipal democracy.

In sum, the constructive, assertive vigour in early western urban life was not necessarily displayed in the somewhat conservative, civic political institutions. It lay far more in individual entrepreneurs and the advancing business community. Municipal government might be a useful public sounding board, and was certainly necessary to provide police and fire protection, street improvements, water and light or even street railways. But the citizenry usually remained content to leave such matters to a relative few, and rely on their sense of public service. The new western cities did not produce an upsurge of democracy. In their élitism they were remarkably like the older eastern ones. But there still was a significant degree of difference here, just because they were new. There was thus both a greater cost of development and greater pride in it, greater confidence instilled when it succeeded. The city had to grow, by popular will; and every individual citizen – in his private capacity – could and must share in making it grow. In this there was a special strain of democracy and individualism in the western city – perhaps derived, after all, from the newness and potential of a frontier West.

IV

Once more, much could be added about other institutional forms of life in the cities: the courts and law enforcement, schools and beginnings of higher education, religious, cultural and recreational associations, class and ethnic structure and mobility within it. But once more it is time to move on to a final aspect, which I can only call "urban ambiance," an immaterial quality of atmosphere encompassing a city, which can be felt, if not measured, and certainly is real enough. This urban "feel," to coin another useful, if awkward phrase, is a composite of many things arising from the physical and human environment: actual physical layout and construction, in streets, parks, buildings and architectural practices; occupational and residential patterning; social amenities and social awareness; life style, cultural interests and climate of opinion. As usual, in the scope of this paper, I can only touch on just a few of these in passing – but sufficiently, I hope, to express the ambiance or "feel" of the young western cities.

First, their physical appearance was full of contrasts, chiefly the result of rapid and virtually uncontrolled growth. Humble little frame structures of village years stood by the heavy, brick and ornamental stone elegance of the 1890s; simpler workaday brick stores and warehouses of the 1880s beside the new secular, classical temples of banking that went up in the 1900s. Nevertheless out of rawness and internal contrasts each of the four cities had soon produced a definite central business district, while well before 1914 one could identify a graded pattern of residential districts whereby occupational and income groups increasingly lived separate from their place of employment. This separation, so typical of the modern industrial urban community, developed with remarkable speed in these all-but-instant cities. But then they were the product of the over-night process of city-building made possible by steam and technology.

Furthermore, they had space to build on, and from the nineties onward, the electric street railway. Urban sprawl was already inherent in the western city before the further technology of the automobile made its full impact, to produce a wider urban expansion, or explosion, across the surrounding landscape. And it was significant that the automobile did arrive in the first decade of the twentieth century in all four cities; perhaps significant as well that Vancouver could lay claim to Canada's first gas station, established in 1908.[14] In any event, given the confident hopes of city greatness and the major industry of real estate promotion, one might expect excessive spread into grandly-named mud pastures; exhibited, for instance, in the conquering annexations that more than tripled Edmonton's area between 1904 and 1914.

Winnipeg, indeed, in 1903 was looking to "swiftly whirling trolleys" to tie the outlying areas into the city's heart.[15] That year its paper, *Town Topics*, commented on the "almost magical transformation" that had occurred in this Chicago of the North. "Where lately we waded in mud, today we walk on stone pavement. Where a short time ago unsightly wooden business blocks reminded us of pioneer days, today stately buildings and modern conveniences fill the eye."[16] Certainly all four cities had come a long way by 1914 in achieving an urban co-ordination out of the seeming confusion of old, new, and the welter of construction; of streets half paved and half dug-up in Edmonton and Calgary, of skyscrapers rising in Winnipeg and Vancouver.

Civic amenities were growing. Vancouver had its Stanley Park, opened in 1888, happily transformed from a military reserve. Winnipeg already had six parks by 1903, and the public library founded by its Historic and Scientific Society in 1881 became the nucleus of the fine new Carnegie Library opened in 1906. Libraries, rinks, sports grounds, opera houses (a generic name that covered very little opera), were there for recreation, along with older rooted amusements like taverns, race tracks and bawdy houses. Even urban planning raised a tentative eye by 1914, as in Vancouver's negotiations for the False Creek harbour area development, or the abortive Mawson report of 1914 in Calgary for rendering it the city beautiful.

In each case, by 1914, the city had acquired a structured physical character, identifiable despite its own internal contrasts. No doubt much of the identity simply derived from setting: Vancouver's sea and mountains, Calgary's back-drop of the Rockies, the soaring river-bank front view of Edmonton, and even Winnipeg's waterside location at the forks of the Red and Assiniboine. No doubt, too, Vancouverites were willing to claim civic credit for their mountains, and Winnipeg to take a perverse hometown pride in its winter rigours. The fact remained that the inhabitants of the western cities did identify ardently and proudly with their communities, as visitors often remarked. And they even had their own local building characteristics, as in Calgary's grey sandstone public and commercial structures, or bungalow residences of a Pacific coast variety – which its local press in 1910 lauded as "elegant and cosy."[17]

Western urban pride easily became boosterism, as a testament of civic faith. Thus for example, Vancouver's slogan of the boom years after 1905, "In 1910, Vancouver then, will have one hundred thousand men."[18] Or thus the admission by *Town Topics* in 1902 that "Winnipeg in fact has been rather given to the practice of announcing from the roof tops that she considers herself some potatoes."[19] Or thus even the intercity rivalry that brought the Vancouver *Province* to note unkindly in February, 1913, "Winnipegers are congratulating themselves on the fine winter and are looking forward with great expectations to an early spring in the next five or six months."[20] The reference might be light-hearted; but the belief of the western urban dweller in the innately superior blessings of his own city could be much more fully documented, and was a basic attribute of the early urban West.

The belief in manifestly destined progress that could only be thwarted by malign forces like the C.P.R. or the undue political influence of rival capital cities (Victoria to Vancouver, Edmonton to Calgary) informed the climate of opinion in western urban centres and even added a distinctive ingredient to their lifestyle. Otherwise that lifestyle was none too different from the urban East. Though the noted actress

Lilly Langtry might make the prejudiced and prejudicial comment in Calgary in 1913 that, "Everyone in Edmonton is either an Indian or a squaw,"[21] the busy bowler-hatted inhabitants of the northern city bustling about their new concrete-and-steel McLeod or Tegler Buildings, looked and acted much the same as those who thronged King and Yonge Steets in Toronto. The mansions of Vancouver's West End set similar standards of material achievement and conspicuous consumption as those of Sherbrooke Street in Montreal.

Winnipeg's slogan of 1913, "Do it out of rush hours,"[22] showed that the urban traffic problem had arrived in the West no less than the East. And social pretensions in Calgary were all too similar to those in older, more ritualized eastern cities – a fact Bob Edwards was particularly adept at satirizing. Of course there were the signs and survivals of a pioneer past – as well as of a changing future, in the greater freedom and larger role which women were achieving – but lifestyle in the western cities had very soon become largely a counterpart of eastern.

This simply indicated the common conditions of modern urban living, for the urban West had virtually become contemporaneous with the urban East by 1914. What were basic differences lay in the expansion of space and the compression of time. The western centres felt they had all God's room to grow in – although this, on the other side of the ledger, was the liability of distance and the nagging problem of transport. At the same time, they had in a few short decades compressed a century or so of eastern urban growth, from which came their pride, expectations and frustrations, their rawness and internal contrasts.

They had also been able to achieve this sudden growth through the application of industrial technology, chiefly exemplified in the railway – which takes us back almost to where we began. It has been held that the general historic process of urbanization may be expressed in terms of four great factors: the environment, the population that occupies it, the technology and organization that mediate the relations of the first two. In this frame of reference, the western natural environment had been occupied at certain nodal points on traffic routes by considerable concentrations of population homogenous to the degree of still being largely English-speaking in language and culture. The young western cities generally did not have influential non-Anglo-Saxon components much before 1914, even though immigrant elements had certainly made their urban presence known: Asians in Vancouver, Icelandic, Mennonite or Jewish groups in Winnipeg. The original predominantly homogenous society, whether derived from eastern Canada, Britain or the United States, had readily transferred urban institutions and municipal organizations from the older East to the West – so that the organizational factor was not of much innovative importance in the latter case. Much more important, naturally, was the technology of transport which had also been transferred.

This was the prime mediating factor between environment and population in the ecology of the urban West, the most vital urbanizing force there. Sprung from and tied to eastern metropolitanism, railway technology essentially integrated the new western cities into a continent-wide metropolitan pattern. They would build their own regional metropolitan domains within this pattern. They would contend against its overriding controls. But most of all, they would require a great deal more examination than I have been able to give them here.

Endnotes

1. R.J. McDougall, "Vancouver Real Estate for Twenty Five Years," *British Columbia Magazine* (June, 1911), p. 607.
2. R. C. Bellan, "Rails across the Red – Selkirk or Winnipeg," *Transactions of the Historical and Scientific Society of Manitoba*, Series III, No. 18, 1964.
3. Edmonton *Journal*, March 18, 1911.
4. Calgary *Daily Herald*, *Magazine Supplement*, August, 1910.
5. *Ninth Annual Report of the Winnipeg Board of Trade for 1887* (Winnipeg, 1888), p. 17.
6. Malcolm Melville (J.W. Dickson), *Edmonton's Progression* (Edmonton, 1908), p. 3, 15.
7. W. Playfair, "Vancouver and the Railways," *British Columbia Magazine* (June, 1911), p. 498.
8. Grant MacEwan, *Eye Opener Bob* (Calgary, 1957), p.171.
9. M.L. Foran, "The Calgary Town Council, 1884-1895: a Study of Local Government on a Frontier Environment," unpublished M. A. thesis for the University of Calgary, 1969.
10. W.L. Morton, "The Significance of Site in the Settlement of the American and Canadian Wests," *Agricultural History*, 1951.
11. Vancouver *World*, January 1, 1898.
12. H.C. Klassen, "An Intellectual History of Early Vancouver," unpublished paper, University of British Columbia, 1955, at Provincial Archives of British Columbia, p. 11.
13. Winnipeg *Commercial*, December 25, 1893.
14. J.S. Matthews et al., "Early Vancouver," typescript, Archives of British Columbia, p. 307.
15. Winnipeg *Town Topics*, May 30, 1903.
16. *Ibid.*
17. Calgary *Herald*, *Magazine Supplement*, August, 1910.
18. J.P. Nicholls, "Real Estate Values in Vancouver," typescript, Archives of British Columbia, p. 22.

19. *Town Topics*, December 13, 1902.
20. Quoted in *Town Topics*, February 1, 1913.
21. *Ibid.*, January 11, 1913.
22. *Ibid.*, December 13, 1913.

Rail and industry seen from the east end of Toronto Harbour, 1900s.

Some Aspects of Urbanization in Nineteenth-Century Ontario

In Canada, the rise of urbanism is popularly seen as a twentieth-century phenomenon. Yet one of the most notable features of the nineteenth century in Ontario was the steady advance of urbanization; the growth of urban places in number and size through the concentration of population at particular sites. This theme is already the subject of considerable specialized scholarly study. Still, it seems worthwhile to try a broader approach: to make a selective, reflective inquiry into major aspects of urbanization in Ontario by way of producing a general, if highly qualitative, analysis of the process as a whole.

In pursuing this quest, certain points of reference will be utilized, basically derived from Eric Lampard's conceptual article, 'American Historians and the Study of Urbanization,' but varied to fit Canadian circumstances in the well-tried Canadian way of borrowing.[1] He names four primary factors involved in urbanization: environment, population, organization and technology. The process of societal change that builds urban communities is an interplay of environment and concentrating population, mediated by organization and technology. It is a suggestive formulation that can cover a great deal; but rather than follow it rigidly, this present venture will use the four terms or factors as categories for examination in turn; and it is hoped, for some illumination of aspects of urbanization that significantly shaped nineteenth-century Ontario.

Of course, the physical environment provided the first term for urbanization in Ontario. Land forms and water systems, climate and vegetation, soils, resources and site advantages, all entered into play. Beyond that, they set the underlying conditions for general community development in the whole Ontario region, which first received political definition as the province of Upper Canada in 1791, was reconstituted as Canada West in the province of Canada in 1841, and finally (with subsequent enlargements) as the province of Ontario at Confederation.

The distinctive environment in which this human community took form was preeminently that of the central lakelands, extending downward to the great St Lawrence waterway. While deep in the continental interior, this region was unlike the western plains of Canada in having a broad and basic artery of water transport bordering its full length, although its more broken and forested land mass was initially harder to penetrate than was western prairie or parkland, and the southern edge of the Shield confined its fertile agricultural lands more narrowly than in the expanses of the West. Then, too, unlike the Maritime region, Ontario's main line of water access was sealed off by winter, whereas on the coasts the wintry Atlantic was hazardous but open all the way to Europe. And unlike Quebec, there was no Appalachian barrier along the southern limits of the Ontario region but the St Lawrence and Great Lakes, which provided ready contact with the neighbouring United States from the very start of Upper Canadian settlement. All these features entered into the urbanizing process as it developed in Ontario.

In the first place, urban communities emerged in a long string along the river and lake fronts in the fertile southern Ontario region below the Shield. They were tied to the waterways. It was only slowly that other centres grew up behind them, up rivers into the land mass, or where early roads like Yonge Street penetrated the terrain. It well may be, as T. F. McIlwraith has demonstrated, that the poor roads of Upper Canada before the railway age were still adequate for the spreading of farm settlement and commercial agriculture.[2] Yet it is clear that no sizeable urban places developed in the interior of the province before railways brought all-weather bulk transport, especially in the quite extensive inland reaches of the western peninsula. Urban Ontario was originally oriented to its trunk water system; and really remained so during the nineteenth century, despite the spread of the railway net, for the main cities on lake fronts tended to hold their lead – the railways themselves being directed to their harbours as major transhipping and distributing points. Thus urban life in nineteenth-century Ontario was strongly shaped by ports, a condition not greatly altered till the coming of the automobile highway in the twentieth century.

The 'water-born' nature of so many primary Ontario towns and cities assuredly deserves emphasis, looking as they did to lake horizons or river courses, whereas later inland centres (as in the plains west) essentially were structured on the railway line. Waterside location shaped Kingston, the province's first commercial centre of importance, as the key transshipment point on the St. Lawrence route between lake and river navigation. It founded Toronto, as York in 1793, to be the 'naval arsenal' and seat of the government for the new province of Upper Canada.[3] It supplied prime impetus to Cornwall, Belleville, Niagara, and Hamilton (once Burlington Bay was channeled open in 1832); and even gave Bytown, or the city of Ottawa from 1855, its vast inland lumber empire up the Ottawa river system. Only London, of the earlier emerging concentrations of any size (it was a town by 1848), grew initially as an inland service-centre for prosperous surrounding farming districts. Yet other relatively early inland places, from Peterborough to Brantford to Chatham, flourished first as shipment points on waterways.

Urban growth in Ontario, in the second place, was constantly influenced by close proximity and ease of access to the United States. The same might obviously be said of other regions in Canada; yet there was some significant degree of difference, for many leading Ontario centres from Kingston to Toronto and Hamilton to Windsor were right on the water border, at most a few short hours' passage from American cities across the lakes. Furthermore, the whole southern Ontario peninsula was thrust into the midst of one of the richest and fastest-developing areas of the United States, the Great Lakes basin. Still further, in pre-railway times the chief answer to Ontario's winter isolation, when the lakes and the St. Lawrence were shut, was travel by ice across to the United States. In short, despite the strong Upper Canadian connection eastward with the St. Lawrence outlet to the sea, a pattern of communication and commerce southward was equally inherent, stemming from the very physical position of the region.

The latter pattern was considerably reinforced, in spite of existing tariff hindrances, when the Erie Canal opened water communications between Buffalo and New York in 1825, with feeders subsequently being added directly to Lake Ontario. This man-made feature no less became an environmental force acting on Upper Canada, since much of its grain went out to market via the Erie – especially after the American Drawback Acts of 1845-6 remitted duties on goods in transit between Canada and the United States Atlantic ports. Toronto in particular benefitted from ease of access to the Erie system, for it found itself ideally situated as an entrepôt between American and St. Lawrence routes to the sea, able to use both to advantage, or play one off against the other.

Britain's adoption of free trade and repeal of the Navigation Acts from 1846 to 1849 removed the structure of imperial preferences and restrictions that had worked to channel traffic into the St. Lawrence route for trade with the British market. The new colonial free-trade environment (for such it might well be termed) further enhanced the pattern of north-south connections for Ontario towns. The establishment of reciprocal free trade in natural products by the Treaty of 1854 with the United States was a wholly consistent climax to the development. Quite as significant, however, was the rising demand in the eastern United States for Canadian supplies in lumber and foodstuffs, which made the Reciprocity Treaty less a cause than a result of mounting north-south traffic between the Ontario region and American urban industrial markets.

The coming of the railway age to Ontario in the 1850s again enlarged north-south traffic, as lines funnelled Canadian commodities southward to the United States: the Bytown and Prescott or the Brockville and Ottawa lumber routes; Toronto's Northern Railway down from Lake Huron; and the Great Western, focussed on Hamilton, which provided direct connection between New York rails at the Niagara border and Michigan lines across the Detroit River. Ontario, in fact, became thoroughly tied into the spreading United States railroad net, as a commerce of convenience grew across it between the American mid-west and the Atlantic seaboard. The abrogation of the Reciprocity Treaty in 1866 by no means brought this to an end – although the new 'national environment' of Confederation and subsequently the protective National Policy did add a stronger alternate overlay of east-west connections.

In the whole process, urban centres like Windsor, Sarnia, London, Hamilton, Toronto, and Ottawa gained markedly from the through traffic with the United States, which plainly fostered urbanization at these points. More than this, however, the powerful north-south ties that had been created for Ontario's urban communities also brought American business connections, techniques, and capital for branch plants after the National Policy of 1879. The communications with the south as readily conveyed American books and periodicals in mounting quantity to Canadian towns, touring American road companies and lecturers, American fashions and models to emulate. Granted, the countryside as well as the town felt these influences; but they were strongest in the urban centres that were the foci of traffic with the United States.

Moreover, in the later nineteenth century the north-south pattern grew more extensive, as Americans invested in rising factories in Ontario towns, in rail lines probing further northward for lumber supplies, and, above all, in the new frontiers of development opening in the North – of silver, copper, and nickel mines or pulpwood mills all the way to Lake Superior. The American tie-up, which was conditioned by environment from the start of Ontario's urban development, was thus a far larger factor by the close of the century. In one sense, urbanization and Americanization had proceeded together.

In regard to population, the essential fact prevails that it is the concentrating of people, in whatever environment, which produces an urban centre. This in itself is not enough, of course; a mere crowding together of numbers might constitute a rural slum with no particular urban functions – or a prisoner-of-war camp. Function as well as number is involved. The people must compose a community engaged in services or activities that can be designated as urban: which normally mean those of a commercial, financial, industrial, administrative, cultural, or informational kind, which are not generally part of primary production and are carried on in close contiguity with considerable differentiation of labour. A further point worth noting is that the concentration of population should be seen in relative terms. What matters is the size of the closely populated centre in relation to its whole society; indeed, in regard to the age and kind of society as well. Thus Kingston could be a significant urban concentration in 1817 with 2250 inhabitants in a thinly settled pioneer Upper Canada, whose total population was around 100,000. Likewise, in 1851, in a rural Canada West of some 950,000 people, Toronto could loom fairly large with 30,000 – about the size, incidentally, of the highly important town of Bristol in the English Middle Ages.

To trace this urban population growth in Ontario across the century, one may begin with the estimate (for want of reliable figures) of an average rate of increase of over two percentage points a decade from the 1820s to the fifties, during the period when waves of British immigrants were pouring into Upper Canada, chiefly to settle its agricultural frontiers but stimulating town development as well. By 1851 the urban proportion in Canada West stood at 14 per cent; by 1861 it had reached 18.5, an increase of 4.5 points in the era of the first great railway-building boom. By 1871 the proportion stood at 20.6, a solid 4.1 advance. But in 1881 the urban segment had risen 27.1, up by 6.5; and in 1891 to 35 per cent: a soaring growth of nearly eight points, reflecting the rapid industrial development of the eighties. Moreover, the increase by 1901 to 40.3 per cent still indicated a continuing rise of 5.3 despite the state of depression during the mid-1890s.[4] Obviously, then, urbanization had taken off in the later nineteenth century in Ontario, although its mid-century growth was substantial, and even its course in the earlier decades was definitely worthy of attention. For it bears noting that in this early era, that is generally treated as a time of frontier and rural settlement, urban centres were nonetheless steadily increasing their proportion in the total provincial community. In this respect, they were growing faster than the populating countryside itself.

Several factors were involved in this early period of urban growth. To begin with, small service centres appeared inland, as immigration pushed out farm frontiers, supplying a tavern, general store and mill, blacksmith's shop, and probably a log church. Concurrently, there was the corresponding advance of older places on the fronts, from crossroad or waterside hamlets to well-settled villages and towns serving a much bigger hinterland, each with several mills, warehouses, stores, and churches, and with lawyers, doctors, clerics, and teachers, and soon little newspaper offices. Thus, as Peterborough emerged in the 1830s in the Otonabee backwoods, Cobourg grew on the lakefront as key to the Otonabee district, or Hamilton as a marketing centre for new hamlets in the Grand River Valley. There was also a 'multiplier effect,' most apparent in the larger towns. Increasing urban activities in variety or size tended to produce additional activities as spin-offs. Timber production at Bytown in time led also to towing companies, shingle mills, and sash factories. In the forties, the growth of wholesaling in Toronto brought the specialization of retail trade out of it for the flourishing local market, while the overall expansion of the city's business community caused the establishment of more newspapers and printing offices. And all this meant more jobs and people in urban centres.

In addition, some of the immigrants themselves did not go to the country but stayed to swell the towns directly. Incoming settlers halted there, while arranging and preparing to take up a farm, and often to find work to pay for stock and supplies. The age saw such a stop as temporary – and certainly transiency was a marked feature of the town population. But often the halt became quite permanent. Some immigrants stayed because they found better prospects in the urban setting; others because they had scant prospects at all. Those best equipped with capital or work skills or those least advantaged with only unskilled labour to offer – and often ill-nourished, sick or unadaptable besides – either might remain to add to the urban population. The result was the heightening of class differences and a growing urban concentration of poverty. The scale of urban misery, with attendant problems of degradation and disease, alcohol and violence, was nothing like the size it would become in the later century. Still, it began there: Toronto had its slums by the 1840s. But social problems would long be left to private charity or church effort, with little urban community action beyond providing constables and a workhouse: the latter by 1837 for Toronto.

In the mid-century years of the fifties and sixties, immigration declined and agrarian expansion came up against the intractable line of the Shield. A period of intensive more than extensive growth ensued, but there was much to be done in filling in and consolidating. Indeed, this led to greater urban concentration, in the rapid economic development stimulated by the export boom of the fifties in wheat and lumber, by reciprocity, and, above all, by the coming of rail transportation. Railways brought land speculation, and glittering schemes in towns for each to rule a new transportation empire, as well as high wages, free-flowing money, jobs, and hopes of jobs. People poured in. Expensive private and public buildings went up, such as the imposing town hall Cobourg erected in visions of becoming a grand railroad capital. Hamilton's population shot up from 10,300 in 1850 to 27,500 in 1856, London's from 5000 to 15,000. Toronto's property values more than doubled in the period, while present-day landmarks like the St. Lawrence Hall, University College, and an enlarged, reconstructed Osgoode Hall rose then in the city's lavish building boom.

The railway fever broke in 1857 along with the world depression, leaving a heavy load of civic and private debt, and even declining population in some cities. Hamilton, for example, fell to 19,000 by 1861. But many of the urban gains remained solid, and the new trade surge rising during the American Civil War quickly recovered lost ground. Moreover, towards the close of the sixties, railways were again being promoted, aided by the government of the new province of Ontario established at Confederation in 1867 – which also, of course, made Toronto a political capital again. Any setbacks which that city had suffered in depression had more than been made good; indeed by the seventies it was in the midst of another, still mounting boom. It had expanded its industrial, commercial and financial facilities greatly, founding the Toronto Stock Exchange in 1852, the powerful Bank of Commerce in 1867. It was the principal Ontario educational, publishing, and newspaper centre, with a dominating hold on the shaping of provincial opinion. Consequently, its population had climbed in keeping with this increasing metropolitan stature and diversification of activities: from 30,000 in 1851 to 44,000 in 1861, and 56,000 ten years later.

As for rural Ontario in the period, it had evolved a stable, well-knit agricultural society, still based mainly on an export wheat economy, but with other specializations appearing, such as dairying and stock-raising. Accordingly, this was the hey-day of the country market-town set in prosperous agrarian surroundings. Outside of cities like Hamilton and Toronto, or in some respects in the lumber world of Ottawa, manufacturing industry was not yet of much significance in Ontario's urban life.

The next period, however, from 1870 to the end of the century, brought the mounting impact of factory industry. Urban population continued to grow for many of the older service-providing reasons, but the main new factor added was that of industrial production. True, the forest frontier went on extending northward, creating new lumber centres from Muskoka to Kenora, and Sudbury was increasingly mining copper from 1887. Nevertheless, major development of the forest and mineral resources of the vast Northern Ontario region was only beginning in the 1890s, and its effects on urban Ontario belong mainly to the twentieth century. In the later nineteenth century, instead, the rising theme in population concentration was industrialization.

Of course, the National Policy's protective tariff of 1879 had much to do with the noteworthy spread of factories and factory towns. Yet industrial enterprise had been growing in Ontario during the seventies, despite depression after 1875. In fact, heavy industry had appeared in the Toronto Rolling Mills in the sixties to meet railway needs for iron rails, in Hamilton's extensive car shops, or Kingston's locomotive works during the fifties. And steam power had been applied at least from the forties in some flour or saw mills where water-power resources were not adequate for rising demands. None the less, the rapid growth of factory industry in the later century was certainly impelled by the size of the markets now available for home manufactures, in a much more populous Ontario, in the Maritimes since Confederation, and in the Canadian West that opened particularly after the completion of the Canadian Pacific in 1885. All these, moreover, existed as protected markets by the eighties.

The consequent growth of industry – in textiles, agricultural machinery, milling and food processing, in clothing, iron ware, wood products, and leather goods – was much too extensive to be detailed here. Suffice it to say that urban centres were widely affected, and that some in particular emerged as distinctive manufacturing communities producing for much more than merely local hinterland consumption; notably places in western Ontario on good rail communications, like London, Brantford, Galt, Guelph, and Berlin (later Kitchener). Obviously, population concentrated still further at these factory sites, as it did also in Hamilton and Toronto. In fact, as time went on, the workings of economies of scale and multiplier advantages of the bigger industrial centres – more subsidiary operations, more financial and commercial services at hand, larger pools of labour, broader transportation facilities – tended to enlarge the size of factory operations and again concentrate them more and more in major places. The result could be seen by the 1890s in the decline of small village industries, along with fewer but larger manufacturing units in the chief centres.

One indicative instance of the trend was the movement of the Massey agricultural machinery plant from Newcastle to Toronto in 1879. Another was the fact that Toronto had, in round numbers, 930 industrial establishments in 1881 with 13,200 workers, and in 1891, 2400 units with 26,200 workers.[5] But then over the nineties its number of units became reduced to 847 by 1901, while the much smaller manufacturing centre of Kingston saw a still greater reduction during the decade, from 401 to 42.[6] In general, this consolidation meant more concentration of people at the leading places. It was, in fact, another mark of urbanization – as exhibited in the growth of Hamilton from 35,000 in 1881 to 49,000 in 1891, and Toronto in the same decade from 86,000 to 181,000, then to 208,000 by 1901.[7]

A final mark of urban concentration to be noted for the period was the corresponding emergence of rural de-population. No longer were cities growing chiefly because of immigration from abroad (though there was some revival of it in the eighties) or from the surplus of a still-increasing agrarian society. From this point on, rural society ceased to grow in size, and even began to lose ground to urban population. The movement from the country to the city developed from the 1870s onward, particularly of young females, which would produce a feminine dominance in urban numbers, as well as leave a persisting degree of rural bachelorhood. But farm society, as such, did not decline in size during the later nineteenth century. The loss thus far came mostly in rural non-farm elements – an additional indication of the decline of local village industrial and service occupations, as more and more industry and services were concentrated in the larger towns and cities. This movement out of the country became most evident from the mid-eighties, but can be traced back earlier, for many rural areas had reached their population peaks at the census of 1861. Thus Peel County, for example, declined from its maximum numbers in 1861 by 21 per cent in 1901, and its Chinguacousy Township, in which was the rising town of Brampton, fell from 6129 in 1871 to 5476 in 1881, and to 4794 by the end of the century.[8]

In sum, the major effects of modern urban population concentration were manifest in Ontario by the time the nineteenth century had closed, including the social strains and problems produced by people crowding into cities. Indeed, the very size of the complex of problems thus created led in the later century to the framing of provincial and municipal social policies and institutions to cope with baneful urban conditions, But this brings us to another aspect of urbanization – organization.

The human organization of urban centres has so many facets that it is impossible to do more here than select one or two, while leaving out a great many of equally valid interest. Those chosen – municipal framework and social structure – do not include such major considerations as religious and educational institutions, occupational and family patterns, spatial distributions and streetscapes, social and physical services, and much else besides. But they do illustrate distinctive features of Ontario's urban growth, and that is their reason for choice.

Municipal institutions developed slowly and piecemeal in early Upper Canada, an expression of the frontier state of its society and the prevailing conservative context of rule by oligarchy. Though a representative assembly was there from the founding of the province, the fact that administration at the centre was by appointed officials not under popular control was naturally reflected in the localities also. Hence, in spite of the existence of minor locally elected officers in townships, the real power over the countryside was wielded by the appointed district magistrates sitting in Quarter Sessions, from whose authority the incipient urban centres were not excepted, not even the little capital of York.

The growing population of these places, however, and the resulting problems with which they had to deal, did gradually bring them distinctive though limited grants of authority. Some of them secured 'police acts' from their district Quarter Sessions (not the modern connotation of 'police,' but rather the power to regulate) enabling them to deal with street improvements, nuisances, and fire prevention: Kingston first in 1816, York in 1817, Niagara in 1819. But as fuller, more effective powers grew necessary, agitation rose for some form of municipal government in the 1820s. This was largely frustrated by the sharp divisions in the legislature between Reform exponents of popular power and Tory defenders of appointed right. At last a provincial act of 1832 established an elected Board of Police for Brockville, setting a precedent that partly broke through the old control of the appointed magistrates. A number of other police-board towns followed all along the front, including Hamilton in 1833, Belleville, Cornwall, and Port Hope in 1834, Cobourg in 1837. But York took a long leap forward, achieving incorporation as the city of Toronto in 1834 under its own elected council and mayor – who was, however, chosen by the council from its members.

The Rebellion of 1837 and the stresses that followed brought a temporary check to the evolution of municipal organization. Still, Kingston, which had sought incorporation since 1828, managed to become an incorporated town in 1838. In any case, the towns' needs were pressing, and the provincial mood was clearly changing by the forties. When the oligarchic power of the Family Compact at the centre was uprooted, the local oligarchies were foredoomed as well. Furthermore, the Reformers' drive for responsible government in the province during the decade also involved the establishing of municipal self-government. Thus the road led naturally from the partially elective District Councils Act of 1841 to the Municipal Corporations Act of 1849, defining a complete series of incorporated, elected rural and urban municipal authorities: on the urban side, from police village to city, the latter being equal to a county in status, but separated from the county's jurisdiction under its own mayor and council.

Even before this general Act, which remained the basis of municipal organization in Ontario until almost the present day, particular enactments had carried individual towns forward. Hamilton and Kingston were both incorporated as cities in 1846. Bytown and Brantford became police-board towns in 1847, each, too, with a mayor and council. Moreover, the structure given all these places was modelled on that first developed for Toronto in regard to taxing powers, a ratepayers' franchise, and the like. Consequently, the Act of 1849 simply generalized a pattern that was already being worked out in urban Ontario to fit its needs and attitudes, a pattern set in its fundamentals by the 1850s, and one which would be of lasting significance.

It was a combination of North American circumstances and precepts of British Victorian middle-class liberalism. Based on rule by elected representatives, it by no means went as far as popular democracy. A still engrained conservatism, the set habit of looking to an élite, distaste for party politics in municipal affairs, the fear of 'Yankee' boss rule and corruption, all militated against any further move to full democratization. Though mayors became directly elected from the late fifties, no basic change in the character of Ontario urban political organization occurred through the rest of the century. Hence the structure of public life in the towns, the kind of places they became, continued to differ significantly from American counterparts across the border, in the lesser play of popular power, the greater degree of social control from above – and, one might add, in less evidence of confused and corrupt administration.

The kinds of places that Ontario towns became equally expressed the social structure which they developed during the century. On the one hand, their expanding wealth and economic dominance produced a newly powerful capitalistic and entrepreneurial middle class that was displacing the older urban élite of officials and large resident landowners even in the 1840s. On the other hand, the very concentrating of population shaped a much larger urban working class. The rise of factory industry in the later century added greatly to its mass, while no less adding a strong component of industrialists to the ruling urban element of wholesalers, shippers, railway directors, and bankers. In sum, the old graduated range of social orders in the towns, from unskilled labourers through artisans and shopkeepers to gentlemen, became much more plainly polarized into two main class groups representing either numbers or power. One accordingly could see the indicative organizing forces at work in the establishment of Boards of Trade (in Toronto in 1844), of manufacturers' associations (at Hamilton and Toronto in 1858, and more lastingly in 1871), or in the growth of the labour movement: the Trades Assembly set up at Hamilton in 1863, at Toronto in

1871, and Ottawa the next year, leading to the enduring Trades and Labour Congress founded in 1886.

The degree of class polarization still must not be over-emphasized. At one end of the social scale there continued to be an aristocratic leaven. Originally this had much to do with the presence of officers of the British garrisons, but it lasted particularly in towns like Kingston and London, and to some degree Toronto, supported by the continuing imperial fount of honour and prestige, and the strength of social conservatism and British loyalty. Further down the scale, the still numerous 'respectable' artisans and tradesman elements served to bridge and blur sharper class identification; and they were often quite prominent in civic politics and Orange lodges. Finally, the strong sectarian religious ties that cut across class lines were frequently the more in evidence, particularly when deep-rooted Protestant and Catholic antipathies divided the working class itself.

In ethnic terms, this was a remarkably homogeneous urban society, with virtually no non-English-speaking immigrant groups till late in the century, where there was a widespread preponderance of British ancestry, and most were proud of it. It was the result, of course, of the long continued migration from Britain: as late as 1861 more than half the inhabitants of Toronto had been born in the British Isles, and their children would have constituted a large part of the remainder. Nearly every wholesaler in the city of the fifties was a native of the United Kingdom,[9] and at least to the end of the century Toronto's influential business élite came largely from that sort of background: from England, the Gooderhams and Worts; from Ulster, William McMaster and Timothy Eaton; from Scotland, Robert Hay and John Macdonald. Much the same might be said of most of the other urban centres. To a less but still highly influential degree their dominant middle-class elements also had a strongly British orientation, in background, outlook and sentiment.

As for the lower classes, the case was not greatly different. In Ottawa, it is true, they were largely Catholic Irish or Catholic French Canadian. Hamilton had a sizeable Catholic Irish minority; one quarter of Toronto was Catholic by the later century – chiefly Irish also. Yet in general the towns were Protestant British in complexion; and with a strong coloration of Ulster Irish, as in Toronto, that was exemplified in the power of the Orange Order in their midst. Moreover, the Catholic Irish stressed religious more than national identity. Hence the towns could well be called focal points for Victorian British attitudes in nineteenth-century Ontario: another important offset, in the realm of organization, to American influences in the urbanizing process.

The significance of technology for urban development is so fundamental and pervasive that once again only a scant selection can be made here from the varied aspects of technological change that bore upon the growth of Ontario centres both from without and within. Yet one particular aspect stands out as obvious for discussion: changes in the technology of transport, from the steamboat to the railway, that so signally affected the nineteenth century everywhere.

The steamboat came to Upper Canada with the launching of the *Frontenac* on Lake Ontario by Kingston enterprise in 1816, and spread rapidly in the next few years, along the lakes and up navigable waterways. Its impact on an embryonic urban society living by water transport was sweeping. It not only made passenger traffic far more swift and sure, but also brought steam towage, whether for timber rafts or barges filled with freight or immigrants. It made coping with rapids on the St. Lawrence and the use of new canals far more effective, especially with the introduction of more powerful propeller craft that supplemented the paddle-wheeler in the forties. And it led increasingly in the little Upper Canadian ports to investment in steamboat building or steamboat and harbour companies, one of the first significant developments in local capital accumulation and business organization in these emergent urban places. Finally, it implanted in them a knowledge of steam technology, exemplified in marine machinery works at Niagara or in Kingston's shipyards. Well before the arrival of the railway, Upper Canadian towns could produce boilers and engines, which were applied as well in early 'steam mills'. In many ways, indeed, the steamboat was the harbinger of the nineteenth century for Ontario.

It was, however, still only one part of advances in water transport that quickened the whole pace of economic development for Ontario towns in the first half of the century. There was also the widespread introduction of the lake schooner, that efficient work-horse of the Lakes, or the improvements of harbours and of aids to navigation. Beyond this, there were the canals – and the telling impact of the Erie that has previously been noted. The Welland Canal not only cleared the way to the Upper Lakes; the water power and shipping facilities it offered fostered new urban centres along its course; for example, St. Catherines and Thorold (once Stumptown). The Rideau brought lumber traffic down to fatten Kingston at its western entry, and at the other created Bytown, the canal construction headquarters, which had a single cabin on its site in 1826 and 1500 inhabitants when the work was finished in 1832.[10] As for the chain of St. Lawrence canals, finally completed by 1848, the lower shipping rates and heavier imports they engendered widely affected the urban centres of Ontario's commercial life.

In regard to land transport, the earlier part of the century did see some improvements with the introduction of macadamized and plank roads that undoubtedly aided towns in acquiring larger or more effectively held rural hinterlands. Thus the Port Dover plank road gave young Hamilton an advantage over nearby rivals like Dundas, while the macadamizing of stretches of Dundas and Kingston roads or Yonge Street (almost to Lake Simcoe in the thirties) much enhanced the spreading inland dominance of Toronto, which was already 'a fledgling metropolis' by the time of the rebellion of 1837.[11] But the projecting of railways in the 1840s and their implementation in the fifties, led to a transformation in land transport technology that would command the second half of the nineteenth century for urban Ontario: the building of its rail communications net.

The opening of the Great Western in 1854, inspired and backed by Hamilton enterprise, made that city headquarters of one of the most successful early Ontario lines. Moreover, Windsor rose fast as its western junction with the United States, Niagara Falls as its eastern, and London advanced no less rapidly when its rails went through that town in 1853. Toronto's Northern, opening in 1855, created Collingwood as its port-terminus on Georgian Bay, and gave the Lake Ontario city a much greater northern hinterland, reaching even into the Upper Lakes. Toronto, in fact, became a major lumber port, as timber resources up to Georgian Bay were drained by rail to its harbour, leading in the seventies to the extension of the Northern into Muskoka to exploit its wealth of forests. Other lines served Ottawa or Cobourg, Port Hope or Brantford.

But the greatest of all was the Grand Trunk, running westward from Montreal to Toronto by 1856 and on to Sarnia by 1859. Though this transprovincial system became a costly failure for its private investors, a heavy burden on the public purse, and a dire entanglement for governments, it none the less tied the southern Ontario region together with one through, all-weather iron highway, and inevitably had profound influence on urban centres all along its path.

Places in the inland west like Guelph or Berlin were decidedly stimulated by the new line of transport. Port towns along the upper St. Lawrence and Lake Ontario, however, were often hit by the rail competition that carried through traffic along behind them but not to their harbours. Kingston, for instance, had no expanding hinterland to tap in its corner of the province, and could not become a sufficient focus of rail traffic to benefit much from the Grand Trunk. In contrast, Toronto certainly gained. It did become a major rail focus, what with its large hinterland, its own Northern, and also the extension of the Great Western from Hamilton – which actually allowed the larger city's interests to penetrate into the southwestern reaches of the province. In consequence, the Grand Trunk to Toronto meant even better access east and west, and more spokes in the railway hub it was building up. Rail technology was completing a metropolitan pattern that could bring the whole Ontario region under the economic dominance of its chief city.

The main outlines of the pattern had been drawn when the first railway-building boom collapsed in 1857. When construction rose again in the early seventies, it largely filled the pattern further, with more lines across the western peninsula or fanning northward out of Toronto and Hamilton. But by 1880 it was approaching a new phase, entrance into Northern Ontario. The building of the Canadian Pacific Railway from 1881 westward across Northern Ontario provided stimulus for a line to reach it from the south; above all, so that Toronto could tie into the transcontinental traffic, which otherwise would go far above it, eastward to Ottawa and Montreal. Between 1884 and 1886 the Northern and Pacific Junction Railway was built from the Northern rails in Muskoka to reach Callander, then on to North Bay. By this time the CPR route was fully open from Montreal to Vancouver; and as well the Ontario rail net was linked with it. Furthermore, the Canadian Pacific line itself had brought about the uncovering of the mineral resources at Sudbury, the beginning of western grain shipments from Ontario's Lakehead, and the building of a branch completed in 1888, across Algoma to Sault Ste. Marie.

By the nineties, then, the railway had begun to raise urban centres in Northern Ontario as well, through conquering its formidable distances and opening up inland resources as nothing could have done before. Meanwhile it had greatly stimulated the manufacturing growth of the south, making Hamilton in particular a city of heavy iron industry, with its first modern blast furnace in 1895; concentrated whole complexes of factories at focal points on the transport network (especially, of course, at Toronto); yet equally had brought decline to many a smaller manufacturing centre from Dundas to Bowmanville. The depression of 1893 was only a brief setback; recovery spread fast from 1896. As the century closed, rail transport was moving on to big new designs: the Ontario government's Temiskaming and Northern Ontario line from North Bay, announced in 1900, and soon two new transcontinentals across the northern Shield.

Moreover, rail technology had now developed a wholly new instrument affecting the growth of cities, the electric street railway. Electric traction, first displayed in Canada on a little line to Toronto's Exhibition grounds in 1885, came into use in St. Catherines in 1887, and spread rapidly in the early nineties in Toronto, Hamilton, and Ottawa. Its effect on the internal organization of Ontario cities was about as profound as the influence of steam traction had been on their external organization within the regional community as a whole. For one thing, it invited urban spatial expansion, or even explosion, since the same period of travelling time could carry the town dweller much further from home to job by way of the electric street car than by horse car, or assuredly, by foot. For another, it greatly advanced the sorting-out of residential from business or industrial districts, already under way, as whole new residential districts developed with the tram lines. And still further, electric rail technology notably affected urban land values and land use, just as railways had done, while raising similar issues of privileged, franchised private corporations in contention with public interests in mass transport. Yet the full impact of this latest technological factor to impinge on urbanization in Ontario would not become plain until the early twentieth century, by which time the next great transport revolution, the automotive upheaval, was already in preparation.

Accordingly, it is time to call a halt. Let it merely be said, in conclusion, that the nineteenth century in Ontario had witnessed a multiplicity of developments in technology, as in organization, that intricately affected the relations of population and environment in the urbanizing process. If this examination has only outlined some of the complexity and sweep of that process in nineteenth-century Ontario, that will be accomplishment enough.

Endnotes

1. E.E. Lampard, 'American Historians and the Study of Urbanization,' *American Historical Review,* LXVII, Oct. 1961, 49-61.
2. T.F. McIlwraith, 'The Adequacy of Rural Roads in the Era before Railways: An Illustration from Upper Canada,' *Canadian Geographer,* XIV, 4, Dec. 1970, 344-58.
3. G.P. de T. Glazebrook, *The Story of Toronto* (Toronto 1971), 11.
4. L.O. Stone, *Urban Development in Canada* (Ottawa 1967), 19, 29.
5. D.C. Masters, *The Rise of Toronto, 1850-1890* (Toronto 1947), 174.
6. J. Spelt, *Urban Development in South Central Ontario* (Toronto 1972), 173.
7. It has not been thought necessary to give citations throughout for population figures taken directly from published census tables. It should be noted here, however, that Toronto's jump to 181,000 over the eighties was partly due to annexations of suburban areas.
8. S.A. Cudmore, 'Rural Depopulation in Southern Ontario,' *Transactions of the Canadian Institute,* IX (Toronto 1912), 262.
9. D. McCalla, 'The Toronto Wholesale Trade in the 1850s' (typescript, Department of History, University of Toronto, 1965), 41-3.
10. R.F. Leggett, *Rideau Waterway* (Toronto 1965), 205.
11. F.H. Armstrong, 'Metropolitanism and Toronto Re-Examined, 1825-1850,' Canadian Historical Association, *Papers,* 1966, 30.

PART FOUR

Other Themes

Introduction

PICKED FROM THE VARIED CONTENTS of my remaining work, the themes of this last section are labelled "other" in that they do not fall clearly into categories already covered, although they certainly do relate to those subjects which have chiefly held my attention in Canadian history. Take the subject of identity, as treated in the article that heads the group below; that is, "Limited Identities in Canada", which I originally gave to a session of the American Historical Association when it foregathered (to honour Canada's centennial) in Toronto in December 1967, but which was finally published in the *Canadian Historical Review* for March, 1969. I acknowledged then, as I do now, that the actual term so apt in Canada, "limited identity", had come to me from an old friend and colleague, Ramsay Cook. But my concern with identity, as involved in metropolitanism, nationalism or regionalism – and whether ethnic, class, urban or rural in its nature – did, in fact, go back much earlier in my own intellectual history. For instance, a paper I delivered to the Canadian Historical Association in Winnipeg in 1954, "Canadian Nationalism – Immature or Obsolete?" (not included here), touched on the power of metropolitan controls over Canadian national responses to the surrounding world, and furthermore dealt explicitly with problems of identity, specifically referring to an influential essay collection of the day, *Our Sense of Identity*, edited by Malcolm Ross.

Moreover, in 1969 I also published "Nationalism and Pluralism in Canadian History" in the journal *Culture*. There is no room, or need, for that to be included here either: my "Limited Identities" study seems to have proved somewhat the more effective in indicating qualifications for too-simple nationalistic treatments of Canadian history. Still, it must be said that neither article, nor any other pronouncements of mine, should be taken as at all denying a Canadian national character: itself expressed through the very limiting and pluralizing of aspects of identity in this country. To my mind, the resulting historic product represents an entirely distinctive Canadianism. Francophones and anglophones, native peoples and recent immigrants, communities of east, centre, west or north and containing élite or underprivileged class elements – the total complex of their mutual limitation and continual interaction has indeed described a manifest Canadian identity.

Let that rest now, for the sake of brevity, as we move to the second item set out below, "'Waspishness' and Multiculture in Canada". This was first read to an Ottawa symposium of the Royal Society of Canada and published in 1975 in *Preserving the Canadian Heritage*, edited by K.J. Laidler; though it has been somewhat revised for the present volume. Basically, this piece carries on with matters of identity, by attempting to trace how processes of history worked to weave fabrics of ethnic pluralism in Canada notably different from the context of the United States. And this despite the apparent hegemony of Anglo-Canadians, here denominated WASPS – but the dubious nature of that acronym is remarked upon within the paper. It suggests, at any rate, that Canada's path to multiculturalism was at least forecast (if all unintended) from as early as the 1770s.

The third selection that follows, "The Emergence of Cabbagetown in Victorian Toronto", may be seen as continuing a theme of ethnic identity; but in another way and on a very different basis, by analyzing one locality or neighbourhood within a particular urban community. This enterprise was, however, also part of a project multicultural in nature, which produced the volume in which the essay was published, *Gathering Place, Peoples and Neighbourhoods of Toronto, 1834-1945*, edited by Robert Harney. The volume itself was a response to Toronto's sesquicentennial year, 1984, put out under the auspices of the Multicultural History Society of Ontario. I gladly joined in the endeavour. I had been first chairman of the board of the Society for some five years from 1976, and my own book published in 1984, *Toronto to 1918*, displayed my interest in the city's history. Yet the essay I submitted for the Harney volume was not only Toronto-urban or ethnic-multicultural in bearing. It also made use of demographic census material to substantiate the "Victorian

Cabbagetown" identity – a small one, but still a building-block in city, region, or even nation. And in its handling of enumerative immigrant, and environmental neighbourhood data, I feel that this item does belong under Other Themes.

The last item of all looks still more miscellaneous in kind, and is admittedly placed here to provide a lighter note by way of conclusion. In truth, "Submarines, Princes and Hollywood Commandos: or At Sea in B.C.," originated as an after-dinner address at a conference on British Columbian history in Victoria; though with further work it appeared in the Spring issue of *B.C. Studies* for 1980. Nevertheless, it always was more to me than a casual, would-be digestive for a banquet, since it also reached well back into my intellectual development and related to significant features in my work. That is to say, this was something of a reversion to an interest in military and naval history which I began at school and carried on at university, where I came to observe the force of strategic command over communications, particularly as exercised at sea. That recognition would surely enter into my thoughts on metropolitanism, whether attested in sea-route dominance on the North Atlantic or by the rise of commanding land bases that became key cities in an emerging Canada – Quebec, Halifax and more. Still further, I found myself after Harvard at Naval Service Headquarters in Ottawa, studying and reporting on Canada's initial cruiser force in the Second World War (the *Prince Robert*, *Prince David* and *Prince Henry*) under the wise and witty guidance of Gilbert Tucker, then a Canadian professor returned from Yale, but later to settle at the University of British Columbia. In consequence, I learned something of Canadian naval history especially – which I used again, if newly examined and documented, nearly forty years afterwards for the final article given below. It seems almost full circle! But then I incline to believe that history goes around, not up: in intersecting cycles, not by linear progress. Probably the Greeks were right.

Immigrants in the inner city, Toronto before the First World War.

"Limited Identities" in Canada

A SUITABLE TEXT FOR THE present disquisition may be found in a review article by Professor Ramsay Cook discussing some works of 1967 that deal with Canada's perennial problem, its lack of national unity and identity. On this topic Professor Cook remarks: "Perhaps instead of constantly deploring our lack of identity we should attempt to understand and explain the regional, ethnic and class identities that we do have. It might be just that it is in these limited identities that 'Canadianism' is found, and that except for our over-heated nationalist intellectuals Canadians find this situation quite satisfactory."[1] What follows here, then, is a commentary on this theme in twentieth-century Canada: if one nation, eminently divisible.

Canadian historiography has often dealt too wishfully with nationalism – and *ergo,* with unification – thus producing both expectations and discouragements out of keeping with realities. We may be somewhat past the colony-to-nation epitome of the Canadian story ("and with sovereignty, everybody lived happily ever after – see Africa"), but we are still considerably hung up on the plot of nation-building. There are the good guys and the bad, the unifying nation-builders and their foes; though one trouble is that the characters often change hats and whiskers in the

French-language version. There are also the good eras and the bad, largely seen in terms of nation-building. In this sense, during the twentieth century, Canada's years before the testing of World War I were golden years of national expansion; the twenties a decade where blotchy prosperity was further marred by the federal government abdicating national leadership; the depressed thirties a time of crisis in federal, more than class, relationships; the forties an era of national triumph arising out of national trial; and the booming fifties a new noonday of nation-building, unity, and harmony – after which the darkening discord of the sixties follows as a decided shock.

Now I would not seek to deny a good deal of validity even to this oversimplified, partial version of the nation-building account. I mean rather to say that it is merely one assessment, which does not necessarily have to be equated with the working out of historical destiny for Canada. This is not to condemn it as too readily subjective – and thereby enter into the bottomless debate as to whether there is objective history. It is to assert instead that the theme of nation-building has an unfortunately teleological cast. One looks for the end to be achieved; one measures developments, pro or con, in terms of the goal – a strong, united nation. One anticipates the re-enactment of the American success story and, when it does not come, particularly blames the presence of the huge American neighbour itself. Again this is not to deny all validity to that account. Obviously, a transcontinental Canadian union has been established and has been constantly subjected to powerful American influences. But it still can be contended that the nation-building approach to Canadian history neglects and obscures even while it explains and illuminates, and may tell us less about the Canada that now is than the Canada that should have been – but has not come to pass.

Viewed in a different context, accordingly, the years of the early twentieth century can appear as the period when a vigorous new western region emerged to join the existing coterie of Canadian regions; the twenties, as a time when forces of modern industrial society began to shape the present powerful provincial empires; the thirties, when class and ethnic strains proved at least as potent in disrupting the Canadian political fabric as the constitutional decisions of the Judicial Committee of the Privy Council; the forties, when external crisis no doubt brought resurgent national sentiment, but two nationalisms in two Canadas; the fifties, an era when rapid industrial and urban growth greatly strengthened regional orientations and ethnic pressures – and helped bring on the divisions of the sixties as a natural result.

This is not an attempt to replace a success story with a failure story: nor is it very new, since it essentially puts forward elements long recognized. What may be newer, however, is the notion that if the Canadian people have fallen short of the Canadian dream (held, that is, chiefly by historians and intellectuals) it could be because their interests were elsewhere – and that they nevertheless shared in a viable Canada, if not that laid up in heaven for them. In consequence, it might be worth investigating what their Canadian experience was, observing that it did not greatly focus on Ottawa and the deeds of hero federal politicians, or on the meagre symbols of some all-Canadian way of life.

How, then, is this Canadian experience to be discerned and defined? Some of it is doubtless common to all as citizens in one political sovereignty, with many economic and social interconnections besides. But much of it surely lies in the "limited identities" of region, culture and class referred to by Professor Cook. These represent entities of experience for Canadians no less than the transcontinental federal union; indeed, it is largely through them that Canadians interpret their nation-state as a whole. Of course – emphatically – regional, ethnic, and class factors apply in other national histories; and of course they have scarcely gone unnoticed in Canada as well. But what still is needed is more study of their roles in this country of relatively weak nationalizing forces: a land of two languages, pluralized politics, and ethnic multiplicity, yet all so far contained within one distinctive frame of nation-state existence.

It is impossible to do more here than sketch some outlines of this study or, because of the limitations of space, to go much beyond one aspect of the limited identities, the regional, while touching on ethnic and class factors in passing. It may be hoped, however, that enough can be done to make plain the significance of such a view of Canada throughout its development as a nation-state.

In taking up a theme of regionalism, one is conscious that it may suggest a somewhat dated environmentalist approach by analogy with the history of the United States. There, it can bring to mind implications of Turner and the frontier school: of the pouring of people into sectional moulds to harden in the frontier's advance across the various physiographic regions of the continent. Through the inevitable workings of revision in American history, from critics of Turner who urged other factors than the moulding power of the frontier environment down to Louis Hartz, whose special stress on cultural importation leaves little to the landscape, a regional treatment can come to seem rather *passé*, tending perhaps to the parochial or antiquarian.[2] This may be so to some extent, for a giant country where national forces have worked mightily, the powers of One Big Market, One Big Government, and the Americanizing Dream having proved so paramount. But the Canadian context is almost antithetical. Whether one moves, accordingly, with Turnerian or Hartzian waves, the experience of regionalism remains prominent and distinctive in Canadian history – and has tended less to decline than to develop down to the present.

Most of the reasons here are oft-given and obvious: the geographical segmentation and encumbrances of this difficult land; the north-south orientation of many of Canada's regional economic patterns and the related problem of sustaining its east-west links; its Anglo-French duality; and the lack of a positive popular commitment to a strong federal union, despite the intentions of the framers of Confederation. Whatever their ideas or assumptions, in fact, the union of 1867 was in large degree a coming together of regions, and so has remained: regions articulated or integrated under a central régime, but surely not reduced or unified thereby.

Yet there are other factors that must also enter to explain this persistence of regionalism. After all,the United States had a mass of geography too, not all of it advantageous, and a strong American union was not born but was made in history, in the very growth of popular commitment. Nor can the Anglo-French duality in Canada, however intrinsic, be found sufficient reason in itself for *e pluribus non unum*; there are also several English Canadas, not just one. A further fact, instead, is that the social patterning of Canada particularly tends to favour regional commitment. There is a relationship here between regional identification and broader social values that deserves investigation.

John Porter makes the essential point when he observes: "Unlike the

American value system which has always emphasized the idea of the equality of peoples within a new nation, the Canadian value system has stressed the social qualities that differentiate people rather than the human qualities that make them the same."[3] Porter discusses the point chiefly in regard to the persistence of immigrant groupings in Canada, where ethnic fragmentation is more the mode than assimilation and is expressed in the ideal of the mosaic instead of the melting pot. But this Canadian tendency to treat people as groups and communities rather than as individuals and citizens pertains to more than the fairly recent development of the ethnic mosaic. Its roots run deep in history.

French Canada's social values found their origins in the corporate authoritarian traditions of the seventeenth century. English Canada's were shaped in the organic, pragmatic Victorian liberalism of the nineteenth century. In other words, one may follow Louis Hartz on the power of transferred cultural fragments to mould new societies, yet contend that for English Canada the formative power lay not in the weak remnants of eighteenth-century American empire but in the swamping force of earlier nineteenth-century British immigration. At any rate, neither French nor English Canada knew eighteenth-century rationalist democracy as did the United States, with its generalized precepts on the equality, rights, and powers of men as men. In the Canadian scheme of values there was no all-embracing sovereign people but rather particular societies of people under a sovereign crown. They were exclusive rather than inclusive in viewpoint. Their guide was adapted organic tradition more than the innovating power of the popular will. And they stressed the nearer corporate loyalties of religious and ethnic distinctions – Scots, English, and Irish, as well as French – instead of broad adherence to a democratic state.

Though self-government came, it developed in terms of the Canadian perception and experience, as did federal union. And while the Fathers of Confederation might devise a strong union under the crown, designed indeed to counter claims for states rights, they could not invoke for it the power of the American belief in the sovereign people. As subsequent demands for provincial rights arose, federal leaders dealt with them pragmatically, rather than seek some broad, national counter-response. In fact, Canadian particularist habits of mind largely favoured impulses to state sovereignty over sovereignty of the people – so that, in the Canadian union of the twentieth century, one might almost witness the gradual victory of the long defunct Confederate States of America.

Furthermore, the crown, whose supremacy the fathers of 1867 might count on to obviate pretensions of founding power in the provinces, had its place within the spheres of provincial government as well as federal. Drawing on the traditional symbol, provinces might well aspire to the rank of co-ordinate kingdoms; and most had existed as entities under the crown before the creation of the federal state. In the twentieth century, the growing demands on government in an industrializing, urbanizing society of course greatly enlarged the activities of the provinces; but, not less significantly, the process strengthened their identification as well as function. It is not only evident that federal-provincial conferences have acquired something of the atmosphere of diplomatic exchanges between states, but it is also not inexpressive of Canadian conditions that heads of powerful provincial régimes may use the title of prime minister for their office – as in the current advance of the kingdom of British Columbia to co-equal dignity.

Consequently, while it would be absurd as well as unnecessary to deny historical evidence of Canadian sentiment for the union and the country as a whole, the fact remains that basic schemes of values in both English and French Canada accord more readily with smaller, differentiated provincial or regional societies. In French Canada, too, sentiment is far more strongly focussed on the corporate Quebec community than on the whole extended French-Canadian segment of the union; it is even a question whether separatism is not best conceived as the very height of Quebec communalism. As for English Canada, the habitual emphasis on particularized social groupings rather than mass citizenship, on pragmatically nearer community interests instead of some generalized, idealized, national way of life, effectively ministers to strong identification with regions or provinces as delineated by geography, economics, and history.

That pervasive twentieth-century process, urbanization, has also reinforced regional identities in Canada. It was after World War I that the Canadian population became more than 50 per cent urban; by the 1960s the proportion was over 70 per cent. One might conjecture that the long decline of an older, more isolated rural Canada, one of the most notable features of this century, would foster nationalizing forces – and no doubt this has been true in some degree. But the significant aspect for this study is the way in which the rise of dominant urban centres or metropolises has also aided regional orientation and the shaping of provincial power structures.

One may note that all across the country major metropolitan centres have organized broad regional hinterlands about themselves, thanks to their dominance of communication nets and of market, manufacturing, or financial facilities that serve the region. Again, this is a world as well as North American phenomenon, and has been going on in Canada itself for quite some time. Even in the relatively static Atlantic provinces, Halifax achieved metropolitan dominance in Nova Scotia in the later nineteenth century, largely through the building of railways; and through railways Saint John widened its commercial sway in New Brunswick. As for Quebec, another old port city – of hallowed antiquity by North American standards – its political role and cultural hold as the capital of French Canada maintained its special regional dominance, however much it continued economically to fall behind its upriver rival, Montreal. Leaving Montreal for the moment, Toronto was fully established as the metropolis of prosperous agricultural and industrial southern Ontario by the end of the nineteenth century; and in the twentieth, it added control of the huge mineral resource area of northern Ontario, so that successive opulent suburbs of Toronto spell out a veritable progression of northern mining booms.

In the West, Winnipeg's hold spread across the prairies with the wheat boom of the early twentieth century and the long transcontinentals that funnelled down to its rail yards. Its growth was slower after World War I, as the opening of the Panama Canal route tapped off some of its western hinterland to the Pacific. But the city retained an influential position as a major regional focus, even when newer western metropolises developed: Calgary especially with the oil boom after World War II; Edmonton through its drive to the northern hinterland of the Peace, or by air, railroad, and barge to the very margins of the Arctic. Westward again, there was Vancouver, the transcontinental outlet, soaring with its own ever-larger Pacific hinterland of lumber, minerals, and hydro-electric power.

All these cities were centres of regional dynamism, identified with the economic leadership and welfare of vast sections of the country; centres, often, of political as well as of business élites, foci of public opinion in their regions, of chief media instruments like newspapers and television, seats of major provincial educational or cultural facilities. And the continually growing pattern of urban concentration in the highway and apartment age has simply strengthened the focussing of the major Canadian regions around their chief metropolitan cities.

To admit the obvious once more, the metropolitan centres of the United States have grown in similar fashion – to still greater wealth and size – yet the result has not really been comparable in the regionalizing of the nation. The fact is, however, that while the phenomenon of metropolitan-regional growth is wholly apparent in the United States, there are offsetting factors in that country; and it is these that are notably less evident in Canada.

For one thing, the American urban pattern is far more complex, containing many counter-pulls; with more sizeable cities and tiers of cities, more regions and subregions, and also more states. There is not the relative simplicity of the Canadian scene, where a few large cities dominate huge sweeps of territory, sometimes within one provincial jurisdiction, and that perhaps centred within the city itself. For another thing, the overmastering role of the chief or "national" metropolis is not really comparable. In times past, Montreal has been Canada's closest equivalent to New York, the greatest head-office centre, key to the national transport system, the final capital of the country's economic life. This in general has been so in economic terms. But in socio-cultural terms – and in "national regard," if one may use the phrase – Montreal is not a single great metropolis but the split capital of two bilingual Canadas: for the one, yielding to Quebec in some aspects; for the other, to Toronto and elsewhere; and perhaps finding over all national regard only at some extraordinary occasions like Expo. In brief, Montreal does not fill the metropolitan headship role held by the huge American conurbation of New York. People in Canada do tend more to look to their regional metropolitan centres than to Montreal – or else even to New York, Chicago, or Los Angeles. As for Ottawa, as a thoroughly political national capital, a weaker Washington in a less consolidated country, its presence does not greatly alter this Canadian particularist tendency to focus on to regional metropolises instead.

In the main, therefore, the growth of urbanism and metropolitanism has largely worked to confirm regional identities in twentieth-century Canada. One can identify the West-Coast culture of Vancouver, for example, far more explicitly than the traits of national culture; just as one can more easily depict an Albertan or a Maritimer than a Canadian. About the only strongly identifiable national urban propensity, in fact, is the wide eagerness to scorn Toronto, which is nevertheless consoled by an inherent belief that all Canadian cities truly do aspire to be Toronto, if they are good.

One could go on noting still more factors that make for regional identification – the ethnic mosaic, for example, particularly built up in waves of twentieth-century immigration. Each region has a largely distinctive ethnic composition of its own, according to the proportion and variety of immigrants it has received, with consequent effect on its political as well as cultural responses. Once more this might also be said of the United States, where assimilation may have been the ideal more than the complete achievement. None the less, how different is the degree, when in Canada the ideal, or plain acceptance of fact, is the survival of ethnic diversity, where there is a declared distinction between "founding peoples" and later arrivals – and where "ethnic" has vulgarly become a noun to signify a member of one of the contingents of the non-French, non-British third force in Canada? Of course, acculturation has nevertheless proceeded among immigrant elements, from the mid-nineteenth century "famine Irish" to the mid-twentieth-century Hungarian refugees. Still, the ethnic persistence fostered by Canadian socio-cultural values plainly intensifies regional differentiations, quite aside from the special French or English identifications of Quebec and Ontario. Compare the largely "old-Canadian" make-up of the Maritimes, for example, with the strong non-British, if English-accultured component in Plains society; the significance of Ukrainians in Manitoba, of Italians in urban Ontario, or the still more cosmopolitan mixture of West-Coast society.

Then too, class patterns may be observed as varying from region to region in Canada; no doubt complying with differing regional economic scales. At any rate, industrialism and urbanism have not yet here created strong national awareness of common class interests. Socio-economic strains have tended to be expressed in largely regional terms, or at most in non-enduring regional alliances of disadvantaged elements. This may be said of Progressivism in the twenties, a class-oriented movement which foundered amid regional diversity; of the CCF of the thirties and forties, which largely failed, beyond its western bases, to make lasting inroads on the eastern working classes; of Social Credit in the fifties and after, which essentially stayed dependent on sure provincial bailiwicks in Alberta and British Columbia. And today class discontents are still largely expressed in regional or provincial stances, as in the Maritimes, or in Quebec communalism. As for socialism, one might feel that if the hopefuls of the Second International ran headlong into nationalism, so in Canada its proponents still have to face the divisive force of regionalism.

These threads, of course, should be followed further; but for now one may assert that regional, ethnic, and class identities have all tended to fit together more than to develop national identification in Canada. The ultimate conclusion, indeed, might seem to be that the true theme of the country's history in the twentieth century is not nation building but region building. But here it is necessary to make one final point. All this *does* add up to a characteristic and persisting Canadian pattern, largely differentiated from the United States – and the whole may indeed be greater than the sum of its parts, producing through its internal relationships some sort of common Canadianism. At least this is the final contention here: that the distinctive nature of much of Canadian experience has produced a continent-wide entity identifiable in its very pluralism, constraints, and compromises.

A key word is articulation. What has been sought, and to some degree achieved in Canada, is not really unification or consolidation, but the articulation of regional patterns in one transcontinental state. In this process, it may be said that, the implicit aim of every regional community has been the maximum autonomy for itself consonant with the maximum advantage to be gained from an overriding central régime. In this, indeed, these communities were simply manifesting the historical behaviour exemplified in Canadian relations with British imperial power, where the essential process followed was the gradual maximizing of autonomy, rather than a doctrine-based conflict over sovereign independence. But the concept of autonomy involves notions of both practical adjustment and continuing association. The analogy may not be precise between the external and internal processes of development in Canada (at any rate, in honesty, one knows where the former led), but the real fact is, it does fit the particularist, pragmatic tradition of the historical Canadian communities

And the result may be that each of them, in whatever varying degree, could exhibit something common to be called Canadianism, as they viewed the whole country from their own regional, ethnic, or class position: seeing it largely in their own perspective but accepting its limitations and need of continual adjustment, while also feeling the shared benefits it provided. All, indeed, have tended to make a virtue of their own regional or provincial willingness to "sacrifice" to maintain Canada, and most have found the concept of the general union necessary as a context for their own aspirations and desires. In any case, by pursuing a line largely of socio-cultural enquiry, one may hope to uncover satisfactions in the limited identities named by Professor Cook that have added up to some positive balance of satisfaction with Canada itself.

Endnotes

1. G.R. Cook, "Canadian Centennial Cerebrations," *International Journal*, XXII (autumn, 1967), 663.
2. Louis Hartz, et al., *The Founding of New Societies in the History of the United States, Latin America, South Africa, Canada and Australia* (New York, 1964).
3. John Porter, "The Human Community," in J.M.S. Careless and R.C. Brown, eds., *The Canadians*, 1867–1967 (Toronto, 1967), p. 396. See also John Porter, *The Vertical Mosaic* (Toronto, 1965), pp. 60–73.

Urban recreation: golf up the Don Valley in the 1890s.

"Waspishness" and Multiculture in Canada

IN DEALING WITH THE BRITISH component in the Canadian multicultural heritage, one runs into problems of definition at the very start. Just who were the "British-Canadians", historically speaking? Canadians whose origin lay in the British Isles, presumably; yet this wide category not only covers the three different national communities of English, Scots, and Irish, but also two notably divergent kinds of Irish, the mainly Northern Protestants and the Southern Catholics; and let us not forget the Welsh either. The Southern Irish, besides, might not thank you for the description "British", although probably at the time of their main nineteenth-century influx into Canada many of them would then have accepted it. Still, at least all these settlers from Britain could be described as English in a broad linguistic sense? Scarcely the Gaelic-speaking Scots Highlanders, or many of the Irish and Welsh! The major British immigrant groups, in fact, could be no less nationally, religiously and to a great extent linguistically distinct and separate among themselves as share in one collective British category.

But apart from the foregoing caveats, can British-Canadians even be loosely defined as those who emigrated to this country from the British Isles? What of the United Empire Loyalists whose arrival after the

American Revolution from the former Thirteen Colonies did much to shape the very outlines of a British Canada? They certainly regarded themselves as British – as loyal British Americans in contradistinction to traitorous American rebels – but they included sizeable numbers of German origin, not to mention Dutch or Gaelic Scottish, while those of English stock among them had often been well settled in America for a century or more. Then, too, what of the many migrants from the United States who followed in the wake of the Loyalists and who continued to enter in waves or in trickles onward to the present? They have generally fitted readily into the English-speaking community; their descendants have largely come to consider themselves, and be considered, part of the British-Canadian segment. Yet like the Loyalists – or even more so – they stemmed from a considerable variety of ethnic backgrounds. Some of them, including those New Englanders who had settled in Nova Scotia even before the Loyalists, had been out of Britain since the days of the *Mayflower*; others in later migrations had not had British forebears in the first place. In short, the British-Canadian heritage has sprung from a fairly heterogeneous community of peoples, and however the term "British" be used as a convenient label, it should always convey the evident fact of ethnic variety, not some willfully imagined racial or cultural monolith.

We might be better off, indeed, to talk of "British Americans" in order to refer to this prominent and historically dominant culture group in Canada. One can recognize, however, that by now some short-forms such as "BRAMs" is not too likely to replace "WASPs", White Anglo-Saxon Protestants, as a popular catchword to denote their powerful presence. True, WASP is an American transfer of terminology that does not wholly fit the Canadian situation, like a good many American transfers. For it is obvious that the Canadian British were by no means all Anglo-Saxons or Protestants in themselves. Nevertheless, their ruling élites were pre-eminently Protestant, and their ethnic values tended to exalt presumed "Anglo-Saxon" stock, tradition and character – whose excellence other breeds should properly endorse, and whose admirable guidance in Canada they thus should surely follow. Hence in a figurative if none too friendly way, these other breeds might conceivably picture British-Canadian WASPs as living high on the national tree in strong, well-defended nests, ready to sting any who rose up to challenge them. Besides, if they were not exactly banded black and yellow, they sometimes wore striped old school ties as emblems of their influential kinships, usually got more than those below, and sought commonly and combatively to maintain their sway. Though this insect analogy is a partial myth, it does still suggest a sense of WASPishness quite widely perceived by those outside the British-Canadian ethic segment; and it does express the fact that this significant group, for a long time the actual majority of the Canadian population, is still clustered in many of the top controlling sectors of the Canadian society and economy.

Accordingly, WASPs and WASPishness seem very indicative words to use in examining the British-Canadian share in the heritage of a multicultural and bilingual Canada. In particular, there is much historic evidence that WASPishness also had as one of its leading features the desire or expectation that other cultures in Canada should eventually assimilate; that everyone should and would in the long run become just like *us*, absorbed in One Canada, which would turn out to be remarkably WASPlike. Here an identification with American WASPism does look valid, for in that country emphasis on "think American" and "the American way" traditionally have meant that immigrant outsiders should adopt the standards and outlook of the possessing native WASP elements and become assimilated to them. So in Canada, too, WASPishness has frequently seemed to mean assimilation and uni-culture, not the acceptance and development of multicultural heritage.

But *has* WASPishness in Canada really worked out in such a way? Has the British-Canadians' contribution to multiculturalism essentially been that negative: to deny it, oppose it, and strive against it? I do not think so. Whatever the WASPish aims and desires for dominance and absorption, which assuredly have been present, I would contend that in the larger reach of history, the British-Canadian element has actually operated (if often unwittingly) to found and develop a multicultural environment. This did not emerge by accident, though some of it did by necessity. But the essential point is that the British-Canadian community, being multicultural itself in many respects, served to foster a multi-cultural heritage. It was not as WASPish as it tried to be. That, then, is what the rest of this paper seeks to illustrate: the ways in which, in Canada –

unlike in the United States – our own British-Canadian WASPs contributed all but inevitably to the growth of ethnic pluralism and the patterns of popular multicultural existence.

In the first place, ethnic identity is often powerfully buttressed by religious distinction. One need not labour this general, worldwide proposition, illustrated by the historic role of Greek Orthodoxy in many Slavic nations, Roman Catholicism in Latin countries, national Protestant churches in northern Europe, or Hinduism, Islam and Buddhism in Asian lands. The much more specific proposition contained here is that in British-dominated Canada – for all its ascendant Protestantism – the legal and constitutional guarantees given to Roman Catholic inhabitants provided through the course of history a built-in basis for ethnic differentiation. Whether these rights were sufficiently fair or full as granted is not under consideration now. What matters instead is that, from the Quebec Act in the eighteenth century to the Ontario separate school laws during the nineteenth, the public aid and recognition awarded to Roman Catholic communities in varying degrees across the country meant that church and state were never as constitutionally separated as in the United States; that a principle of state-supported religious division was acknowledged here, behind which cultural distinctions could shelter and maintain themselves. Plainly, this was of great consequence for French-speaking Canada, for the Catholic Irish who otherwise formed part of English-speaking Canada; and who is to say that Italians or Portuguese in Ontario today do not find the separate school of positive value in preserving their own ethnic identity?

Unquestionably these religious supports for ethnic differentiation have not applied equally and everywhere to the whole range of distinctive culture groups in Canada; although their example has proved capable of extension well beyond the situations out of which they originally emerged. Yet religious minority rights, as granted within a mostly British Canada, meant that its Roman Catholic elements came historically to occupy a much stronger position, politically and socially (if not necessarily economically) than their counterparts long did in the neighbouring United States. In that republic, Irish Catholics until far into the present century were attacked by nativist WASPs as posing an alien menace of papistry and state-church connection to American religious liberty and equality, as were German Catholics, Polish Catholics, Italian Catholics and others in turn. Assuredly the same sort of charges were recurrently and vehemently raised among Protestant British-Canadians; but the situation and the rules of the system were different. Between the Quebec Act of 1774 and Confederation in 1867 the Canada that was so largely led by WASPs enacted a series of special religious entitlements; whether or not it did so reluctantly, for plain expediency, or through political bargaining. In consequence, Canadian WASPism was constantly to be qualified by Catholic co-recipients of power in its very midst. (Notably we had our first Catholic Prime Minister, Sir John Thompson, in 1892: a long time before John Kennedy's presidency in the United States). And so the British-Canadian heritage came to incorporate a potential pattern for future pluralism, based on the state-established religious rights initially confirmed for French-Canadian or Irish-Catholic communities.

In the second place, Canada's long-enduring British colonial connection (which British-Canadians generally upheld and which only gradually disappeared) was not, I would argue, necessarily a barrier to multicultural development, but in many ways a positive encouragement. There is indeed a certain popular assumption that if only Canada had had a nice clean break from its British imperial past, perhaps featured by a formal pronouncement of independence, things would be much better for everyone, especially the non-WASP elements. Perhaps so: I do not seek to examine the whole complex case here; but rather to point out that in ex-colonial countries that do "begin anew", that declare clear-cut independence and a fine fresh start, cultural minorities often are the first to get it in the neck. The mass of citizens are supposed to conform to some new national pattern, generally that of an ascendant uni-culture, to be taught, imposed, and required with patriotic fervour. For divergences from this national norm are seen as dangerous, if not treasonous; above all, if independence comes accompanied by violence and revolutionary explosion. And least of all, then, is there time and place for those who would cherish and conserve a differing older heritage, especially one imported originally from outside.

But Canada, historically, has been linked with the other side of revolution: the continuing, conserving side. This other side of the American Revolution produced the Loyalists who helped to shape British Canada, by defending legal colonial institutions and traditional ways. The French-Canadians who faced the British Conquest of 1760 (and that decidedly was a revolution for them) similarly expressed their own desire to conserve what had grown up out of their earlier colonial heritage. And since, as it is often stated, Canada thereafter advanced gradu-ally to national status by evolutionary rather than revolutionary stages, older modes and patterns were adapted rather than disrupted or discarded. Our constitution consequently has been one of the oldest, unbroken forms of government in the world. Our ties with a transatlantic past were maintained, and not replaced by self-consciously new political and cultural designs. We did not, as did revolutionary America, look with distrust on whatever was not truly American or indigenous to the New World – what ever that might be. I think it is not without significance, indeed, that our federal parliamentary buildings, symbols of the Canadian political entity, would be Victorian British adaptations of the Gothic tradition of medieval Europe, whereas the American republic largely took up an idealized neo-classicism for its own young national and state capitols.

The upshot of all this is, that if it was right and desirable for French and British to retain old heritages, so it would be for other ethnic groups who later joined them in Canada. There was no revolutionary patriot tradition in this resolutely colonial country which said "you must be born again." Granted, the two older Canadian groups still might display alarm over incoming alien elements as dilutants of their own heritages; but they had no overall moulding pattern to impose instead. For the French, on the whole, the immigrant tide might best go away, or at least move beyond their cherished native patrimony of the St. Lawrence, westward into British Canada. For the British, "foreign" newcomers should no doubt adopt a duly British-Canadian way of life: but just what was this Canadian way? Actually, it *was* there; an historic pattern of gradual adaptation and of conserving change which over time did work to integrate immigrants as Canadians, without cutting off old roots. Yet that was hard to conceptualize or present as an explicit ideal. And so – very much because Canada had emerged but slowly out of British colonialism, without definite proclamation of some overriding new national model – ethnic pluralism based on the continued recognition of past cultural traditions was itself enabled slowly to develop with the increasing influx of non-British, non-French peoples into this country.

The long-lasting colonialism of British-Canadians, (a willing colonialism that was seen essentially as a guarantee against absorption by the mighty United States) was thus an influential, long-term factor that made for a multicultural environment in Canada. Of course, the British-Canadians also talked glowingly of the greatness of the British "race" – of its Law and Liberty, its Parliament and Empire. In that regard, particularly in the later nineteenth and earlier twentieth centuries, they went through an effusion of sentimental, racist-sounding imperialism – though this, as has been effectively noted, was also an expression of an incipient British-Canadian nationalism striving to promote Canada as the brightest jewel in the worldwide British imperial diadem.[1] None the less, they still had to accept the truth that the vast empire they lauded was composed of many races, creeds and colours; and why should not Canada be so comprised itself? If the great ideal was globe-girdling variety, all within a frame of free British institutions, then it was logically difficult not to accept such a pattern within Canada, too. The very "empire-consciousness" of the British-Canadian habit of mind, plus its almost instinctive anti-American leanings, impelled it on into our present era to assert as presumed fact that continental European immigrants were freer to live their own lives and carry on their own customs within the flexible, British-derived Canadian system, than they were within a monolithic American nationality that sought to make everyone conform to it. The Canadian British may have really wanted to see assimilation; but their own imperial heritage brought them, at policy levels, to affirm the mosaic (actually arising in the Canadian West) as superior to the American premise of the melting-pot. Imperialism consequently also pointed towards multiculturalism in Canada.

This – to underline the point – was very much the British form of imperialism, arguably more ready to accept multicultural existence in its holdings than were Spanish, French or perhaps Czarist Russian empires. Such cultural tolerance certainly did not preclude political mastery or economic exploitation; but the fact remained that British imperialism on the whole considerably permitted ethnic differences within a common political power structure; and this often recognized fairly extensive special minority rights, from the Quebec Act (a striking imperial departure in its eighteenth-century day) to the Morley-Minto reforms in early twentieth-century India. I would hazard the proposition that some of this historic imperial procedure inevitably left a mark on the British-Canadians. They came to develop in Canada a nation-state that was based on a common political and economic power structure, but with wide internal diversity – not cultural unity.

Beyond doubt, the French-Canadians also had more than a little to do with this national result. They successfully resisted varied attempts to deny their own cultural existence, largely through gaining a share of control of the political structure itself. Thus they ensured the persistence of dual, legally recognized cultures in Canada. (And where there are two such chartered ethnic partners, call them Founding Peoples or not, it is hard to avoid three, four or more in some degree: let alone to ignore the native peoples forever, who, oddly enough, just might have some claim to being Founding Peoples themselves). In any event, as for the French-Canadians, however much they had to strive to gain or extend their cultural rights, it is important also to recognize that the British-Canadians by no means simply stood in opposition to that determined effort. There were those among the latter element who consistently sought a partnership of the dual peoples in Canada, who looked for a common pattern of parliamentary institutions, within the British imperial model, to hold the two big cultural communities together. That concept did not always work out; it was not always sincerely pursued; but the intention and the endeavour can be repeatedly documented through history. In fact, the aim in Canada when our present federal union was erected in the 1860s was essentially to create a "political nationality", which – it was said by leading spokesmen for Confederation – would include four much older nations: the French, the English, the Irish, and the Scots.

What else was this but a recognition at a crucial stage in Canadian development of the idea of ethnic plurality within political unity? One can see it visually, moreover, in the original Canadian ensign after Confederation, which carried emblems of the four peoples on its field – or in the still existent arms of the City of Montreal, again emblazoning the rose, lily, thistle and shamrock. Small things, possibly; but culturally indicative. Admittedly, also, the symbolic emblazoning, thus, of four culture-groups hardly proves a readiness to add Italian, German, Polish and further armorial bearings to some Canadian coat of arms that would nearly have to rival the other kind of Canadian Shield in monumental size. No, all that needs to be suggested here is that, if in our past not just two charter peoples, but four component ethnic communities could be seen as co-existing within one overall self-governing entity, then it would be the more difficult in the future to deny that other ethnic groups might similarly come to co-exist within the national frame. Certainly a once-large and powerful British-Canadian majority might want, and even expect, to retain its ascendancy as a collective body. Yet that very collectivity had in its own heritage not the principle of the bloodstream nation as a unified folk, but that of the political nation embracing several folk.

Furthermore, from initial settlement until well into the later nineteenth century, the British elements who came to Canada widely lived under what might almost be described as tribalized, as well as localized, conditions. Scots and Irish in particular tended to settle in ethnic blocks in the earlier colonies of British North America: no less than did Icelanders or Ukrainians on the western plains thereafter. From the Scottish Highlanders of Cape Breton to the Lowlanders on the Huron Tract, from the Catholic Irish of Montreal or Ottawa to the Ulstermen of Toronto or Hamilton, there were close-bonded ethnic communities all across English-speaking Canada. Moreover, while persons of English origin tended to congregate less (though some still did so) they did not form the greatly preponderant sector in the total British-Canadian collectivity that they constituted in Great Britain itself. There was a different British mix here. Aside from the leading cities – or until English migrants became by far the largest component of the British influx in the early twentieth century – the British stocks in Canada were markedly weighted on the side of the Scots and Irish. And these were peoples strongly oriented to clan and extended family relationships who had often functioned within quite parochial environments at home. They consequently created their own ethnic mosaic in this country, even if it was far less multiple and varied than is our present one.

Note, too, that in so doing these incomers still remained acceptably

British in a British colony. In the United States, WASPs might come to denounce the immigrant trait of ethnic hiving as un-American, a threat to the established Anglo-Saxon integrity and conformity of the republic. But Canada in history (at least beyond New France) grew up with this accepted degree of ethnic, or almost tribal, diversity. The original Loyalists had exhibited it themselves. The real test of collective conformity for colonial Canada was loyalty to Crown and empire. In this regard some of the Catholic Irish might at times arouse suspicions of harbouring disloyal Fenian sentiments over Ireland's wrongs; but in politics in general they complied readily enough. A nineteenth-century Canadian might thus be a Saint John Loyalist or immigrant Irish timber driver, a Lunenberg schoonerman of German ancestry or an American merchant who had first settled into Victoria during the Cariboo gold boom of the 1860s: as long as their British loyalty was duly manifest, other differences could be lived with. In short the uniting pattern of "British" collectivity could best be found (much like that of the British empire itself) in group, clan, or familial ties to the ultimate headship of the Crown. And the Crown was especially venerated when it was worn by an emphatically family figure, Victoria, the Queen-Mother.

Once more a comparison with the United States is instructive. There, the Revolution had established the Sovereign People, of which each citizen, ideally, formed an equal part. But in Canada, the people were self-governing yet not sovereign. The Sovereign was both an individual and a symbol, distant but almost mystical in the reverence it could inspire. Under that monarchical form, to which all owed allegiance, British subjects could and did retain their own local differences and distinctions as members of varied organic cultural or ethnic units; whether as upholders of the Orange Order, the St. George or St. Andrews Society, or as good Irish Catholics who still rendered – as their clergy taught – due obedience to a heretic monarch in those things which were Caesar's.

I do not mean to paint some nostalgic romantic picture of medieval order and contentment under a benign regal sway in bygone Canada. The aim is merely to indicate that the British-Canadian pattern of authority and political perception then favoured the maintenance of group identities and even their exclusiveness, while the American promoted the merging and conforming of groups within a would-be egalitarian society.[2] The former bonussed internal differences without at all opposing the liberty either of individuals or communal units; the latter underwrote democratic equality for all, but, theoretically at least, on the basis of mass conformity within the Sovereign People. Theory and perception do not always work out in practice and conduct; nevertheless, they have their powerful influences. Hence it is still my contention here that the British-Canadian experience, as it developed into a major Canadian heritage, had within it strong propensities that made for the continued growth of multiculturalism in this country. Whereas in the United States, it is only quite recently that its people have awakened to the fact that not everyone becomes assimilated; that the problem of ethnicity remains of vital significance, not merely for blacks and Chicanos, but for a wide assortment of other cultural elements as well.[3]

Coming closer to the present in Canada, one should observe that succeeding waves of British immigrants, from before the First World War up to the 1970s, could by and large no longer be described as tribalized or parochial in their make-up, arriving as they did from a highly industrialized and urbanized British society. The same of course, had long been true for those who came and still come here from the United States. Moreover, it is quite a time since we have had stalwart peasants in sheepskin coats arriving from continental Europe, and most recent Caribbean or Asian immigrants to Canada have not been simple agriculturalists either. Yet, to revert to the British-Canadian element, what matters chiefly is the heritage which they had already built up well before the present era of our modern, urban, industrial Canada – prior to the final withering away of the British empire, and the cosmopolitan (yet equally regional) condition in which this country and the world now finds itself. The British-Canadian component has today changed vastly; and not least from now becoming but one more of the minorities in the total Canadian population, large and potent as it does remain.

Where is WASPishness today? In its would-be assimilative aspects we still hear from it: from those who still talk of One Canada to which no "hyphenated-Canadians" need apply, from self-styled Loyalists in Ontario, New Brunswick or Alberta who are not the U.E.L.'s of yesteryear; from those who think it would be so patriotic and simple – as indeed it would – if we all spoke English, thought English, and conformed to one hundred per cent Canadianism – without saying what is in that hundred-proof bottle! It is seen also in attacks on the creeping menace of bilingualism in high places (how slow can you creep?), and at least in some of the alarmed reactions to the immigrants' presence in our cities, when they are held to foster poverty, crime and violence in the same way the Irish were as immigrants, back in the 1850s.

There is, no less, the other side to WASPishness which I have endeavoured to set forth here. And in my view this comprehends a much more vital and significant part of the historic British-Canadian heritage: its empirical acceptance of diversity, thereby affording factual consent if not intellectual approval to ethnic variety; its manifest record of acknowledging minority rights and internal community differences under law; and the sense it has repeatedly shown, however tacitly, that within a common political allegiance, regional and ethnic differences can be maintained and protected – so that the resulting integration, not unification, of the various component groups in Canada can serve each or all together as the best means of their living and growing within a free society. This last may be preaching; but I seek to preach. I do believe that the British-Canadian heritage has something to offer all Canadians that is not just represented by power or wealth. Nor is it the case that French-Canadians and many other Canadian groups have always appreciated the value of live-and-let-live; even though they may assuredly have suffered as minorities themselves. In truth, minorities need to practice tolerance, accept differences, resist their own internal conforming pressures no less than do majorities. Now that the British-Canadians have also become a minority in our present state of multiculturalism perhaps they may assert as much. That side of WASPishness is worth marking and remembering, at any rate.

Endnotes

1. Berger, Carl. *The Sense of Power: Studies in the Ideas of Canadian Imperialism, 1867-1914.* (Toronto, 1970), *passim* and especially Chapter 10.
2. Careless, J.M.S. "Limited Identities in Canada," *Canadian Historical Review,* (Toronto), Vol. L, No. 1, March 1969, pp.4-6.
3. Glazer, N. and Moynihan, D.P., ed. *Ethnicity: Theory and Experience.* (Cambridge, 1975), Introduction especially.

Streetcars in downtown Toronto, carrying passengers to and from Cabbagetown.

The Emergence of Cabbagetown in Victorian Toronto

LIKE MANY ANOTHER URBAN NEIGHBOURHOOD, Cabbagetown has gone through various transitions since it first took shape in the later nineteenth century. Set at the eastern end of the original city of Toronto and extending to the Don River, the area was scarcely occupied before 1850, for the main thrusts of expansion had moved westward along the harbourfront or northward around Yonge Street, the central route inland.[1] Hence the easternmost city territory for a considerable time had stayed little more than a fringe of humble cottages and vegetable plots. But that changed with the growth of a railway and industrial Toronto from mid-century. The area increasingly became a populous residential district for urban workers, bordering a new rail and factory complex at the Don end of the harbour, which offered jobs, soot and smells together. Thus Victorian Cabbagetown characteristically developed as a domain of small, cheap houses on minor streets. It had little in common with the handsome estates of Rosedale rising beyond Bloor Street on its north, or with the big mansions on Sherbourne and Jarvis to its west. And the poor, the working class and lesser members of the middle class who filled this unadorned preserve stemmed overwhelmingly from the flow of Anglo-Celtic immigration. Consequently the community that had consolidated there by the late nineteenth century was all but homogeneously English-speaking, pre-eminently Protestant (though with a sizeable Catholic Irish minority), and highly British, and Orange, in feeling and tradition.

This was the historic Cabbagetown to be examined here. Yet one may go on, briefly, to note later transitions. Around the First World War, as still newer areas arose in the enlarging city, aspiring residents began moving out from the district. Poorer elements crowded into its houses, sometimes two or more families in each. These flimsily constructed, largely rented homes readily leaked and deteriorated, and landlords found decreasing value in keeping them up. The grim years of the 1930s deepened the decline; but it no less marked a process of neighbourhood decay continually repeated across urban America. Cabbagetown's life-quality, cohesion and morale went downhill together. In due course, Hugh Garner in the preface to his novel *Cabbagetown*, first published in 1950, would thus term the locality he had earlier lived in for some three years "a sociological phenomenon, the largest Anglo-Saxon slum in North America." That, however, is the kind of sweeping verdict which catches the eye yet also expresses literary licence. The same licence was exemplified when Garner went on to say that, "Following World War II most of Cabbagetown was bulldozed to the ground."[2] Actually, most of the area's Victorian cityscape then stayed in being, despite several big clearance projects, whereby the state and the developer erected highrise towers of sinister proportions and other handy blocks for breeding social alienation. Still, Cabbagetown went on changing from the 1950s, as an influx of newer ethnic elements brought a very different diversity, and then as gentrifiers swept in, extensively and expensively remodelling its humble houses. Again these are typical processes in urban North America. In any event, today it may be said that little beyond the physical layout remains of the old Cabbagetown community. It is now scarcely more than a heritage myth, hazily invoked by real-estate agents busy merchandising quaintness.

But Cabbagetown did exist: as a working, well-knit neighbourhood of Victorian Toronto. Its community life in that era is substantially conveyed in the reminiscences of the city journalist, J.V. McAree, who was born within it in 1876 to Ulster immigrant parents, and grew up at the shop he describes in his book *Cabbagetown Store.* The account undoubtedly displays nostalgia and later, selective memory; yet allowing for these, and with corroborating evidence, one may broadly deem its picture valid. This Cabbagetown was a place of small-town family and neighbourly focuses, of mutual aid and accepted, bonding obligations. It was equally a place of arduous work, often in adjacent industries; of stringency, layoffs and all-too-frequent hardship; of contending constantly with dirt, cold and disease.[3] In fact, the record presented reads like many another urban immigrant story in a developing communal area, whatever the language spoken there, the religion or traditions upheld. At any rate, this community on the whole strove determinedly to stay decent, ordered and self-respecting. Here by no means was a slum; a haunt of degradation, social apathy and personal breakdown. Whatever it later became – and Gardner's verdict surely remains an excessive overstatement – Victorian Cabbagetown was a vigorously functioning segment of the contemporary civic society, in which it played no insignificant part.

Since Cabbagetown was not an officially demarcated territory, but really represented a perception shared both by those within it and without, its recognized bounds might vary with beholders. None the less, there was, and is, a wide consensus that this community ran east from Parliament Street to the Don (not beyond it), and spread northward from Queen Street on the south to reach roughly to Bloor at its fullest extent. But points of contention immediately arise. On the south, the dwelling area below Queen and across King towards the harbour industries was intimately linked with Cabbagetown. There was a similar pattern of settlement and employment; the housing and populace had much in common; in fact, to some extent Cabbagetown simply grew northward out of this adjoining sector. On the west the same kind of lesser streets with little homes generally extended on past Parliament to Sherbourne and its larger properties; while to the north, if some oldtimer purists would hold that Cabbagetown proper just went up as far as Gerrard, others would take it on to Winchester. Yet here too the same residential setting and communal life in time expanded virtually to Bloor. Only the eastern boundary of the Don seems beyond much dispute, for there rolling valley slopes and the wet, open flats that bordered the river at the bottom marked a plain physical limit.

Accordingly, we can merely make the best approximation of bounds which indeed were sensed, not designated. So, we will take Queen Street on the south, but make required transgressions across it, down to King at least; will certainly endorse the Don riverline to the east, and take Parliament Street to the west – with other small transgressions. As for the north, Bloor seems the best ultimate boundary, though more precisely this was set by the grounds of St. James Cemetery that intervened before that limit, and by bigger residences that came to edge the Bloor ravine, beyond which lay Rosedale. It is also worth adding that the territory so delimited fell within one Toronto civic division, St. David's Ward, for much of the period under study, and between 1873 and 1892 was nearly coterminous with it.[4] This not only gave Cabbagetown some political framework and voice at city elections, but furnished census data on that community during its central decades of growth, because wards at that time served as urban census units. Though the neighbourhood entity and its covering city ward were not the same thing, and not at all before 1859 or after 1892, St. David's in the years between did supply the territory with a kind of municipal realization.

After 1892 Cabbagetown lay mostly in a big new Ward Two, which extended down to the harbour and up through wealthy Rosedale to new districts above. Politically and statistically, the neighbourhood in effect was swallowed up; but socially and culturally, it certainly continued.

I

We can now turn to the actual settlement story of Cabbagetown. Both the initial layout of an urban community at Toronto, and the basic nature of the terrain at its eastern end had a lot to do with the way in which this particular area was subsequently occupied. When the city's predecessor, the little town of York, was plotted out in 1793, it scarcely reached from the harbour margin north to Queen Street (then Lot Street), and only from George to a Parliament Street (now Berkeley) on the east. East from here lay a Government Reserve, on which provincial parliament buildings were erected: thus present Parliament Street acquired its name when it was opened beyond Berkeley. And north of Lot Street, up to existing Bloor, hundred-acre "park lots" were surveyed to provide estates for government officials and, hopefully, well-to-do landowners. The first two park lots, between Parliament and the Don north to Bloor, were further reserved for government purposes, originally with a probable eye most likely to naval timber supplies in woods accessible from the Don. The first provincial governor, John Graves Simcoe, established his Castle Frank estate overlooking the river in the northern portion of this official tract, long referred to as "the Park". In 1819 some of its land was granted off for hospital purposes, and later for cemeteries, then for private development. Yet this whole sector, to be the home of Cabbagetown, was definitely backward in being taken up. Even Parliament Street had not a house upon it before the early 1830s.

In part, this lack of growth reflected the government clamp upon the Park area. Its properties were not available to common citizens, or only through official thickets discouraging to venture. True, the parliament buildings were relocated to the western quarters of the town in the 1820s; but with them went government officers and potentially prestigious home sites, which only reduced the appeal of the Park further. Yet far more inherent in its slow development was the nature of the land itself. Through it Taddle Creek meandered to the harbour: a separate stream from the Don, it cut off the extension of Queen Street eastward for years (until buried in sewers) by interposing a glum, swampy area known as the Meadow. Moreover, the placid, larger Don spread still wider marshes around its own mouth; while neighbouring Ashbridges Bay was similarly marsh-choked, and a fostering ground for mosquitos and fever. Nor was the area's soil that good, even where not overly wet. In comparison with better land to westward, it was less suited to gardens and orchards than root crops and cabbages. Accordingly, physically more difficult to develop as well as none to prepossessing, the Park acquired a reputation as a backwater, despite initial hopes that it would be the home ground of the provincial political élite.

After the little government and port town of York became the advancing commercial city of Toronto in 1834, its eastern growth still stayed retarded, even though construction rose vigorously west, north and centrally.[5] Yet gradually, and scarcely heralded, poorer elements in the community began to spill beyond the build-up eastern streets of original York, now a declining district where they found cheap shelter.

They spread along both sides of King Street East, and on vacant lands to northward were scattered squatters' shacks and cabbage patches. Quite probably, popular tradition is right in attributing the later-received name of Cabbagetown to proliferating little fields like these, associated as the term was also with poor Irish settlers of the day (both Protestant and Catholic) who traditionally raised the humble green vegetable. Yet it should be kept in mind that such a disparaging label for a local area of low esteem was more generic than specific. Urban places in nineteenth-century North America had their full quota of similar Shantytowns, Paddytowns, Corktowns and so on. Nevertheless, a loosely applied nick-name of this sort could become an enduring badge of identity for a recognized neighbourhood community: and so it had become for "Cabbage Town" (at first two words) by the time that title appeared in printed works on Toronto in the early 1890s. And however the name evolved, or when, it would stick; as "the Park" did not.

In any event, the easterly population trickle was sufficient by the 1840s to cause the establishment of a second Anglican parish in Toronto, separate from that of St. James, the church of the dominant civic élite. In 1843 Trinity Church, or Little Trinity as it has come to be known, was built on the south side of King just across from Power Street – a block east of Parliament. This attractively designed Victorian Gothic structure was funded by wealthy Anglicans such as Messrs. Gooderham and Worts, leading city millers, distillers and merchants, to serve the largely Ulster-Irish Anglican working populace of the east end.[6] Just south of Little Trinity, in 1848, the philanthropy of brewer Enoch Turner erected the first free schoolhouse in Toronto, again to help serve the disadvantaged residents of the area. And across King, north on Power Street, the Roman Catholics of the city had had St. Paul's from the late 1820s, in its case ministering to the increasing Catholic Irish lower class in this quarter. In consequence, the east end community was acquiring structuring points even before the precincts of future Cabbagetown were widely entered.

The easterly population flow swelled beyond a trickle in the 1850s, after a fresh tide of overseas migration surged into Toronto between 1847 and 1854, chiefly from an Ireland devastated by potato blight, famine and ruthless evictions. While Irish immigrants, more notably

Protestant Ulstermen, had been numerous since the 1830s in Toronto's annual intakes – together with English and Scots – impoverished Catholic Irish now formed the great proportion of the arrivals.[7] Many died tragically in the typhus and cholera epidemics that flooded with them to the city of the closing forties, and left destitute, debilitated survivors in their wake. Still, the large majority did survive and settle, engendering formidable problems of welfare, employment, social adjustment and, most simply, population pressure.[8] Inevitably, many of the newcomers collected in the poorer, eastern fringe of the city. A closely settled Irish area that was dubbed Corktown developed around the focus of Catholic St. Paul's, roughly centring between King and Queen. But many Protestant Irish, along with poorer English and Scots, also gathered further in the east end vicinity, spreading north past Queen to start the real urban settlement of Cabbagetown. Thus it was that the lands in this direction were so much in process of being occupied that the eastern wards of the city took in the former fringe tracts called "liberties" in 1859.

At the same time, the immigrant population push accorded with crucial economic developments in Toronto. From 1850 a new era of prosperity brought expanding enterprises with more jobs and above all, railway building. By the 1860s, when this first rail construction boom had passed, the city had all but been transformed into a regionally dominant railway centre commanding track access to the Upper Lakes, across Ontario to Montreal or Detroit, and down to New York. But more than that, the steam and iron transport growth opened the way for industrialization. Rail traffic spread along Toronto's harbourfront, bringing with it engine and machine works, coal-yards, iron-moulding and forging plants, and steam-driven factories.[9] In particular, many of these activities clustered around the southeastern edge of the city, around the harbour's end and near the Lower Don, where little-used land was cheaply available and accessibility both to docks and incoming rail lines was excellent. This growing industrial concentration in eastern St. Lawrence's Ward featured such sizeable units as the big new gas works, put up in 1855 south of Front past Parliament, the Grand Trunk Railway workshops, the truly massive Toronto Rolling Mills erected in 1857 to supply rails for that line, and the impressive Gooderham and Worts distillery, newly housed in five-story stone buildings in 1859. Moreover, the Don as a water route had early attracted mills and small industrial concerns up its course. These grew in size and number also, so that the eastern industrial development was enlarged by other processing operations, such as wood or hardware manufactories, tanning and meat-packing houses. Altogether, working opportunities in the city's east end by the 1860s could readily urge on its settlement, which hence began to rise rapidly north from Queen, within St. David's Ward.[10]

Maps, directories or city assessment returns can demonstrate the ensuing growth in the Cabbagetown area.[11] For example, a map of 1858 shows an extensive street layout there, with a new Toronto General Hospital built on a Gerrard Street property in 1856, and St. James and Necropolis cemeteries towards the northern end of the locale. But a map of 1862 illustrates a good deal of subdivision proceeding in its southern portion, where small building lots were being parcelled out. Somewhat ironically, the low esteem in which this Park region had long been held eased the way for the creation of such a district of small residences, ones that workers could afford; though adjunct industries and packing plants no doubt helped keep up the area's poor repute. Wealthy landholders and bigger developers, who elsewhere promoted subdivisions and house plots across the park lots of an expanding city, in the main left the Park to little men. Some of the latter improved on early shacks, put up their own houses or in time enlarged them. But mostly it was minor speculators who opened streets in Cabbagetown and erected lines of utilitarian frame houses, largely covered over with roughcast plaster. Numbers of these structures were later bricked, or received a share of showy Victorian gingerbread in fretwork and cast iron, as did more solid brick edifices like local hotels, schools and churches. Overall, however, the Cabbagetown streetscape took characteristic form as plain rows of narrow, gabled residences up to seventeen feet wide, one, or more usually, two stories high and with attics above; perhaps as well displaying a front bay window or an added rear wing; but thinly built, lacking central heating, and boasting privies out behind. Most houses were detached, and had sufficient backyard space for vegetable patches; although there were some attached terraces, notably on older, southern streets of the area. At any rate, by the standards of the time these looked broadly desirable, practical homes to those with little money and few pretensions.

And so this neighbourhood spread onward, filling up with houses from 1860 to 1890, especially as industries continued to spring up in east-end Toronto. The city of the late sixties and early seventies witnessed another economic boom. Then a long period of world-wide deflation set in that brought hard times and business failures through the gloomy later seventies; but Toronto's manufacturing growth picked up powerfully in the eighties; and despite some severe downturns, in general made a major advance in scale on into the nineties. There were more, and larger, factories now to hire the people of Victorian Cabbagetown. As well, they worked as rail and civic employees, in the large stores and big press houses now prominent in the central city to the west, as cabmen, labourers and domestics, or as local artisans, shopkeepers and clerks.[12]

The development of Toronto's streetcar system – horsedrawn from 1861 to 1892, electrified thereafter – may be said to have forwarded the process of residential segregation into income-determined neighbourhoods, whereby the affluent hived off to roomier, suburban retreats opened by streetcars, and the poor collected near to downtown workplaces at lower travel costs. But the extension of carlines no less gave many Cabbagetown dwellers greater mobility in getting to jobs, and fostered the enlargement of their own neighbourhood, while knitting it up more closely. In this respect, the King Street route was carried out to the Don in 1874, when a line was also run up Sherbourne, then east along Carlton and north on Parliament to Winchester. In 1882 tracks were extended from Parliament out Gerrard to the Don, and connected with the Queen crosstown route – which in 1887 was sent on over the river. In 1889 a now thrivingly commercial Parliament Street was double-tracked.[13] Even in the horse-car days, Cabbagetown was thus effectively tied into the city street transport network. The coming of the electric car in the early nineties gave it still more track extensions and much faster service.

Important also in the onward expansion of this neighbourhood was the renewed immigration to Toronto of later Victorian times. The strongly Catholic Irish influx had dwindled away in the mid-fifties and was not to soar again.[14] But a migrant stream from Britain grew once more in the later sixties; and while it did not reach anything like previous flood proportions for a now far larger city, it went on, with varied fluctuations, across the rest of the period. Notably this newer intake derived more largely from England, with fewer Irish and Scots among it.[15] And those it brought were no longer country dwellers or semi-rural cottagers, but inhabitants of an urbanized, industrialized Britain. Consequently they were generally adapted to city occupations, industrial and store employment – and many would move into the developing Cabbagetown as a well-suited residential quarter. Along with Canadian-born inhabitants, chiefly the offspring of earlier Anglo-Celtic arrivals, they consolidated a now maturing neighbourhood, and naturally reinforced its British composition and character. Down at least to the turn of the twentieth century, there were scant non-British, non-English-speaking traces in the neighbourhood, for the smaller wave of continental European migration to the city that rose in the new century came after Cabbagetown had essentially been occupied. In any case, the later Victorian British inflow fitted into that district, continuing its motherland ties, imperialist loyalty and "Anglo-Saxonism." Furthermore, its Protestant predominance was sustained.

Anglican churches in particular arose beyond Little Trinity in the area: St. Peter's in 1866, All Saints in 1874, St. Simon's in 1888 and St. Bartholemew's by 1889. The erection of their parishes in itself illustrated the progressive filling in and structuring of Cabbagetown. Less numerous were major Methodist and Presbyterian churches, such as Berkeley Street Methodist (1871) or St. Enoch's Presbyterian (1891); while the Catholic Church of the Sacred Heart (1888) then stayed a minor focus in contrast to the strongly Catholic convergence around long-established St. Paul's in Corktown below Queen, with its big charitable House of Providence nearby (1857). Moreover, this district version of Toronto the Good, the city of churches, was decidedly evangelical in its dominant tone. Independent chapels of ardent fundamentalist faith, missions, earnest prayer meetings and outdoor revival gatherings also featured the majority Protestant community and further evidenced its outlook.

The population growth that had built up this very identifiable neighbourhood by the 1890s may be substantiated from the census records for St. David's Ward from the 1870s, in terms already noted. In 1871 (allowing for the western section of St. David's of that date which did not form part of Cabbagetown) the population of the latter locale might reasonably be estimated at around 7,000 in a city of some 56,000.[16] In 1881, St. David's, now nearly coterminous with Cabbagetown, held 11,000 in rounded numbers within a city of 96,000.[17] And in 1891, when even more coincident, it had over 22,000 inhabitants in a Toronto of 181,000.[18] The most obvious fact is the doubling of population in the Cabbagetown area over the eighties – a basic product of climbing industrialization and immigration during the decade. Thereafter, the district's own demographic record is submerged within the new and different civic ward system implemented in 1892. For by the early nineties the Cabbagetown locale had clearly been taken up and its community had acquired firm outlines, whether or not out-migration or more crowding-in would subsequently affect its numbers. We have seen when and how it became settled during the Victorian era. It now remains instead to examine the society and life of this emergent neighbourhood.

II

One major aspect of Cabbagetown society was its religious patterning, at a time when Toronto's church ties were pervasive, whatever class ranks, and taken pretty seriously. Census statistics for the seventies affirm the area's notably Protestant complexion, yet tell more. The figures for extended St. David's in 1871 show about 7,400 inhabitants belonging to the chief Protestant denominations to some 3,000 Catholics.[19] And though it again has to be observed that this ward then still reached west to Jarvis Street and so included others besides Cabbagetowners, there is no cause to think that the religious ratio would have been greatly different if we had just the Cabbagetown section to go on. The census returns of 1881, for a St. David's reduced much more to our area, may be considered in more detail. They report 2,410 Catholics to 3,937 Anglicans, 2,095 Methodists and 1,449 Presbyterians, which (with 632 Baptists added) give a main Protestant majority of 8,113, even without other small sects.[20] Finally, the 1891 returns in a St. David's which by then virtually coincided with Cabbagetown show 3,992 Catholics to 7,166 Anglicans, 5,081 Methodists, 4,200 Presbyterians and 1,088 Baptists: or a main Protestant majority of 17,535 in a far more populous local community.[21] Three points stand out: the Catholic element had grown by less than a third over the eighties; the Anglicans had nearly doubled, and remained much the largest single denomination; while the Methodists and Presbyterians had more than doubled.

The process that in consequence produced a still more Protestant Cabbagetown can surely be linked to the relative decline of Catholic Irish immigration since the 1850s and to the continued flow of English and Scots into Toronto, even though natural increase of native-born and movement from the countryside to city jobs also affected the neighbourhood. Here we need a closer look at the ethnic origins and birthplaces of its members, and for that must focus on the 1881 census by wards. The ethnic figures for the St. David's Ward of 1871 are risky to apply specifically to Cabbagetown, while the 1891 census did what censuses too often do, change category units, rendering it of little value for a relevant comparison on nationalities.[22] At any rate, statistics for 1881, in the midst of the area's principal growth period, showed for St. David's 4,562 residents of English origin, 1,305 of Scottish, and 4,548 of Irish stock. The last-named group of course comprised both Protestant and Catholic elements. Since in that day Toronto's Catholics were overwhelmingly Irish-derived, it seems meaningful to subtract the contemporary Catholic component given for St. David's in 1881 from the Irish ethnic total, which gives a figure of 2,138. Almost certainly, this to a great extent represented the Protestant Irishmen of the ward. In other words, probably close to half the Irish residents in Cabbagetown of the eighties were of Orange rather than Green affinity. Beyond these main ethnic groups, only about 260 each of French or German origin were then reported for the area, 6 "Russian-Polish," 10 Swiss, 5 Scandinavians and 18 "Africans."[23] There were no Italians, Jews, Dutch or Chinese listed. An Anglo-Celtic bailiwick indeed, if neither English nor Irish entirely.

As for birthplaces, the English element in 1881 contained the largest number of homeland-born, 1,924 or over 42 per cent.[24] The Irish correspondingly displayed nearly 34 per cent of similar overseas origin, the Scots about 32 per cent. Totalling these segments against the area majority of Canadian birth (but Anglo-Celtic stock) gives to the neighbourhood of 1881 a non-native component of around 40 per cent, still a high proportion when one considers that this comes just after the migration lull around the close of the seventies when hard times ruled Toronto. And since the city's British intake swelled again over the eighties into the nineties, it is altogether probable that Cabbagetown did maintain its large immigrant ingredient throughout the rest of the period. It remained, in short, both an Anglo-conformist stronghold and a home of migrants from the United Kingdom. That it held only 379 of United States birth in 1881 indicates that any American component was very limited. Yet it did play host to another small and rather different group of newcomers: French Canadians, about 250 by 1881, who had been brought there to work in a local tannery. They formed the nucleus of the Sacred Heart Catholic congregation, but hardly affected the ethnic nature of the community.

Another socio-cultural aspect of the Cabbagetown neighbourhood appeared in the schooling of its young, traceable from city educational records.[25] The public school system, that became free in the 1850s and compulsory in the early seventies, was naturally paramount in this Victorian quarter, where Catholic separate schools then played a very minor role. Among the main public schools of the area were Park School (1853), Parliament Street (1872), Winchester Street (1874), Lord Dufferin (1877), Rose Avenue (1884) and Sackville Street (1888). Park particularly had a tough reputation, but a survey of the school inspector's reports shows that the most evident and endemic local school crime was absenteeism, in which Park at times ranked high for all Toronto.[26] Absenteeism, however, was a widespread problem in poorer city schools of the seventies and generally declined thereafter. It was largely ascribed to pupils being kept home through family poverty and sickness, long distances to travel to school over unimproved roads, and needs for children to supplement household earnings. More schools, streets with sidewalks, stiffer truancy measures, child labour restrictions – and, hopefully, better living standards and health services – made regular school attendance far more the rule by the 1890s.[27] In any event, Cabbagetown's schools were by no means at the bottom of the educational record. On the whole one gets the impression that our neighbourhood was hard-working and earnestly striving after respectability in education also. There do not seem to have been rowdy blackboard jungles in this morally conservative family community.

The trustees who represented the area on the city's public school board are worth some comment.[28] Two were elected annually for the St. David's Ward, until school districts replaced wards as designated units in 1892. These representatives during the period came from the locality's limited élite – professionals and businessmen who maintained homes, offices or firms in the area. Three trustees who served repeated annual terms and in the time became board chairmen were E.P. Roden, a newspaperman, Edward Galley, a confectioner, and the physician Dr. R.A. Pyne. Roden, in fact, held office from 1874 to 1897 while being a reporter or editor on successive city papers such as the *Leader*, the *Mail* and the *News*, and later a city hall official. The eldest son of a large family of Protestant Irish immigrants, he eventually had a school named after him. Galley, trustee from 1873 onward, was an alderman for St. Thomas's Ward just to the west through the later eighties, while Pyne, who replaced him on the school board in 1884, by the early twentieth century sat as a Toronto Conservative member in the provincial legislature, and became a Minister of Education.

This community acceptance of rule by its upper crust was plainly witnessed in municipal politics also. Those who constituted St. David's aldermen through the seventies to nineties were area business and professional men, along with some industrial figures and successful artisans advancing as employers.[29] Among them were the ward's longest serving aldermen, William Adamson (1873-1885), the manager of the Toronto Tea Company, and the lawyer John Blevins (1875-1884). Others with several terms included Thomas Allen, a brewer residing on River Street; James Martin, proprietor of the Ontario Engine Works; William H. Gibbs, a painter-contractor; John C. Swait, superintendent of the Toronto Harbour Works; and Daniel Lamb, owner of a blacking and glue factory, who kept a large home on Winchester Street and sent his children to Rose Avenue school. Lamb was subsequently an alderman for Ward Two. As for Robert F. Fleming, who ran a coal and wood business on Parliament in the eighties, then moved into real estate, he rose from alderman to be mayor of the city in 1892 and 1896, and thereafter manager of the Toronto Street Railway Company. Wholesale importers and upholsterers, more manufacturers and lawyers, might be added to the list; yet it all makes plain that proletarian voices or labour radicals were not noteworthy in Cabbagetown civic politics of the day. By and large, public affairs were left to a British-cast, conservative-minded (and Protestant-engrained) leadership element, which had some degree of affluence and social prestige. And if they lacked the wealth of the really rich found in other areas, their rule was not very different from that of Toronto politicos elsewhere, with whom they were well integrated.

Inherently linked both with the politics and the dominant sentiments of this society was the Orange Order. A recent work on the Order in Canada, by Cecil Houston and William Smyth, demonstrates that its membership was widespread across later Victorian Toronto, with lowest density in the upper-class residential tracts of Jarvis Street and Rosedale, but highest in Cabbagetown. No doubt the numerous Ulster Irish in that neighbourhood had much to do with the case. Yet Houston and Smyth confirm that the Order drew widely on English and Scottish stocks also, and it had strong followings in all three major Toronto Protestant churches, Anglican, Methodist and Presbyterian, especially the first two – which were also the largest in Cabbagetown. Smaller Protestant denominations like Baptists or Lutherans were much less evident in Orangeism, as they were also in Cabbagetown.[30] At the same time, the Order crossed class lines, and kept a substantial middle-class component, even if the bulk of its members came from the lower classes. "Orangemen were not a segregated minority confined to either economic or ethnic ghettos."[31] As much could be said of the Cabbagetowners in Victorian Toronto. Their Orange hue was markedly bright, one they shared with the Protestant city about them.

Orange lodges pervaded the district, but a main meeting place for their members was the eastern Orange Hall on Queen. Here was a forum for their views on public issues, and a headquarters for political transactions. The Orange vote in Toronto mattered, municipally, provincially and federally. Orangemen were perennial among civic politicians and plentiful in city employment, whether at city hall, the works department or in the police force, for all of which Cabbagetown residents offered a goodly quota. It is unnecessary, however to view this as some dark conspiratorial net, a King Billy underground. Orange ties, for better or worse, operated pretty openly; and it would have been hard to impugn the respectability of the Order's stands on British loyalty and Protestant freedom to majority Toronto then. Cabbagetowners marched on the Orange celebration day, 12 July, but almost as virtuously as in a temperance or trades union parade. Granted there were fights and uproars in Toronto associated with the Glorious Twelfth or Hibernian St. Patrick's Day; still, violence chiefly occurred in more turbulent and crowded areas of the city. For our neighbourhood, Orangeism broadly implied order rather than disorder. Furthermore, it has been pointed out that Toronto's denser residential districts really contained religious admixtures, and there were no great separate, terraced confines of either Protestants or Catholics, as in Belfast, mass citadels for religious warfare.[32] In Cabbagetown, assuredly, Protestants had many Catholic street-neighbours; the converse was equally true in adjacent, prevalently Catholic Corktown south of Queen and on below King. There hence was not the same tight territorial basis for major sectarian combat. Sparring there might be, as when an Orange band trumpetted and coat-trailed into a largely Catholic street; yet this local version of "chicken" was a fairly minor fringe sport.

If the Cabbagetown community was not an ethno-religious enclave, for all its Orange display, or a politically sequestered compound, then was it set off as an economic precinct of poverty? Obviously it was one of the poorer areas of Toronto. City assessment records for St. David's Ward from the seventies to the nineties broadly show it as near the bottom in ward returns for the value of real and personal property. Nevertheless, they also demonstrate an overall rise in property worth for St. David's across the period, despite some depression downturns. Expansion of settlement and the rise of bigger industrial units in the district would explain some of this increased value; but at least the general trend was strongly upward. In 1874, the first full year after St. David's was cut back to quasi-Cabbagetown limits, it returned a real-property assessment of $1,737,646, a personal-property one of $88,005. In 1881 the respective values were $2,952,543 and $100,300; in 1891, $7,827,138 and $322,650. And the total assessment for the ward (also including land income) advanced between 1874 and 1891 from $1,857,201 to $8,195,096, a more than fourfold gain in a largely deflationary period.[33] The rise was not astronomical, but it was significant. Cabbagetown was amassing dollar and tax value, not declining slum-ward. Besides, though it was unquestionably an area of small, lower-priced houses, these were regularly being improved, while home ownership was growing. And there were some larger dwellings, as both political and assessment records illustrate, along with a middle-class presence that was not only politically ascendant, but also widened the social context from that of a purely working-class quarter.[34] In brief, if Victorian Cabbagetown predominantly held wage-earners and many on the subsistence edge, it was not simply a proletarian conflux, but had an essentially wider economic and social make-up.[35]

Middle-class values dominated the area's schools, as they did its political life, and largely its churches and social mores. Conceivably, too, if a Cabbagetown workingman came to detest an obdurate factory boss, he was more likely to impute personal faults than those of the economic system. He could keep up his own hopes of upward mobility when he was himself only a generation (if that) away from immigrant arrival – by which time he seemed already to have made a place in the land of opportunity, where diligence, thrift and honest toil would surely pay off. Hence conscious class conflict was no more a distinguishing feature of the neighbourhood society than was explosive religious warfare. That is not to depict it as a docile, peaceable kingdom: it had its angers, unruly spirits and share of social crime.[36] Yet it cannot be regarded as seething with deprivations and repressed discontents. It kept its own lid on, hoped soberly but rootedly, and made the best of daily living, as sound Torontonians should.

Daily living meant still coping with common facts of Cabbagetown existence: the nevertheless drab environment as blemished by industrialism, and the struggles which the bulk of residents repeatedly faced against sickness and want. Drabness appeared in monotonous little streets of box-like, meagerly built homes. Blight stemmed from the dirt, debris and fumes of factories close at hand, their industrial dumps and coal heaps – not to mention stockyards, livery stables, cow barns, and all their refuse. Some of these offences were right in the district, but other major offenders lay not too far off on the south, such as the reeking hog pens of the big William Davis Company's meat-packing plant, or the cattle herded at Gooderham and Worts to feed on used brewing mash.

All these posed serious threats to area health, compounded by dangers from choked privies, overflowing cesspools and contaminated wells, in a district thinly served by the civic water system.[37]

Health conditions, however, improved from the early eighties, when Toronto's pioneer medical health officer, Dr. William Canniff, took up the tasks of sanitary reform. Deadly epidemics such as typhus and cholera had departed, in spite of a scare in the 1860s. Canniff's work checked the ravages of smallpox, though diphtheria, tuberculosis and pneumonia remained killers in Cabbagetown. Still, the worst "public nuisances" were progressively brought under control; water mains and indoor plumbing spread (though more slowly than in better-off districts); and overall death rates curved steadily downward toward the end of the century. Pasteurized milk and civic water safe from sewage contamination had yet to be assured; but the incessant burdens of sickness were lessening.[38]

The burdens of want continued for most, with recurrent ups and downs. None the less, enlarging city welfare activities, local self-help, and patterns of communal assistance gave varied but altogether valuable measure of support. Welfare agencies were more than local; but notably present for the area were the Irish Protestant Benevolent Society, the Girl's Home established on Gerrard in 1871, the Boy's Home to the west on George beyond it, and the Catholic House of Providence south of Queen, which sheltered Protestants as well.[39] The Toronto General Hospital on Gerrard, two medical schools and the Ontario Medical College for Women, built on Sumach in 1891, together afforded some doctoring and dispensary services. With regard to self-help, the neighbourhood poor all too plainly expressed it in their yearly contests with the cold: collecting firewood from the broken crates at the St. Lawrence Market, picking over the ash heaps at the gas works for stove coals, liberating still more from factory stockpiles. And as to communal aid, here the small grocery stores of the locality played a crucial role. Each was a centre of neighbourly transactions, news and gossip; each had its own few street blocks of family clientele. Collectively, they sustained their customers with store credit between pay days, and often over far longer spans of illness or unemployment. Many an overextended storekeeper certainly went down, taking his ledger losses with him; yet by and large debts were faithfully honoured by customers, with more than practical necessity as their motive. Mutual help further gave comfort in times of sickness and death. The neighbours stood close: a statement of simple reality, not wishful sentiment. For joint, informal obligations were intrinsic in neighbourhood living.

Community life found a relieving side, however, in recreations. One great benefit Cabbagetown did have was ready access to the open expanses of the Don Valley on the east. Its slopes may largely have been too abrupt to build on, its bottom too dank, even when not subject to flood. But here still was room: bush for children to explore, flats for lacrosse and football, water reaches for summer boating and bathing, for winter skating, shinny and curling. This was an unkempt parkland, but it was Cabbagetown's. Its grass and trees, its play and rambling space, offset the bleak confines of the adjoining built environment. Then the opening of Riverdale Park in 1880 brought lasting official designation to the open tract, wherein a municipal Riverdale Zoo (fathered by Alderman Daniel Lamb) became another district attraction from 1894. In any event, the outdoor engagements of the parkland, the indoor recreations of choirs, church dinners and bazaars, of the Orange Hall – or many a bar and pool hall – showed that the neighbourhood surely did not take its leisures glumly. And festal days like the Glorious Twelfth (of course) or the Queen's Birthday on 24 May were enthusiastic mass celebrations. Austere, withdrawn Puritanism was hardly an attribute of this lively local society.

III

Where, in summary, does one place nineteenth-century Cabbagetown in Toronto's ethnic and communal development? It definitely was not some kind of a WASP ghetto. It could not be, when it formed part of the city's "social majority," and was effectively tied into the prevailing Anglo-conformity in political as well as social terms – even in its very Orangeism. It was equally not a slum, despite bleak spots of blight, or living conditions that could better be called pinched than poverty-stricken. The local populace displayed cohesiveness, vitality and confidence; they had rising property values, improving health and environmental controls, mostly separate housing; and freely attainable recreation space. Nor was this an economic enclave either. While chiefly occupied by wage-earners lacking capital, it also held influential middle-class components, and by no means functioned as a consciously proletarian district. Finally, though its immigrant origins were as apparent as its resulting ethnic and religious composition, the community was not clearly characterized by language and cultural differences, by problems of heritage defence and adaptation, or by traits of temporary sojourning, so common to many other urban immigrant experiences in Canada or the United States.[40] What then was this Cabbagetown?

A neighbourhood. A locality with perceived limits and identity, with internal bonding, a built environment and a history of its own; thereby comprising an integral but distinctive part of the larger urban society. The study of neighbourhoods such as this one is an essential ingredient of urban history. Not the least of its value is the salutary check it brings when generalizations or models applied to the urban sphere come up against local realities. The emergence of neighbourhoods, most obviously, cannot only be viewed in the light of immigrant segregation, even in a land of migrants, nor as the result alone of geographic apportionment, economic sorting or class separation. All these and other factors have their various mixes and impacts – including timing, opportunity and human evaluation. But neighbourhoods come in different shapes and weaves. The record of Toronto asserts as much; and the specific case of Cabbagetown decidedly illustrates the point.

This is not to conclude that particularism is everything. Common aspects of local Toronto experience surely existed also. Our specific neighbourhood was quite typically built by newcomers, the products of immigrant intake, and went on receiving them across its building years. Its Protestant churches and chapels were as focal as the homeland churches and synagogues which later arrivals established in other forming localities. The Orange lodges were its own equivalents of national and benevolent societies, while the street store-circle was as basic to local joint-survival. Still further, the community faced hard physical conditions and disparagement from outside, yet not only persisted, but also developed property-holders, a local middle class and leadership of its own.[41] No doubt European migrants slightly later in "the Ward" area just west of the downtown city core found a much rougher road ahead of them: still worse housing and living conditions, language and cultural barriers, and prejudices much deeper than disparagement that attributed social evils, crime and violence to their clustering, far beyond any poor repute known to Cabbagetown. Still, the affinities were real. They were, in fact, parallel themes in the development of newer, poorer Toronto neighbourhoods. Cabbagetown does not stand unique in a story that runs from early Corktown to the Ward, and on to "the Junction" district of today, in the continued expansion of a teeming city.

Endnotes

1. For basic background on the spatial, social and economic growth of Toronto of the period, see Jacob Spelt, *Toronto* (Toronto, 1973), esp. chapter 4; D.C. Masters, *The Rise of Toronto, 1850-1890* (Toronto, 1947); and P.G. Goheen, *Victorian Toronto, 1850 to 1890* (Toronto, 1970), chapters 1, 3, 4, 6, 7.
2. Hugh Garner, *Cabbagetown* (Toronto, 1950, reprinted 1968). The preface quoted is in the 1968 edition, p. vii.
3. The account in McAree's *Cabbagetown Store* (Toronto, 1953) may be enlarged and substantiated from contemporary newspapers, civic archival records, social statistics and city directory analysis. In drawing the picture of Cabbagetown – and throughout the article to follow – I have been much helped by the kindness of Mr. George Rust D'Eye who allowed me to read his now published work, *Cabbagetown* (Erin, Ont., 1984) in manuscript, which contained a good deal of very valuable information.
4. For the history of the changing territorial limits of St. David's Ward, and neighbouring St. Lawrence's Ward, see maps and records at the City of Toronto Archives (hereafter TCA), particularly the typescript on the "Development of the Ward System."
5. F.H. Armstrong, "Toronto in Transition, 1828-1838" (Ph.D., University of Toronto, 1965), pp. 12-17, 23-30, 43-4. See also F.H. Armstrong and Gordon Pitts, *Toronto: The Place of Meeting* (Toronto: Windsor Publications, 1983).
6. Masters, *Rise of Toronto*, p. 30; Eric Arthur, *Toronto, No Mean City* (Toronto, 1964), pp. 80-81.
7. Nearly 90,000 migrants from the British Isles entered at the port of Quebec in 1847, the great famine year, of whom over 54,000 were Irish, some 31,000 English and 3,700 Scottish. See H.I. Cowan, *British Emigration to British North America* (Toronto, 1961), appendix B, table 1, p. 289. By early 1848 more than 30,000 in this wave had swept on to, or through, Toronto (*British Colonist* [Toronto] 8 February 1848), when the city's resident population was then only about 23,000. Through 1853 Irish entries were greatly preponderant, though in 1854, the last sizeable year in this migra-

tion phase, arrivals at Quebec stood at approximately 18,000 English, 16,000 Irish and 6,000 Scots (Cowan, *British Emigration*, p. 289).

8. D.S. O'Shea, "The Irish Immigrant Adjustment to Toronto: 1840-1865," graduate research paper, University of Toronto, 1972, pp. 18-38.
9. See *Globe* (Toronto) 12 February 1866, for descriptions (including work forces) of major industrial establishments.
10. A map in Goheen, *Victorian Toronto*, p.129, "Distribution of Employment in Toronto, 1860," graphically illustrates the dense clustering of chiefly industrial jobs in the southeastern corner of the city.
11. Contemporary maps and assessment records are found at TCA. Toronto yearly directories which not only show residential spread but occupations of residents, are far more usable when they give a street-by-street treatment, as most do at least from 1868.
12. Directory information from the sixties to nineties provides the basis for this general summation.
13. L.H. Pursley, *Street Railways of Toronto, 1861-1921* (Los Angeles, 1968), pp. 7-10.
14. For example, in the migration ebb of the later 1850s, Irish landings at Quebec fell from a low 4,100 in 1855 to a minute 410 by 1861, while English entries led with 6,700 and 7,700 at the same respective dates (Rounded numbers: see *Government of Canada, Report of the Department of Citizenship and Immigration, 1860-61* [Ottawa, 1961], p. 28.) Of course Irish landings rose somewhat in the renewed phases of British migration to Canada over the late sixties through eighties, which had their own lulls interspersed. But the Irish proportion of the whole intake did not regain preponderance (*ibid.*)
15. Immigrant arrivals just for Toronto, as available over the later Victorian years, make the pattern evident. For instance, the numbers listed of English, Irish and Scots entrants to the city (in that order) were for 1869: 7,275, 811, 1,548; for 1874: 7,694, 1,530, 1,995; for 1878 (example of a depressed year): 2,706, 646, 979; and for 1880 (time of partial recovery): 3,982, 2,288, 1,225. (See Ontario Archives, "Immigrants' Arrivals to Toronto, Statistical Returns, 1868-1881," XLVI, n.d. handwritten.)
16. *Census of Canada, 1871*, I, p. 114. The total figure for the St. David's of that year was 11,229. In view of the much older and denser development of the western, non-Cabbagetown section of this ward at that date, to assign its larger but newer Cabbagetown portion around 60 per cent of the count seems safety conservative for 1871.
17. *Ibid., 1881*, I, p. 73.
18. *Ibid., 1891*, I, p. 174.
19. *Ibid., 1871*, pp. 114-15. If anything, the Protestant ratio for Cabbagetown alone might have been a bit higher; since the older western section of St. David's in 1871 likely held more Catholics – as is strongly suggested by the

denominational charts compiled for the settled city of 1851-61 in Shea, "Irish Adjustment," appendices. In any event, it is unwise to use the 1871 census figures for St. David's to convey much more than the general but sizeable Protestant ascendancy in our locale that was attained by that time. Closer applications concerning specific church numbers run into too many uncertainties of linkage between the total ward figures and the Cabbagetown community itself. The same is true regarding statistics of birthplaces and national origins: the 1871 census is not a sufficiently indicative key to them, since the fit between the St. David's of the day and its Cabbagetown content was still too loose before 1873.

20. I*bid.*, *1881*, I,pp. 174-75.
21. *Ibid.*, *1891*, I, 282-83.
22. Regarding the census of 1871, see note 19 above. As for ethnic patterns later than 1881, it could be noted that the census of 1901 did at least present "origins" by wards, and here it may be somewhat illustrative to mark the wide Ward Two that from 1892 included most of Cabbagetown. For what it is worth, the 1901 statistics for this successor ward enumerate (rounded) 15,000 of English ancestry, 11,800 Irish, 5,800 Scottish – and specifically, 1,153 "Germans," 299 Jewish, 61 "African" and 42 Italian, among other small components. But the 1881 census affords the closest analysis.
23. *Ibid.*, *1881*,pp.276-77.
24. *Ibid.*, pp. 374-75.
25. The Educational Centre Archives of the City of Toronto (hereafter ECA) provide primary materials here, while H. M. Cochrane, ed., *Centennial Story: The Board of Education for the City of Toronto, 1850-1950* (Toronto, 1950), gives a secondary account of public school developments.
26. ECA, Annual Reports of the Inspector of the Public Schools, 1873-91.
27. Cochrane, *Centennial Story*, pp. 70-71, 80, 86. See also ECA, Annual School Reports which also show an improving teacher-pupil ratio for most area schools over the 1880s. Winchester, for example, went from 72 pupils per teacher in 1881 to 49 in 1892, Parliament from 62 to 38, though others altered less.
28. For trustees of the area, see Annual School Reports and biographical information available at ECA.
29. For aldermen elected in St. David's Ward over the period, and their occupations, see a convenient appendix provided on city council members in Victor Russell, *Mayors of Toronto, I: 1834-1899* (Erin, Ont., 1982), and biographical files at TCA.
30. C.J. Houston and W. J. Smyth, *The Sash Canada Wore: A Historical Geography of the Orange Order in Canada* (Toronto, 1980), pp. 108, 104.
31. *Ibid.*, p. 106. This book criticizes the view of G.S. Kealey that the Order of Toronto was "overwhelmingly working-class" ("The Orange Order in To-

ronto," in G.S. Kealey and P. Warrian, eds., *Essays in Canadian Working-Class History* [Toronto, 1976], pp. 13-35), and effectively shows how it bridged classes and contained a wide occupational mix.

32. *Ibid.*, p. 109; Shea, "Irish Adjustment," pp. 19-21.
33. TCA, Appendix, Minutes of City Council, Commissioner's Assessment Returns for St. David's Ward, 1874-92. Figures given are for original assessments.
34. This can be well discerned from city directories as examined from the later sixties to mid-nineties. For example, the house occupants listed for the streets of the locality in 1878, a well reported year (See *Toronto Directory for 1878*, Might and Taylor, Toronto, 1878), show residents who were porters, teamsters, rail and factory workers, carpenters and other skilled tradesmen, firemen, book-keepers and so on. But also listed are commercial travellers, retailers, wholesalers and insurance agents, builders, company superintendents and factory owners, plus professionals from physicians and clerics to civil engineers. No doubt but few in the upper ranks grew highly affluent, and no doubt they gathered more on "better" streets like Winchester than, say, Sumach. Still, their local presence was widespread; and checks carried to 1895 reveal little essential change.
35. McAree notes few white-collar workers in his store's vicinity (*Cabbagetown Store*, p. 65), but also observes, "few of our customers were conscious of poverty" (p. 9). In general, his view of a community that yet showed little class polarization or worker self-awareness is borne out by George Rust D'Eye's research, and by the sources used for our study.
36. While statistical civic reports on "crime committed" are found at TCA in Council Minutes, relevant police records for the Cabbagetown area over the period have been lost or damaged. Nevertheless from what is left, but mainly through newspapers and other impressionistic accounts, one may infer that Cabbagetown did not stand out from other areas for crime and violence in the general city mind, and certainly was not regarded as a distinctive threat to public order and morality in the way that the Ward would be.
37. See Heather McDougall, "Health is Wealth: Development of Public Health Activity in Toronto, 1834-1890" (Ph.D., University of Toronto, 1981), chapters 6-7 particularly for sanitary conditions.
38. *Ibid.* See also H. McDougall, "Public Health in Toronto's Municipal Politics, 1883-90," *Bulletin of the History of Medicine*, LV, pp. 186-202.
39. For the significant Irish Protestant Benevolent Society see its records at Metropolitan Toronto Public Library. The main, public-aided, non-sectarian House of Industry lay in the western half of the city.
40. Cabbagetown undoubtedly took in boarders, especially after rising house prices and rents became felt in filling core neighbourhoods during the 1880s (Shea, "Irish Adjustment," p. 21). C.S. Clark's somewhat sensation-

alized depiction of the city's darker sides in the late nineties, *Of Toronto the Good* (Montreal, 1898), notes this trend continuing (p. 3). Yet our district evidenced relatively few boardinghouses and still less tenements in the time-span covered; while its inhabitants were more chiefly engaged in regular city employments, not the seasonal work-gangs of sojourners. Nuclear families in individual houses remained the general rule.

41. McAree's own account displays the ascent of a poor Ulster Irish immigrant family to local middle-class status. They not only ran their store (in a house with indoor plumbing), but also gained rent income from other, small store and house properties (p. 29). That certainly did not ensure economic prosperity since their own store finally folded: another aspect of immigrant precariousness. Still, on yet another side, the rising Ulster alderman from Cabbagetown and subsequent mayor, Robert Fleming, was McAree's uncle – but not an Orange Conservative; instead, a relative rarity, a Toronto Liberal who reached top civic office. Here, too, the particulars of history both confirm and qualify generalizations on immigrant and neighbourhood development.

Prince David with Canadian troops aboard for the "raid" on the British Columbian coast, 1942.

Submarines, Princes and Hollywood Commandos, or At Sea in B.C.

NO ONE COULD QUESTION THE significance of naval history for this ocean-bordered region. But I don't intend to deal with its high strategic import; merely to examine certain lighter aspects of the British Columbian naval story, memorable happenings in two World Wars. This will not be a particularly well-connected narrative of separated events, linked up by some central message – unless this be that only in British Columbia were such things likely to take place. Everything grows so profusely and luxuriantly on this mild and humid coast, even the odder undergrowth of history. You could find it harder to conceive of such doings on the bleaker, more staid east coast. At any rate, it is truly said that wackiness did not begin with W.A.C. Bennett in B.C.

I have two main exemplary tales to offer. The first concerns submarines on the west coast during World War I. But it is really just a curtain-raiser, since I can assume that the learned gathering present has already heard of British Columbia's brief career as a naval power in 1914, with the submarines, CC1 and CC2, the only completely submersible navy of the period – intentionally submersible, that is. Still further, you might already know of an excellent article on the submarines' role and activities written by Gilbert Norman Tucker: my old boss at Naval Service Headquarters in Ottawa for a period during World War II, and later Professor of History at UBC. His own account appeared in the *British Columbia Historical Quarterly* for 1943, but a good story is worth re-telling, and, in any case, the younger historians here may not have worked back into the dim antiquity of the defunct BCHQ.[1] And so I offer a come-on with the First War submarines, before turning to a fuller treatment of some Second War events.

Recall the situation on the North Pacific coast at the close of July 1914 (you will know it well), as Anglo-German conflict was about to break out, and the British Admiralty sent its warning telegram to Royal Navy forces around the world. An elderly British cruiser squadron lay far down in South American waters; a more modern German squadron under Admiral von Spee was at large in the western Pacific, with two cruisers, the *Leipzig* and *Nürnburg*, probably off the coast of Mexico. Actually, the former was in a Mexican port, while the latter was ranging off the Hawaiian Islands. But to defend British Columbian waters, in the event of a quite possible raid, there was only the over-age *Rainbow* of the recently founded Royal Canadian Navy – under-manned and under-armed besides – and within possible supporting distance the small Royal Navy sloops, *Algerine* and *Shearwater*. Victoria and Vancouver were virtually open to assault. Almost anything would help. And there were two new-fangled submarines being built for the Chilean navy in Seattle nearby, on which payments were in arrears, since the Chileans thought them overweight and so of insufficient endurance at sea.

The answer arose out of a meeting held on July 29 at Victoria's Union Club. There a little group of city business men, including Captain W.H. Logan of the London Salvage Association, conferred with the president of the Seattle Construction and Drydock Company, J.V. Patterson, builder of the submarines. They learned that the two vessels just might be available – at a price, that is. Chile was to have paid $818,000 for the pair; Patterson now would take $1,150,000 – he knew a good thing, indeed. The next few days saw busy conferences in Victoria, as Sir Richard McBride, provincial premier, got into the act, along with officers from the Esquimalt naval dockyard and Martin Burrell, federal member for Yale-Cariboo and Minister of Agriculture in the Borden government, who chanced to be on holiday in Victoria at the time. Anxious efforts were made to have Ottawa authorize the purchase of the boats, but the discussion turned on their usefulness in the current naval situation, so that the Commander-in-Chief Esquimalt wired Naval Service Headquarters in Ottawa, who cabled the Admiralty – twice – without immediate reply. Presumably their Lordships were too busy getting steam up in the Grand Fleet at Scapa Flow to give speedy attention to far-off British Columbian waters. At any rate, recognizing that delay until after a British declaration of war could mean that a neutral United States would refuse to release the vessels, McBride resolved to act on his own. He agreed to buy them with provincial funds: the key step to British Columbia acquiring its very own navy.

On August 4 a somewhat cloak-and-dagger mission from Victoria met with Patterson in Seattle to close the deal. It consisted of Logan and Sub-Lieutenant T.A. Brown, RCNVR, the latter disguised as a cook, and evidently intended to smell out any German agents among the construction company's submarine staff. Patterson insisted the price was non-negotiable, but he would deliver the subs to Canadian waters. That night, as the British Empire went to war, the submarines crept out of Seattle harbour on their quiet electric motors (for undersea use), not starting up their noisy diesel engines until safely at sea. By morning light they had reached their rendezvous point, five miles south of Trial Island. Here the Canadian ship *Salvor* met them with Lieutenant-Commander Bertram Jones aboard. A retired Royal Navy officer with several years of experience in submarines, he carried with him a cheque for $1,150,000 drawn by the Province of British Columbia on the Canadian Bank of Commerce. Jones inspected the new craft thoroughly; Patterson, eager to be off, got his money; British flags were hoisted, and the little war fleet proceeded to Esquimalt, arriving there on the morning of August 5.

It almost didn't, for its sudden unexpected appearance caused widespread alarm in Esquimalt that the Germans were on their way. The examination ship on duty outside the harbour dashed madly for safety, with her siren lashed open, bleating continuous alarm. The shore batteries, manned by the Army, had not been told of the arrival and were making ready to fire, but fortunately somebody telephoned the Dockyards first – fortunately, indeed, or the British Columbian navy, with few men trained to dive it (or get back up if they did) might have been eliminated on its first morning.

In actuality, it was to have but a brief provincial existence, as the federal government moved in to take it over. The Admiralty had now replied, approving acquisition of the boats; and Borden on August 5, the very day of their arrival, transmitted that news to McBride along with warm appreciation of the latter's action. A nice touch followed when Naval Headquarters signalled Esquimalt the same day, "Prepare to purchase submarines," and Esquimalt answered, "Have purchased submarines."[2] On August 7 the Government of Canada took on their purchase price, and the vessels became a regular part of the Royal Canadian Navy as HMCS CC1 and CC2, under the Admiralty's overall wartime control.

The submarines' saga was still only at its beginning, however. They yet lacked crews and armament; they were a purely nominal factor in the naval balance. Another trained submariner was uncovered, Lieutenant Adrian Keyes, R.N. retired, then working in the Toronto offices of the Canadian Northern Railway. He was hastily packed off to the west coast to command one sub while Jones took charge of the other. They directed the training of Victoria volunteers for the crews, with only a few old naval hands among them. And 18-inch torpedoes had to be sent out all the way from HMCS *Niobe* stationed at Halifax, jouncing their way by rail across Canada. One by mistake travelled with a filled compressed air chamber. If it had taken off in the mountains, it could have derailed the train and jammed a trans-continental tunnel – as one of the German navy's cheapest inland victories. But the torpedoes arrived intact. And it was not found out till later that the reason the crucial Kingston valves (which controlled filling and blowing the subs' ballast tanks for diving and surfacing) did not seem to work right was that inadvertently a piece of two-inch plank had been left sloshing around inside one tank and a pair of workman's overalls in the other. Such are the countless hazards of life at sea – or rather beneath it. Still, the tricky, crowded and uncomfortable CC1 and CC2 were brought to do their job efficiently; and it was an important job at that.

They became, in fact, effective units of sea defence, able to guard the restricted approaches to B.C.'s most vital coastal waters, her chief cities and main waterborne traffic. Beyond that, however, was their *pres-*

ence, and the knowledge of it. For three years they patrolled out from Esquimalt, until in 1917, with the United States in the war – and Von Spee's fleet long since destroyed by British forces at the Battle of Falkland Isles – they were sent eastward to the Atlantic war zone. Yet perhaps the submarines' greatest role and service was in the opening days of war in 1914. Then their presence mattered highly – for one thing, in stilling public anxieties over the apparent defencelessness of the west coast. When the war broke out, banks in Victoria and Vancouver started sending their funds inland. Citizens bought millions of dollars worth of bombardment insurance – and one Victoria family converted its cemetery vault into a bomb shelter. Moreover, the then Senior Naval Officer at Esquimalt, overworked and overwrought, went rather round the bend, ranging the streets to fight off Germans. The scare might have enlarged to panic had it not been that the press, learning of the submarines' arrival on August 5, thankfully took to spreading the word of the impressive, latest modern instruments of war that had now appeared to save the Far West of Canada. The *Colonist* and *Times* trumpeted the power and merits of the subs. And the authorities were only too happy to have their existence known, not least to enemy designs.

That raises the second point about their presence. Did it deter an actual attack? The evidence is uncertain and will probably remain so. Nevertheless, it is clear that the German cruiser *Leipzig,* pushing onward to San Francisco, learned by radio on the night of August 6 that British west coast naval forces now had "two submarines bought from Chile."[3] Whether the Germans would otherwise have gone on to Juan de Fuca, we do not know. In any event, they did not (and assuredly they did not know the helpless condition of the subs at that precise moment). In sum, we may say that the essential feature of CC1 and CC2 was that they were available – to redress the naval balance and to restore confidence to the B.C. public at a crucial period. McBride had really made an excellent deal.

In their later life the subs completed a gruelling 7,000-mile voyage to Halifax, repeatedly breaking down en route; and there they spent the rest of the war, too worn out to be sent across the Atlantic. Yet they were little coastal submarines, after all; primitive pioneers at that, however brave they had looked off Victoria back in 1914. Their voyage alone, via

Panama, was monumental. British Columbians could well be proud of their three-day navy and grateful for its subsequent years of fortitude and service. Besides, they still have the distinction of being the only Canadian province with a navy – so far. I say "so far" advisedly, since Alberta might well acquire one, as soon as it has bought an ocean. It already has an air force, of course. . . .

But now for something entirely different – to coin a phrase – Princes, Commandos and World War II. Such an acute audience as this has probably already recognized that the Princes are ships (we'll get to commandos later) – specifically, the Royal Canadian Navy's armed merchant cruisers, *Prince Robert, Prince David* and *Prince Henry*, built originally for the pre-war B.C. steamship service of the Canadian National Railways. For where else but in this royally inclined province are you so likely to find sea-going princes among a profusion of floating empresses and princesses, and where even the ferries are queens? To get back on course, as sailor types say, the Princes, for some time in their day the largest, most powerfully gunned warships in the RCN, had been initially designed for west coast waters in the late 1920s as part of the expansive and expensive policies of Sir Henry Thornton, then president of the Canadian National. Thornton had hoped to wrest more of the prime coastal passenger traffic from his great CPR rival, and especially to build up Prince Rupert as his line's northern terminus on the Pacific. Hence in 1930 – hardly an auspicious date – three fast new vessels were delivered to the CN west coast service: the Princes *Robert, David* and *Henry*, built at Birkenhead in England according to lavish specifications that, at a cost of eight and a half million dollars, made them miniature luxury liners.[4] They were nearly 6,000 tons each, 385 feet long and capable of over 22 knots, a high speed then for ships of their size. (By comparison, old CC1 and CC2 had been of some 300 tons displacement, about 150 feet long, and could reach 13 knots on the surface.) The *Prince Henry* was intended for the Alaska traffic, the *Robert* to drum up coastal trade utilizing Prince Rupert, and the *David* to ply the triangle route between Vancouver, Victoria and Seattle.

On arrival, they made a grand impression with their three big raked funnels, sleek lines and rich appointments. But the thirties proved bleak years for Alaska tourism, the triangle trade had too much competition, and no one seemed to want to go to Prince Rupert. At any rate, the handsome-looking vessels languished – as did Henry Thornton who resigned his office in 1932 under a general cloud of criticism. It should also be noted that the Princes had been designed under Admiralty requirements for possible conversion to armed merchant cruisers in event of war. Thus they were overpowered for civilian traffic and hence expensive to run, while their fast lines gave them a rapid roll none too endearing to passengers.[5] Accordingly, unhappy stringencies decreed that while the *Robert* should continue in west coast service, the *David* and *Henry* would be sent to try their luck in the Atlantic, on Maritimes-West Indies runs. Yet times were hard there too, and so by 1936 the *David* was chartered to a New York-based cruise company for trips to Panama and Hawaii. That these cruises again did not do too well is indicated by the fact that she kept a full head of steam up in her ports of call for quick escapes to sea from the company's creditors.[6] The next year *David* was laid up by CN steamships in Halifax. The year following, 1938, *Henry* was sold off to Clarke Steamship Lines for use in their St. Lawrence-Labrador-Newfoundland operations. She was barely making a go of it, as was *Robert* on the west coast, when the coming of world war in 1939 brought on dramatic changes in the careers of all the Prince ships.

Again there was an urgent naval need for the best available ships, to supplement a diminished Royal Navy and an all but extinguished Royal Canadian Naval force. Again there were vast gaps in naval defences against German power – global gaps, in fact. The Princes had speed, and the size to carry larger-calibre guns than existing Canadian warships. They might be used to escort slow-moving convoys, but smaller vessels could fill that role; and in the earlier days of the war there were additional needs to deal with long-range commerce raiders and seize German merchant craft at loose on the high seas. The Prince ships could relieve destroyers for the Atlantic alleys of the U-boat war, while patrolling farther waters against surface raiders or evasive German shipping. And so, in the fall of 1939, *Robert* and *David* were acquired by the RCN for conversion to warships, the *Henry* following shortly afterwards.The *Robert* was taken up at Burrard Drydock in Vancouver and was ready in July of 1940. The *David*, in poorer condition, took until December 1940 to be completed at Halifax, as did the *Henry* at Montreal.[7] All three went through the same essential process. Their two top decks were cut off and replaced with the superstructures of light cruisers, their three funnels being reduced to two squat ones. Hulls were strengthened and sub-divided, and they were each fitted with a main armament of four substantial six-inch guns, with secondary guns, torpedo tubes and depth charges besides.[8] When finished they looked fierce enough to take on a pocket battleship: all three at once, at least.

And yet there were problems. Their main armaments had been supplied out of Admiralty stores saved from scrapped warships of the last war. It was rumoured, wrongly, that their guns dated from the Boer War. In truth, the six-inch had come from old King Edward VII class battleships, their three-inch secondaries out of 1916 vintage cruisers.[9] These were thoroughly sound weapons, but lacking in range and modern fire control. Moreover, the Princes' quick, jerky roll limited their fire power's accuracy and concentration in any kind of sea. Still further, the *Robert*'s working-up trials brought lessons for all three. When she fired her main guns forward the heavy recoil threatened her own charthouse, and patterns of broadsides went wide as the ship rolled merrily. Some "damping down" measures were taken to lessen the trouble, but the message was plain. Don't fire too many guns too often.[10] The Princes were not as formidable as they looked.

Yet once more, they were available, and within their limits would do much. In her first year of naval duty in the Pacific, *Robert* captured the sizeable German merchant liner, the *Weser*, escorted contingents of Australian and New Zealand airmen to Canada for training there under the Commonwealth Air Training Plan, took Canadian forces to Hong Kong – and departed from Pearl Harbour, Honolulu, on the way back to Esquimalt just before the Japanese paid their surprise visit. *Henry* intercepted two German ships off Callao in the spring of 1941 (they scuttled themselves), then patrolled both in the Pacific and the Caribbean into 1942. And *David* worked between Halifax and the West Indies through 1941, sometimes in company with *Henry* in Caribbean waters. Their powerful-looking silhouettes, seen at a distance, may well have inspired free-flowing rumours that Dutch 8-inch heavy cruisers were ranging about the area.[11] At any rate, German commerce raiders with guns better than the Prince ships', but not 8-inches, seemed notably to vanish from the Caribbean. Be that as it may, the success you gain without a battle is surely one of the most pleasant kinds.

But the *David*'s own gleaming moment, also a pleasant one without a struggle, was to occur in the summer of 1942, by which time she too had returned to the Pacific and British Columbia after a voyage via Panama that brought her to Esquimalt late in December 1941.[12] The fact was, of course, that the entry of Japan into the war and the destruction of the American fleet at Pearl Harbour had made the Pacific a vastly more serious zone of conflict; and once again, as in 1914, the British Columbia coasts seemed all too unprotected from attack. (They could even have used the old CC1 and CC2.) So the *David* joined the *Robert* on patrols out of Esquimalt, where the *Henry* arrived also in midsummer. All three ships were to serve in the Aleutian Islands campaign against Japanese invaders that autumn. In a real sense they had come back to their home waters. The *Robert* was from the start heavily manned by British Columbians. The *Henry* and *David* increasingly gained Victorians and Vancouverites in their crews also. And the *David*'s special episode of glamour came off Vancouver Island in July 1942 – when the Hollywood commandos entered too.

Down in Hollywood, California, Columbia Pictures was planning a movie, eventually to be called "The Commandos Strike at Dawn." In the first half of 1942, a grim period when most of Europe was in German hands and the western allies were reeling in defeats from North Africa to the Philippines, one of the few brighter notes to be found lay in the exploits of British commando units raiding the coasts of Fortress Europe. Their attacks had aggressive dash and daring, and, more than that, promised the techniques for lasting landings and the ultimate invasion of Hitler's empire. From Combined Operations by sea and land would stem the Second Front in Europe: that was the hoped-for path. And so it was both good movie business and effective morale boosting to make a major film of a commando operation against the coast of Norway, playing up the strength and spirit of the underground movement as well as the expertise of the raiders from the sea. And where was the nearest Norway but Vancouver Island, with its deep sea fjords and rugged mountains? It all depended upon the co-operation of Canadian military and naval forces on the west coast.

John Farrow, to be director of the film, had the right connections. As a Lieutenant-Commander RCNVR, he had been on loan to the Royal Navy, wounded in the South Atlantic and invalided out, but had retained his links with Naval Headquarters in Ottawa after returning to film work.[13] A capable director, he also had a strong concern for publicizing the war effort and keeping up patriotic enthusiasm. It is fair to say that he wanted a stirring spectacle, but for more than box-office purposes. In any event, he got the response he needed from Naval headquarters and National Defence Headquarters, Ottawa. Canadian forces would provide the troops, both British and German, to the film-makers, together with and most vital – the raiding warship itself. *Prince David* was chosen to become a movie star.

The main human stars were Paul Muni, an outstanding actor with a distinguished set of films behind him, to be the heroic Norwegian leader of the underground; the masterly Cedric Hardwicke as the British Rear-Admiral in command of the raiding expedition; Anna Lee, well-known British actress as the heroine and love interest (playing an officer of the "Wrens," the Women's Royal Naval Service); Lillian Gish, making her movie comeback as a gallant elderly Norwegian patriot; and skilled Alexander Knox as the local Nazi commander, complete with precise, sneering ruthlessness. (Two years later he played President Woodrow Wilson with no less aplomb.) The story was straightforward simplicity. Muni escapes the Nazi clutches to reach Britain with information on a major German air base near his native village. A commando raid is organized, while the hero falls in love with Anna. A Royal Navy cruiser – read *Prince David* – streaks for Norway loaded with commandos, plus Muni, Hardwicke and others, surprises the shore defences at dawn, and lands the troops, who free the village and destroy the base with tremendous battle and explosion. Then the raiders and the *David* sail for home triumphant, along with some surviving villagers, having thoroughly pasted Knox and the forces of tyranny in the process.

The filming on location commenced in mid-July 1942 with Victoria as its base, the actual site of the Norwegian coast being on nearby Saanich Inlet. Plainly this site was very convenient: close to the facilities and flesh pots of Victoria, on the sunny and not exposed side of the island, yet featuring superbly suitable coastal scenery, if one avoided arbutus trees and over-massive Douglas firs. A Norwegian fishing village took shape on Finlayson Arm, while interior sets were built within the main exhibition building at the Willows.[14] Troops in training at Camp Nanaimo were drafted for the action and temporarily encamped in Goldstream Park.[15] And the call went out for a mass of extras from Victoria to be Norwegians, while the Hollywood actors, the film-makers and support staff descended in their numbers on the city. The Empress Hotel throbbed with the expedition from Columbia Pictures, as if six boatloads of Seattle tourists had arrived at the front desk all at once. Victoria was not unacquainted with such visitors from Hollywood – indeed, in the prewar years it had been the setting for a number of "quickie" American movies, which thereby could enter the United Kingdom film market under the quota for British-made products. But there had scarcely been so many celebrated stars on hand together or a production on such a scale before.

Daily the cast assembled at its Empress headquarters to be bussed out to the film site. On one occasion Alexander Knox, late for the bus, stamped briskly through the lobby in Nazi officer's uniform and Iron Cross, followed by jack-booted soldiers of the *Wehrmacht* – and nearly caused heart attacks among the old ladies of the Empress in the shrubbery.[16] No one had told them that the Germans had got *this* far. Then, at the site, the shooting went on (literally), as men from the Royal Rifles of Canada, the Sault Ste. Marie and Sudbury Regiment and the Canadian Scottish, playing commandos, beat down the German defences and captured the dazed, demoralized garrison (the 114th Veteran's Guard). They totally overwhelmed the enemy air base, adjacent to Patricia Bay airport, with sand-filled mortar bombs, thunder flashes and smoke generators, while blank ammunition filled the air. The troops were "dynamic," reported the War Diary of the Royal Rifles: "They gave all they had to the performance, much to the delight of the producers."[17]

These doings took some days; but the *Prince David*'s own role began on July 24, when the filming of the ship sequences got under way. At Esquimalt, a heavy sound truck was hoisted aboard and lashed to the portside of her upper works, along with a portable electric plant, spots, reflectors, and a tangle of feeder cables along the deck, so that she could only present her starboard side to the camera.[18] Admiral Hardwicke arrived to take command. His resplendent gold braid earned him a flurry of salutes on his progress through the Dockyard, which as a veteran First World War officer he solemnly returned. It seemed, he said, "the polite thing to do."[19] Some ninety "commandos" were then marched aboard, as the cameras ground; other troops were already waiting at the site. Then *Prince David* sailed off for Saanich Inlet, looking rather like a holiday-cruise vessel once again. Gazing down from her bridge her commanding officer, Acting Captain V.S. Godfrey, RCN, must have gulped a little to see his trim ship festooned about with cables and cinema equipment, his crew off-watch consorting on deck in the sunshine with sports-shirted cameramen and sprawled-out soldiers, all smoking Columbia's free cigarettes – while the "Admiral" was genially having his picture taken at railside arm-in-arm with various seamen. One shouted, "Take two of this for me: I'll never be as close to a Rear-Admiral again."[20] Nevertheless, the Captain evidently got into the swing of things later, turning out to be "a natural dramatic actor" in his filmed exchanges with a now highly professional Admiral Hardwicke, as the ship steered into action.[21]

The *David* was filmed steaming majestically up Saanich Inlet, guns bristling, steel-helmeted troops peering from her deck, then out again (for the return journey), always showing only her good side. Back into the Inlet, her main armament crashed out in Mill Bay as she engaged the surprised German shore batteries, registering hits and soon silencing the enemy fire – that fire and the *David*'s hits being electrically exploded dynamite charges.[22] Then the assault boats were smartly swung out; the troops slid rapidly down into them, and the craft went boiling away, crammed with Canadian soldiers under Columbia's command. The landing operation was completely successful, except for rope burns suffered by those who slid down into the boats with too much zeal.[23] Otherwise, a good time was had by all. The picture-makers were overjoyed. And the Royal Rifles War Diary recorded happily, "The Commando spirit invaded even the nautical minds of the Navy, as many tars expressed their envy and admiration of this branch of the Army."[24]

Nonetheless, given the ways of the movie world, various shots and scenes had to be retaken or embellished, and so it took a few days more before all the landing operations in the spirited assault on Vancouver Island were dealt with satisfactorily. And after a hard few hours of racing up the rocky foreshore or sweating into the woods with demolition equipment, there were welcome stops for "ice cold beers" supplied courtesy of Columbia Pictures.[25] Here was another nice kind of battle, where nobody shot back with more than blanks; picnic lunches were ready for everyone, furnished by the Empress; the beer was kept chilled; and the only casualty, a Canadian Scottish machine gunner who jammed his hand in his gun's mechanism, got first aid from United Air Lines hostesses who had come along to play WAAFs, the women's unit of the Royal Air Force.[26] *Prince David*'s own part ended when she returned to Esquimalt from anchorage in Patricia Bay late on July 27, and disembarked the soldiery and camera crews. "All Columbia gear landed," the ship's log reported laconically – and thankfully, perhaps.[27]

Work on the film continued into August, with more battle retakes and interior scenes. The irony was that before it had concluded, the real thing happened on a horrific scale: the landing operations at Dieppe on August 19, with heavy losses among the 5,000 Canadian combatants, who were scarcely more experienced than those who had gone ashore on Saanich Inlet. The extent of the losses was hidden at first. Thus Columbia decided to finish the picture speedily and release it while the Dieppe Raid still gripped public attention with speculations on the coming invasion of Europe and the Second Front.[28] And so "Commandos Strike at Dawn" came out during 1942, not in 1943 as initially planned. But meanwhile *Prince David* and her sister ships had gone into the Aleutian campaign. And afterwards they were taken in hand at Vancouver for extensive refitting, to adapt them to new uses in the changing war at sea.

Prince Robert became a powerfully armed anti-aircraft ship, equipped with guns of smaller calibre than her old 6-inch, but with more guns and efficient fire control. In this wise, she was to serve with distinction on the Bay of Biscay in 1943-44, while escorting Gibraltar convoys. The *Prince David* and *Prince Henry* were transformed into heavy landing ships, infantry, with less armament but sizeable space for troops, assault craft and radio command gear. They were to lead their groups in putting ashore Canadians in the invasion of Normandy on D-Day in 1944. Here there was a brighter kind of irony (if such a thing be possible). Among the forces they placed on Juno Beach that day were men of the Canadian Scottish – the same unit that had swept to shore from *David* in the very different Hollywood summer outing on Vancouver Island of two years before.

David and *Henry* went on to share in the invasion of southern France, notably carrying commandos, if French and American this time. Then the *David* took British commandos to raids and landings in Greece, almost re-enacting the role she had established in rehearsal back in '42. She must have been good at the act, for in October 1944 she was chosen to transport the Greek government and prime minister to Piraeus for the re-occupation of Athens: a somewhat more meaningful event than pseudo-Admiral Hardwicke's raid on pseudo-Norway.

Thereafter, the *David* sailed all the way back to Esquimalt, where the *Robert* had joined her by March 1945, to be readied for the Canadian Pacific squadron intended for the final naval operations against Japan. Two of the Princes had come home again. The *Henry* never did. She went instead to Malta, then to Britain to complete her career as a Royal Naval headquarters ship. The *David* had also finished active service; the Pacific war was over before she was renewed to enter it. As for the *Robert*, as usual, she was ready first. In fact, at war's end she was at Hong Kong, and there landed the first party to enter the prison camp containing survivors of the Canadian troops which she had escorted there, so long before, in 1941.[29] War has all sorts of ironies, indeed.

At the close, the Prince ships had journeyed far and seen much since first they had appeared off the shore of pre-war British Columbia. Like the CC1 and CC2 before them, they had markedly contributed to west coast naval tradition – though never more divertingly than *Prince David* in the epic film raid on Vancouver Island. Provincial submarines, Gulf of Georgia light cruisers and Goldstream Park commandos: all had done their part in suitably adorning the uncommon history of the wonderful world of B.C.

Endnotes

1. See G.N. Tucker, "Canada's First Submarines: CC1 and CC2. An Episode of the Naval War in the Pacific, 1914-18," *British Columbia Historical Quarterly*, VII, 3 July 1943, pp. 147-70. Since the account given of the submarines below is drawn from the source, backed by other secondary material, it has not been felt necessary to present a string of *ibids* as citations. All references concerning the submarines come from this BCHQ article; only two quotations taken from it are given specific citation themselves.
2. Quoted in *ibid.*, p. 154.
3. *Ibid.*, p. 166.
4. G.R. Stevens, *History of the Canadian National Railways* (New York, 1973), p. 375.
5. *Ibid.*, p. 376.
6. Public Archives of Canada, Record Group 24, vol. 6717, NSS 8000-412/112. Notes by Cdr. W. Strange, 14 September 1946.
7. G.N. Tucker, *The Naval Service of Canada* (Toronto, 1952), 2 vols., II, p. 520. See this volume for information on the Princes' naval acquisition, conversion and subsequent refits.
8. *Ibid.*
9. *Ibid.*
10. PAC, RG 24, vol. 11838, COPC 8000-314/3. J.O. Cosette to COPC and COAC, 6 November 1940.
11. Personal conclusion of the author derived from signal files while serving at Naval Service Headquarters in Ottawa, 1943.
12. PAC, RG 24, vol. 7549, Ship's Log, *Prince David*, December 1941.
13. Victoria *Times*, 21 July 1942.
14. *Ibid.*; see articles on the movie-making variously, 21 July-11 August 1942.
15. PAC, RG 24, vol. 15230, War Diary of the Royal Rifles of Canada, 1-13 July 1942, Appendix V.
16. *Times*, 29 July 1942.
17. War Diary, RRC, *loc. cit.* It might be noted that the relevant War Diaries of the Canadian Scottish and Sault Ste. Marie and Sudbury Regiments were not available, but the RRC record is full and broadly useful.

18. Evidence from photograph in author's possession. See also Ship's Log, *Prince David, loc. cit.*, July 1942.
19. *Times*, 25 July 1942.
20. *Ibid.*
21. *Ibid.*
22. War Diary, RRC, *loc. cit.*
23. *Ibid.*
24. *Ibid.*
25. *Ibid.*
26. *Times*, 28 July 1942.
27. Ship's Log, 27 July 1942.
28. *Times*, 22 August 1942.
29. Joseph Schull, *The Far Distant Ships* (Ottawa, 1950), p. 386. See this work for the general operations record of the Prince ships in World War II.

Bibliography

A Selected List of the Author's Published Writings

1945

"Confederation", "The United States to 1860", "The United States Since 1860", "Modern Britain", "Canada's Armed Forces", "Newfoundland", "Ottawa", "Royal Military College", *The Canadian Book of Knowledge* (Toronto: Grolier Society). Various years, 1945-1960.

1948

"The Toronto *Globe* and Agrarian Radicalism, 1850-67", *Canadian Historical Review* 29 (1) March, 14-39.

Review of *The Rise of Toronto* by D. C. Masters, in *Canadian Journal of Economics and Political Science* 14 (2) May, 275-6.

1949

Review of *This New Canada* by M. McWilliams, *Canadian Historical Review* 30 (2) June, 170-1.

1950

"The Diary of Peter Brown", *Ontario History* 42 (3) July, 113-51.

"Mid-Victorian Liberalism in Central Canadian Newspapers, 1850-67", *Canadian Historical Review* 31 (3) September, 221-36.

"Who was George Brown?", *Ontario History* 42 (2) April, 57-66.

Review of *The Mohawk* by C. Hislop and *The Mackenzie* by L. Roberts, *Canadian Historical Review* 31 (1) March, 77-8.

Review of *Our Canada* by A. G. Dorland, *Canadian Historical Review* 31 (1) March, 75-6.

1951

"History and Canadian Unity", *Culture* 12 (2) juin, 117-24.

"Letters in Canada, Social Studies, II: The Land and the People", *University of Toronto Quarterly* 20-29. Review articles on regional works contributed annually to 1960.

Review of *The Valley of the Lower Thames: 1640 to 1850* by F.C. Hamil and *The Physiography of Southern Ontario* by L.J. Chapman and D.F. Putnam, *Canadian Historical Review* 32 (3) September, 276-7.

1952

"1925-1939: II", *Trinity 1852-1952*, ed. A. Watson (Toronto: University of Toronto), 153-67. Essay on student life.

1953

Canada: A Story of Challenge (Cambridge and Toronto: Macmillan, 1958; revised ed. 1963, 1970, 1985; Japanese ed.: Tokyo, 1978).

Canada and the Commonwealth (Toronto: Dent). Co-author with G W. Brown, C.R. MacLeod, E. Ray.

1954

Canada and the Americas (Toronto, Dent). Co-author with G.W. Brown, G.M. Craig, E. Ray.

"Frontierism, Metropolitanism, and Canadian History", *Canadian Historical Review* 35 (1) March, 1-21.

"Canadian Nationalism—Immature or Obsolete?", Canadian Historical Association, *Report*, 12-14.

Review of *Three Centuries of Robinsons: Three Centuries of a Family* by Julia Jarvis, *Canadian Historical Review* 35 (2) June, 157-8.

Review of *Our Sense of Identity: A Book of Canadian Essays* by Malcolm Ross, *Canadian Historical Review* 35 (4) December, 353.

"W.K. Rolph" [Obit.], *Canadian Historical Review* 35 (1) March, 92.

1955

Canada and the World (Toronto, Dent). Co-author with G.W. Brown, G.M. Craig, E. Ray.

1956

Review of Pioneer Public Service: An Administrative History of the United Canadas, 1841-1867 by J.E. Hodgetts, Canadian Historical Review 37 (4) December, 365-6.

1957

"The Independent Member for Kent Reports, 1853", *Canadian Historical Review* 38 (1) March, 41-51.

"Letters from Thomas Talbot to John Beverley Robinson", *Ontario History* 49 (1) Winter, 25-41.

"The Political Ideas of George Brown", *Canadian Forum* 36 February, 247-50.

Review of *Daylight Through the Mountain: Letters and Labours of Civil Engineers Walter and Francis Shanly* by F.N. Walker, *Canadian Historical Review* 38 (4) December, 335.

Review of *Sam Slick in Pictures: The Best of the Humour of Thomas Chandler Haliburton*, ed. Lorne Pierce, illus. C.W. Jefferys, *Canadian Historical Review* 38 (1) March, 77.

1958

Review of *The Grand Trunk Railway of Canada* by A.W. Currie, *Canadian Historical Review* 39 (4) December, 339-40.

1959

Brown of the Globe, *I: The Voice of Upper Canada, 1818-1859* (Toronto: Macmillan).

"George Brown", *Our Living Tradition, Second and Third Series* ed. Robert L. MacDougall (Toronto: University of Toronto) 31-54.

Review of *Galloping Head: The Life of the Right Honourable Sir Francis Bond Head, 1793-1875* by Sydney Jackman, *Canadian Historical Review* 40 (2) June, 168-9.

Review of *Problems of Wartime Co-operation and Post-War Change, 1939-1952,* by N. Mansergh, *American Historical Review* 64 (4) July, 941-2.

1960

"George Brown and the Mother of Confederation, 1864", Canadian Historical Association, *Report,* 57-73.

1962

"Government and Historical Resources in Canada", Second Seminar on the Development of Canadian Historical Resources, *Report* (Ottawa). Veritype.

Review of *The Idea of Continental Union: Agitation for the Annexation of Canada to the United States, 1849-1893,* by D.F. Warner, *Canadian Historical Review* 43 (2) June, 153-4.

1963

Brown of the Globe, II: Statesman of Confederation, 1860-1880 (Toronto: Macmillan).

1964

"Introduction", *The Defended Border: Upper Canada and the War of 1812,* ed. Morris Zaslow (Toronto: Macmillan), 1-8.

1966

"Metropolitanism and Nationalism", *Nationalism in Canada,* ed. Peter Russel (Toronto), 271-83.

1967

The Union of the Canadas: The Growth of Canadian Institutions, 1841-1857, vol. 10, Canadian Centenary Series (Toronto: McClelland & Stewart).

"Introduction", *The Canadians, 1867-1967* (Toronto: Macmillan) xiii-xix. With R.C. Brown; also volume co-editor with R.C. Brown.

1968

"Introduction", *Part I of The Canadians, 1867-1967* (Toronto: Macmillan), xi-xii. Co-author with R.C. Brown; also volume co-editor with R.C. Brown.

"Hooray for the Scars and Gripes", *The New Romans,* ed. A. Purdy (Edmonton: Hurtig), 132-4.

"Somewhat Narrow Horizons", Canadian Historical Association, *Report,* 1-10.

Review of *My First Seventy-Five Years* by A.R.M. Lower, *Canadian Historical Review* 49 (3) September, 278-9.

Review of *British Columbia and Confederation*, ed. W.G. Shelton, *British Columbia Library Quarterly* 32, October, 27-8.

1969

The Pioneers, (Toronto: McClelland & Stewart). Co-author with W S. MacNutt, W.J. Eccles, C.M. Johnston. L.H. Thomas, M.A. Ormsby.

"Aspects of Metropolitanism in Atlantic Canada", *Regionalism in the Canadian Community, 1867-1967*, ed. Mason Wade (Toronto), 117-29.

"'Limited Identities' in Canada", *Canadian Historical Review* 50 (1) March, 1-10. An earlier version of this paper was read at a joint session of the American and Canadian Historical Associations, Toronto, December 1967.

"The Lowe Brothers, 1852-70: A Study in Business Relations on the North Pacific", *BC Studies* 2 Summer, 1-18.

"Nationalism and Pluralism in Canadian History", *Culture* 30, March, 19-26.

1970

"The Development of the Winnipeg Business Community, 1870-1890", Royal Society of Canada, *Transactions*, ser. 4, vol. 8, 239-54.

"Donald Creighton and Canadian History: Some Reflections", *Character and Circumstance: Essays in Honour of Donald Grant Creighton*, ed. John S. Moir (Toronto), 8-21.

"George Brown and Confederation", Manitoba Historical Society, *Transactions*, 79-87.

"The *Review* Reviewed or Fifty Years with the Beaver Patrol", *Canadian Historical Review* 51 (1) March, 48-71.

1971

"Introduction" and "The 1850s", *Colonists and Canadiens, 1760-1867* (Toronto: Macmillan). Also volume editor.

"The Historian and Nineteenth-Century Bibliography", Bibliographical Society of Canada, *Papers*, X, 73-84.

Review of *Empire and Nation: Essays in Honour of Frederick H. Soward*, eds. Harvey L. Dyck and H. Peter Krosby, *International Journal* 26, Winter, 274-6.

Review of *Montreal: A Brief History* by J. I. Cooper; *Montreal: From Mission Colony to Great World City* by L. Roberts; and *Nineteenth Century Cities: Essays in the New Urban History*, eds. S. Thernstrom and R. Sennett, *Canadian Historical Review* 52 (2) June, 177-80.

Review of *Illustrated Historical Atlas of the County of York*, [1878]; facsimile ed. 1969, *Canadian Historical Review* 52 (2) June, 177-80.

1972

"The Business Community in the Early Development of Victoria, British Columbia", *Canadian Business History: Selected Studies, 1491-1971*, ed. David S. Macmillan (Toronto: McClelleand and Stewart),104-23.

"Localism and Parochialism in Canadian History", *B.C. Perspectives* 1, 27-38.

"George Bennett", "George Brown", "David Christie", *Dictionary of Canadian Biography, X: 1871 to 1880* (Toronto), 49, 91-103, 168-71.

"D.G. Creighton: John A. Macdonald" and "H.A. Innis: The Fur Trade in Canada", *The Foreign Affairs Fifty-Year Bibliography*, ed. Byron Dexter (New York: Bowker), 412, 417.

1973

"Aspects of Urban Life in the West, 1870-1914", *Prairie Perspectives, II: Selected Papers of the Western Canadian Studies Conferences, 1970 and 1971*, ed. Anthony W. Rasporich and Henry C. Klassen (Toronto: Holt, Rinehart & Winston), 25-40.

"Metropolitan Reflections on 'Great Britain's Woodyard'" – critique based on *"Great Britain's Woodyard": British America and the Timber Trade, 1763-1867* by A.R.M. Lower, *Acadiensis* 3 (1) Autumn, 103-9.

1974

Urban Development in Central Canada to 1850, vol. 17, Canada's Visual History Series, National Museum of Man (Ottawa). Booklet with photographic slides.

The Learning Society, [Report of the] Ontario Commission on Post-Secondary Education (Toronto: Queen's Printer). Co-author and author of the minority dissent.

"Urban Development in Canada", *Urban History Review* 3 (1), 9-13.

"Some Aspects of Urbanization in Nineteenth Century Ontario", *Aspects of Nineteenth Century Ontario: Essays Presented to James J. Talman*, eds. F.H. Armstrong et al. (Toronto: University of Toronto), 65-79.

1975

"Two River Empires: The St. Lawrence and the Mississippi", *American Review of Canadian Studies* 5 (2) Autumn, 28-47.

"Waspishness and Multiculture", *Preserving The Canadian Heritage*, ed. K.J. Laidler (Royal Society of Canada: Ottawa), 141-50.

1976

"Peter Brown", "John Roaf", *Dictionary of Canadian Biography, IX: 1861 to 1870* (Toronto), 88-89, 663-65.

"A History of the Provincial Lunatic Asylum", *City Magazine* 2 (3&4) Summer, 42-44.

1977

"A Few Acres of Snow", Canadian Museums Association, *Gazette* 2. Evaluation of the permanent Canadian Historical Exhibit, National Museum of Man.

"In Praise of Vacant Lots", *The Globe and Mail* (Toronto) 19 February 1977, 7.

Review of *Canada Before Confederation* by R. C. Harris and J. C. Warkentin, and *Illustrated Historical Atlas of Peterborough County, 1825-1875*, ed. A O.C. Cole, *Canadian Historical Review* 58 (1) March, 68-70.

1978

The Rise of Cities in Canada before 1914, no. 32, Historical Booklets Series (Ottawa: Canadian Historical Society).

"Metropolis and Region: The Interplay of City and Region in Canadian History before 1914", *Urban History Review* 7 (3) 99-118.

1979

George Brown, The Canadians Series (Toronto: Fitzhenry & Whiteside).

"The Concept of Canadian Studies and the Multicultural History Society of Ontario", *German-Canadian Yearbook,* V, ed. H. Froeschle (Toronto: Historical Society of Mecklenburg), 1-5.

"Riel Just Bad Hollywood", *The Sunday Sun* (Toronto) 22 April 1979, 24. Review of C.B.C. television dramatic production.

Review of *Victoria: A Primer for Regional Architecture* by Martin Seggar, *B.C. Historical News* 12 (4), 36-7.

1980

"The Place, the Office, the Times, and the Men", *The Pre-Confederation Premiers: Ontario Government Leaders, 1841-1867* (Toronto: University of Toronto), 3-31. Also volume editor.

"How We Celebrate Dominion Day – Canada Day – July 1st", *The Globe and Mail* (Toronto), 1 July, 8.

"Limited Identities – Ten Years Later", *Manitoba History* (1), 3-9.

"The New Fathers of Confederation", *The Toronto Star* (Toronto) 6 September, B-1.

"One Hundred Years after George Brown, What is his Legacy?", *The Globe and Mail* (Toronto) 9 May, 7.

"Submarines, Princes and Hollywood Commandos, or At Sea in B.C.", *B.C. Studies* 45, Spring, 3-16.

"Dominion Day, 1984", *The Graduate,* University of Toronto Alumni, 7 (4), 16-18.

Review of *Mirrors of the New World: Images and Image-Makers in the Settlement Process* by J.M. Powell, *Australian Journal of Politics and History* 26 (2), 319-20.

Review of *The Jews of Toronto* by S. Speisman, *Canadian Jewish Historical Society Journal* 4 (1) Spring, 95-98.

1981

"The Myth of the Downtrodden West", *Saturday Night* 96 (May), 30-34, 36.

Review of *A Canadian Millionaire: The Life and Business Times of Sir Joseph Flavelle, Bart., 1858-1939* by Michael Bliss, *Révue d'histoire de l'Amérique Française* 34 (4) Mars, 627-30. In French, trans. M. Caya.

1982

"Reflections on the Individual in Canadian Society", *Expression* 3, Winter, 5-9.

"James Lesslie", *Dictionary of Canadian Biography, XI: 1881 to 1890* (Toronto), 516-19.

1984

Toronto to 1918: An Illustrated History, National Museum of Man, The History of Canadian Cities Series (Toronto: James Lorimer).

"The First Hurrah: Toronto's Semi-Centennial of 1884", *Forging a Consensus: Historical Essays on Toronto,* ed. Victor L. Russell (Toronto: University of Toronto), 141-54.

"The Life of a New City: Toronto, 1834", The Empire Club of Canada, *Addresses 1983-1984* (Toronto), 285-97.

1985

"The Emergence of Cabbagetown in Victorian Toronto", *Gathering Place: Peoples and Neighbourhoods of Toronto, 1834-1945,* ed. Robert F. Harney (Toronto: Multicultural Historical Society of Ontario), 25-46.

"J.B. Conacher: A Personal Appreciation", *The Gladstonian Turn of Mind: Essays Presented to J. B. Conacher,* ed. Bruce L. Kinzer (Toronto: University of Toronto), ix-xv.

"Upper Canada and Confederation", *The Shaping of Ontario* from Exploration to Confederation, comp. Nick and Helma Mika (Belleville), 241-7.

1986

Review of *Shocked and Appalled: A Century of Letters to the Globe and Mail,* ed. Jack Kapica, *Canadian Historical Review,* 67 (3) September, 440-1.

"Canada before 1800", *Canada: From Sea Unto Sea,* ed. Charles Humber (Mississauga: Loyalist Press), 84-107.

1987

Review of *The Orangeman: The Life and Times of Ogle Gowan* by Donald Akenson, syndicated in Thomson Newpapers, January.

Review of *Canada, 1900-1945* by Robert Bothwell, Ian Drummond and John English, syndicated in Thomson Newspapers, December.

1988

"The Aftermath of Rebellion", *1837 Rebellion Remembered,* ed. D. Duncan and G. Lockwood (Toronto: Ontario Historical Society), 151-64.

1989

Frontier and Metropolis in Canada: Regions, Cities and Identities to 1914 (Toronto: University of Toronto).

Printed on paper
containing over 50%
recycled paper including
5% post-consumer fibre.

Printed in Canada